Alliances with the Real

Flanders Architectural Review N°15

PREFACE

Architecture is linked to all aspects of life. It literally shapes our standing in the world. Now that new insights into social, ecological, economic and cultural sustainability are rapidly gaining ground, architecture is also being asked to bear some responsibility in these areas.

With the ambitious and recently launched project 'New European Bauhaus', the European Union is connecting the sustainability goals of the European Green Deal to architecture. Its vision of sustainability is broad, culturally embedded and based on concepts that go far beyond the energy performance of buildings. It concerns architecture that uses materials prudently, tries to safeguard as much open space as possible, and strives to be meaningful to everyone. Sustainable buildings not only fulfil short-term needs but are also future-oriented and, above all, of enduring cultural value: they become part of a village or city's history. People take them into their hearts and cherish them. Architecture that is cared for is probably the most sustainable story that designers can write.

The fact that in June 2022 the 'New European Bauhaus' Award went to De Korenbloem residential care home in Kortrijk naturally fills me with pride, both as a resident of Flanders and as Minister-president and Minister responsible for the Flemish Government Architect and the Flanders Architecture Institute. Earlier this year, the highly regarded newspaper *The Guardian* published an article on the quality of public buildings in Flanders since 2000. This demonstrates the international attention generated by the architectural level of our designers and clients. These are the fruits of twenty years of sustained Flemish policy governing good business practices and architectural culture. I am delighted to have been able to effect a structural reinforcement of this sector in the recent Arts Decree round.

In so doing, I have tasked various cultural architecture organizations with continuing to feed the social debate about what sustainable architecture can mean for all Flemish people. This fifteenth edition of the *Flanders Architectural Review* is a prime example of this ambition. In addition, critical essays point out where there is still margin for growth. I believe that a mature architectural culture is able to combine this critical reflection with inspiring examples of best practice.

Jan Jambon
Minister-president of the Government of Flanders
Flemish Minister for Foreign Affairs, Culture,
ICT and Facility Management

EDITORIAL

Alliances with the Real

Anyone who surveys architecture in Flanders and Brussels today will immediately notice a contradiction. The global success stories, the selection procedures for public commissions that are the envy of the world and the fact that developers are increasingly gravitating towards interesting designers and thereby opening the door to greater quality in the private market are well documented. The discipline is supported, nurtured and kept on its toes by a lively architectural climate of publications, lectures, exhibitions and education programmes. In the best-case scenario, a critical mirror is held up to the discipline and architecture is offered a space for experimentation and given the opportunity, through various media, of engaging in a broader social debate.

At first glance then, architecture in Flanders and Brussels seems to be thriving. Yet the radical changes taking place in society, many of which have a spatial dimension, contradict this narrative. Architecture faces immense challenges as a result of these changes. Today, however, the discipline seems to be searching. With regard to these new challenges, it appears to be either falling short or reacting too late. In this context, talking about architecture might seem almost non-committal. Nevertheless, it is impossible not to continue the discussion about architecture, among architects certainly, but also with policymakers and the wider public. After all, architecture brings meaning to everyday life and externalizes how we, as a community, deal with the social, digital, economic and ecological upheavals of our time. The tension between the success story and architecture's slow or hesitant response to a range of societal transitions lends new relevancy to the questions posed by Geert Bekaert in the first *Yearbook Architecture Flanders* in 1994: 'Architecture is alive these days. It wallows in its success. But what kind of life does it live? Are architects making a real contribution to the quality of life in our environment, or are they acting like parasites? Are they only good at defending their own prerogatives, cultivating their own atavism and cutting a dash in a coterie that wants to create an image for itself through architecture?'[1]

ARCHITECTURE AS A SOCIAL CONTRACT

The above field of tension was a recurrent and tangible point of discussion for this edition's editorial board. It inspired a process akin to a quest; I would even go so far as to call this edition the 'Architectural Review of Hesitancy'. In the aftermath of the pandemic that dominated social life in the years 2020–22, it is clear that the lockdowns accentuated social and spatial inequalities. With every passing year, climate change becomes more real. The right to housing is a spiralling challenge for which no adequate solution can be found in policy directives. This is what prompted Hashim Sarkis, for example, to advance the question 'How will we live together?' as the overarching curatorial theme for the 17th Venice Architecture Biennale in 2021.

1 Geert Bekaert, 'Parasitic Architecture?' in Dirk De Meyer et. al., eds., *Yearbook Architecture Flanders 1990–1993* (Brussels: Ministry of the Flemish Community, 1994), 184.

In contrast to the Venice exhibition, where future projections based on data analysis and design research set the tone and where speculative scenarios were depicted, the editorial board for this edition of the *Flanders Architectural Review* sought to understand how actual architectural projects deal with these challenges. This exercise confronted us with architecture's slowness, caused by the stringent regulatory framework and the economic conditions that govern its creation. Moreover, the gap between spatial planning and architecture plays tricks on those dealing with these social and climatological transitions. These two design disciplines have developed into autonomous professional fields, each with their own specialized training courses and methodologies. The editorial board noted that the proliferation of knowledge in the planning field – especially regarding climate change and 'spatial equality' – is not filtering through to the practice of architecture in an obvious way.

Take the housing crisis, perhaps the most pressing of all societal problems and the one that also intersects with the widest range of economic, social, spatial and climatic factors. It is a basic human right that impacts every aspect of life. Belgium's housing policy – which mainly revolves around social advancement and discipline – has been determined by property acquisition since the nineteenth century. A home of one's own, preferably outside the city, became a viable option for many in the twentieth century. Provided it remained affordable for the government, and no one shattered the illusion of an endless supply of open space, the principle worked. The formula began to be critiqued within architectural circles in the mid twentieth century; Renaat Braem is perhaps the best-known voice in this respect. Nevertheless, answers to this issue only began to be written into policy documents in the 1990s. By then, unfortunately, there were almost no shared answers to the housing issue to be found in the collective memory, quite the contrary. This is now weighing down Flanders as it tackles the climate and housing emergencies. By late 2021, a staggering 182,000 people were waiting for social housing. Furthermore, 37 per cent of the Flemish population live in sub-standard accommodation. With the Green Deal, the European Union is aiming for all buildings to be climate-neutral by 2050. Yet the renovation policy in Flanders is geared towards those who can afford to invest rather than those with the greatest need. People living in homes that leak energy often lack the resources to tackle the problem. The obligation to renovate existing properties into energy-efficient dwellings within five years of purchase also raises the question as to which kinds of owners can afford this kind of work and whether landlords will pass the costs on to tenants. As a result, the highest renovation subsidies will automatically end up with the group that can most afford the outlay, thereby perpetuating social inequality.[2]

2 Johan Albrecht, *Klimaatneutraal in 2050?* (Ghent: Owl Press, 2022).

We know from work in neighbouring countries, but also thanks to pilot projects in Flanders and Brussels, that collective solutions to the climate and housing crises have the best chance of success. Nevertheless, this approach conflicts with Flanders' space-guzzling spatial planning policies: dispersed housing causes huge transport-related energy losses and prevents the large-scale roll-out of heat networks and green energy production. The building shift – the clustering of housing and manufacturing around cores or nodes with shared transport facilities and access to shared green space – is not a new story in this context. Yet the theme has acquired a new social and climatological urgency. A fresh vision on what constitutes quality of life is vital, as are new collective models. This requires a complete volte-face on the part of residents, policymakers, developers and architects. Residents have all too easily been reduced to consumers in recent decades, a development to which the architectural community has also contributed. Architecture has always trod a fine line between the construction economy, social engagement and cultural ambition; after all, architects are also entrepreneurs. We, the editors, encourage the entire design community to link this entrepreneurship to a genuine commitment to shaping society so that it is better equipped to face the challenges of the future. Architecture thus carries the promise of embodying a social contract.

SEEDLINGS FOR A 'FRIENDLY ARCHITECTURE'

Architecture cannot reverse the systemic errors like found in housing policies. It can, however, feel itself addressed in terms of its social role. Exposing or resisting the prevailing orthodoxy, not to mention the economic or policy imperatives, is what distinguishes architecture from uncritical building. The projects in this book demonstrate what can be done, and often within stringent conditions. Caring and empathy turn out to be keywords in this context.

Once again, the example of housing is telling. The varied and successful residential projects that we have chosen to publish all demonstrate a careful approach towards the pre-existing architecture, one that also extends to materials and site histories; to the housing needs of different generations; to those who fall outside the traditional nuclear family of two-income couples; and to people who might require special care. These are buildings that heed the environment and are habitable in the richest sense of the word. They show generosity and empathy for how people live; provide sufficient protection and opportunities for encounters; avoid abrupt transitions between the private and the public; are places where one can make a life and store belongings; cook and eat together; where there is room to safely store a bicycle; where children can play and adolescents retreat; where there is a play of light, the acoustics are pleasant and there is a view of life outside the home; and where materials and forms are destined to last. These projects inscribe themselves in a longer historical narrative of a place, without nostalgia but with an affinity for how contemporary people live in a world of unprecedented diversity. This form of habitability seems self-evident. The editorial board's many visits to recently completed projects in Flanders and Brussels tended to show the absence rather than presence of these seemingly obvious things.

Visiting the projects thus became a crucial part of a selection process that went far beyond the study of plans, renders and photographs. After the Flanders Architecture Institute issued a call for projects in the summer of 2021, at least two members of the editorial team visited a hundred buildings. By talking to users and clients, by experiencing the spaces, by critically examining and touching the materialization, by empirically investigating how the buildings behave in the city, we often reached conclusions that might differ from the view of an assessment panel for an (international) architecture award. This observation can be reduced to the tension that Geert Bekaert identified in the above citation as early as 1994: superficially, everything seems to be going well, but those who take the time to experience architecture and study it meticulously might draw a very different conclusion.

Mark Pimlott aptly raises the issue of image versus experience in his essay 'In Pursuit of Imagery'. In the current architectural climate of Flanders and Brussels, he discerns a tendency to communicate architecture through a recognizable visual language. While Pimlott does not see this as a problem per se, he observes that the built environment does not always live up to the desired image. The fact that the editorial board has made in-depth visits to projects that have been extensively celebrated in the architectural press but are not shown on international platforms also points to the problematic relation between experience and the representation of buildings, with the latter being difficult to trust. One cannot judge architecture on appearances alone; every architectural criticism – positive or negative – departs from experience. The *Flanders Architectural Review* is thus the result of a slow and intensive process that does not pretend to be objective. It departs, rather, from the intersubjective experience of experts from a range of backgrounds, including urban planning, participation, design practice, theory, image-making and architectural history.

The editorial board looked explicitly at how architecture deals with challenges of our time, such as the housing issue, alternative visions on education, the collective past, open space and care needs. In selecting the projects, we were guided by such criteria as the attitude towards the user, the attention paid to the public aspect of buildings, the position adopted in relation to the memory of places and of one's own discipline, the care for the materials and for all involved in the design and construction process, and the way in which buildings mediate between openness and security. These criteria were not set in advance but were shaped by the editors' many visits to the buildings submitted and an equal number of intensive discussions.

The projects in the final selection all demonstrate how a systemic change in a specific time and place will end up in a concrete architectural project. Just as new plants grow from the seeds of their predecessors, these projects do not arise from themselves. They are nurtured by the interactions of many agents: commissioners, designers, implementers and intermediaries such as city services and quality forums. Like the seedling, they have the potential to grow into meaningful contributions to the built environment. This is already expressed in how the buildings have been appropriated. We invited photographers Sepideh Farvardin and Miles Fischler to capture these appropriation processes. The result is a poetic ode to everyday life within the selected projects.

JANUS FACE OF THE *FLANDERS ARCHITECTURAL REVIEW*

The projects are documented via short texts, plans and visual materials, all of which combine to highlight their various qualities. These project files have a celebratory tone and showcase architecture's capabilities in the year 2022. During the many site visits and conversations, the editorial board also identified issues that are now on the architectural agenda in Flanders and Brussels. They shed light on these matters from a critical standpoint in the essays.

For example, we assessed the results of large-scale urban renewal operations. These are more than just expressions of an approach to the housing crisis; they represent a vision on the public space. Martino Tattara examines where these projects fall short in realizing a truly qualitative urban residential framework and, by way of an interesting range of examples, shows what they can achieve. His text is complemented by Marleen Goethals's contribution, which identifies the quality criteria by which the conversion of the Oude Dokken in Ghent can be judged a successful urban renewal project in Flanders. Marc Martens provides insight into the background to the many other projects that have been initiated since the launch of the Flanders Urban Policy in 2003. He argues that social and spatial issues can no longer be compartmentalized. At the same time, Martens reveals the points at which architecture and urban policy coincide and should therefore be mutually reinforcing. In addition to these three essays, Livia de Bethune focuses on neighbourhood greenery as an urgent necessity if cities are to remain liveable. She analyses whether greenery can be a game-changer in housing quality and spatial justice, a question that became painfully tangible during the lockdowns of 2020–21.

Kiki Verbeeck and Petrus Kemme both consider what empathy and consideration mean in the specialized context of schools and care programme assignments. As with housing, these types of programmes expose both the client and the architect's concept of humanity. The two essays unpack the new typologies that can give vulnerable people – whether because they are young or have special needs – a dignified framework for life. 'Caring' acquires a different meaning in Sofie De Caigny's essay, which explores how architecture can engage in a conscientious and meaningful dialogue with monuments that embody collective memory. In a changing world, and in light of growing awareness of who is visible and who has been erased within the overarching historical narratives, this is a pertinent architectural issue.

The editorial board saw few genuinely climate-proof or sustainable buildings. Of course, they all adhered to the legally binding standards. In addition to the previously mentioned slowness within architecture – it can easily take four to eight years to realize a building – the question remains as to whether the ever-increasing insulation of buildings is the way to go, and where this road will end. Wouldn't a radical change be better, whereby new construction is no longer the obvious starting point? And where the lifespans of buildings are approached in function of as-yet-unknown future programmes? It would entail new kinds of designs, based less on contemporary imperatives and more on what already exists and on future potential. It requires a profound cultural shift on the part of users, designers and commissioners alike. Hülya Ertas discusses three projects that departed from this cultural change, from an 'architecture of means' and a reversal of who adapts to what: the building to the user, or vice versa? It is interesting to note that these projects revert to elements from a centuries-old housing and building culture that disappeared from collective memory in the twentieth century. Certain architects have embraced this cultural shift and focus on social and ecological experimentation. They develop innovative practices that challenge, test and redeploy the role and mission of architecture and design. Maarten Desmet poses the question as to how this social and ecological innovation by designers can be sustainable and how it can be sustained. He arrives at a sampling of socially innovative practices in Flanders and Brussels.

FORM AND COMPLEX HUMANITY

Now that architecture seems to be expanding in all directions, from socially innovative practice to servicing developers, and given that it must actively engage with the pressing issues of our time, a key question arises, namely, What are architecture's mission and strength? Architecture is essentially about designing. What form is needed for this engagement? And what is the most appropriate structure for the interpersonal relations between the various stakeholders? The editorial board is convinced that the projects in this book demonstrate that answers can be found within the profession itself, through the design of spaces and their alliances with the real. A commitment to the assignments of our time seems to demand more rather than less attention to form, materiality, light and composition. This focus on the basic qualities of architecture transcends the delusion of the moment and short-term gain, and in no way excludes commitment. It can produce buildings that are cherished and thus endowed with a long and sustainable life. The matter of architecture's mission thus recalls the late Lucien Kroll's response to a question about what it meant to him personally. He structured his answer around the term 'friendly architecture' and concluded with the reflection that, through his designs, he wanted 'to re-establish that precious connection between form and complex humanity, and then respect for the planet'.[3]

3 Lucien Kroll, 'Respect for the Planet: Notes on Good Architecture', *OASE* 90 (2013): 31.

Sofie De Caigny, on behalf of the editorial board

Coffee roastery and carpenter's workshop, Ghent

Büro Juliane Greb

Two young Ghent entrepreneurs, a coffee roaster and a carpenter, decided to pool their resources and build themselves a new workspace. They purchased a plot on the Wiedauwkaai industrial site, a redundant piece of railway infrastructure recently redeveloped by the City of Ghent, the urban development company sogent, and the national Belgian railway company NMBS/SNCB. The site, which still includes a railway track, is wedged between the residential fabric and the Wondelgemse Meersen, a new green artery with walking and cycling paths between Wondelgem and the city centre. The close proximity of housing, greenery and soft mobility implies a lower level of activity compared to the international seaport, which moved north long ago. However, the clients leaned even further in the direction of 'pleasant industry' when they approached Juliane Greb, a young German architect with offices in Ghent and Cologne, to design the building.

Greb's design makes playful use of the methods and materials typically employed in industrial premises. Like many warehouses, the building mainly comprises a steel structure and prefabricated concrete panels. A lowered corner in the volume, however, quickly reveals the quirkiness of the plan. A courtyard, in the shape of an equilateral triangle, divides the rectangular box (the ultimate starting point for an industrial shed) into three unequal parts. One of the triangle's edges coincides with the centre line of the building, thereby marking off half the volume for the carpentry workshop, where the need for workspace is greatest. The other half is divided, on either side of the triangle, into a double-height coffee roastery and a darkened storage area for the beans. It is this space that explains the building's lowered corner, whose roof, incidentally, forms an outdoor terrace that can be reached from the mezzanine in the coffee roastery. On the other side of the same roof, a second door leads to the carpentry workshop's stairwell.

The entrance lies at the point where the low storage area meets the high stairwell: a triangular cut-out that mirrors the courtyard in the otherwise rectangular grid of concrete panels. A judiciously placed fluorescent light on the axis follows the perspective into the patio, where the sloping façade, yellow doors, aluminium joinery and pink columns behind the glass offer a view as mysterious as it is playful. The triangular opening in the façade is flanked by a pink gate for the delivery of goods, while a slightly larger variant with black-and-white stripes is used by the carpentry workshop. The play of colours continues inside: a purple hue for the roastery's metal structure, white on the balustrades and the spiral staircase to the mezzanine, and a blue lacquered structure in the carpentry workshop. Yellow doors and fluorescent lights are a recurrent feature. The daylight that enters through the patio and various other windows activates the colours yet further.

And yet the bold shapes and colours are not overwhelming. Each design decision has been carefully calibrated in relation to the grey mass (the industrial steel and concrete) that still underpins the project. The building thus succeeds in embracing the industrial construction typology while lending it a personality. How does one account for this? Is it down to the programme, the building's owners, the architect, the environment or a combination of these things? Or, on the contrary, is it the fact that it is so autonomous? To the building, it's all the same. There it stands, oozing self-confidence.

Petrus Kemme

```
COFFEE ROASTERY AND              Design                    Main contractor
CARPENTER'S WORKSHOP             2019                      Morti, Ghent
                                 Delivered                 Technical contractor
Office                           October 2021              Wille Ronald, Ghent
Büro Juliane Greb                Surface area              Technology studies
Website                          1,033 m²                  Emaze, Ghent
www.julianegreb.com              Volume                    EPB reporting
Address                          6,011 m³                  mijnEPB, Ghent
Tapuitstraat 1, Ghent            Total building cost       Photographer
Client                           € 615,000 - excl. VAT     Petter Krag
Vandekerchove & Bar,             Total building cost per m²
Cube4garden                      € 595 - excl. VAT
```

Situation plan

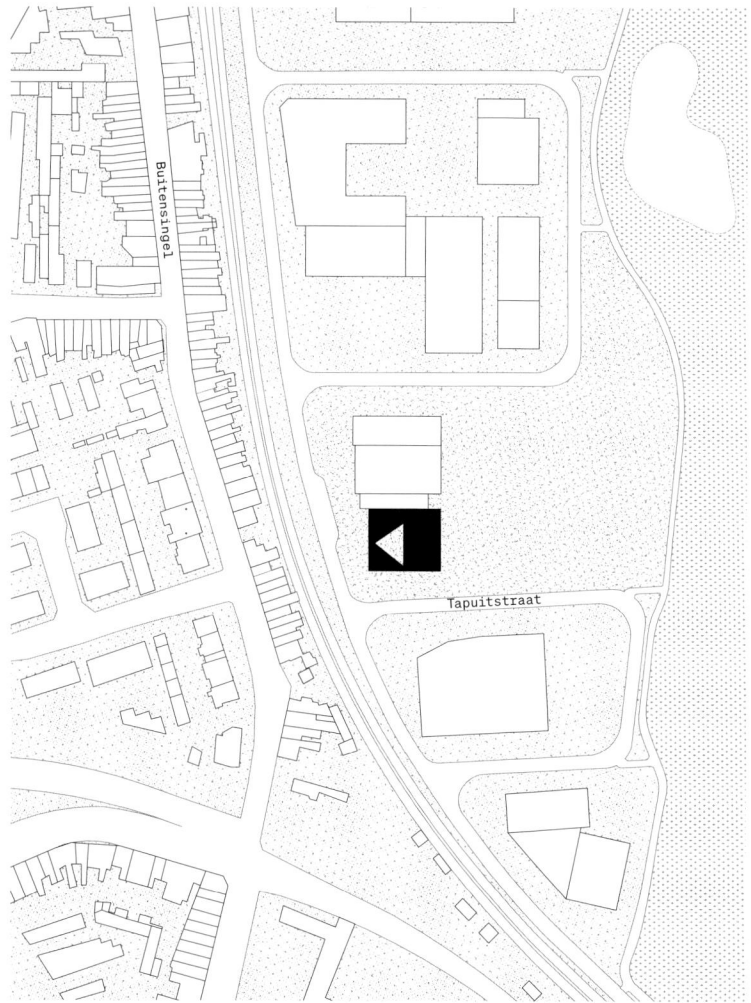

Section Aa

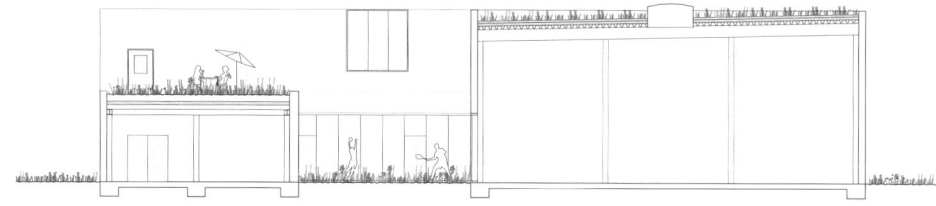

Büro Juliane Greb

Level 1
Ground floor

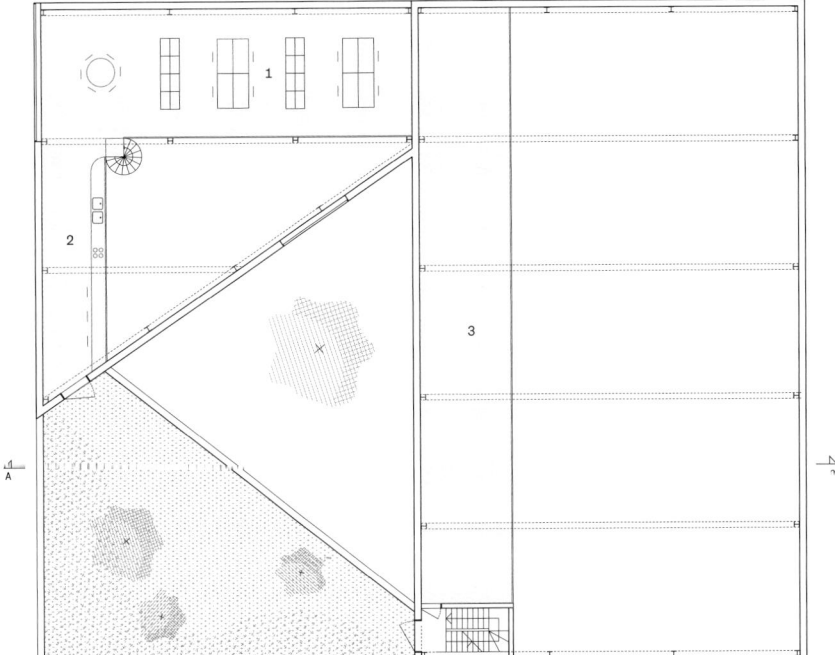

1. Packaging and office
2. Tasting room (cupping)
3. Workshop storage

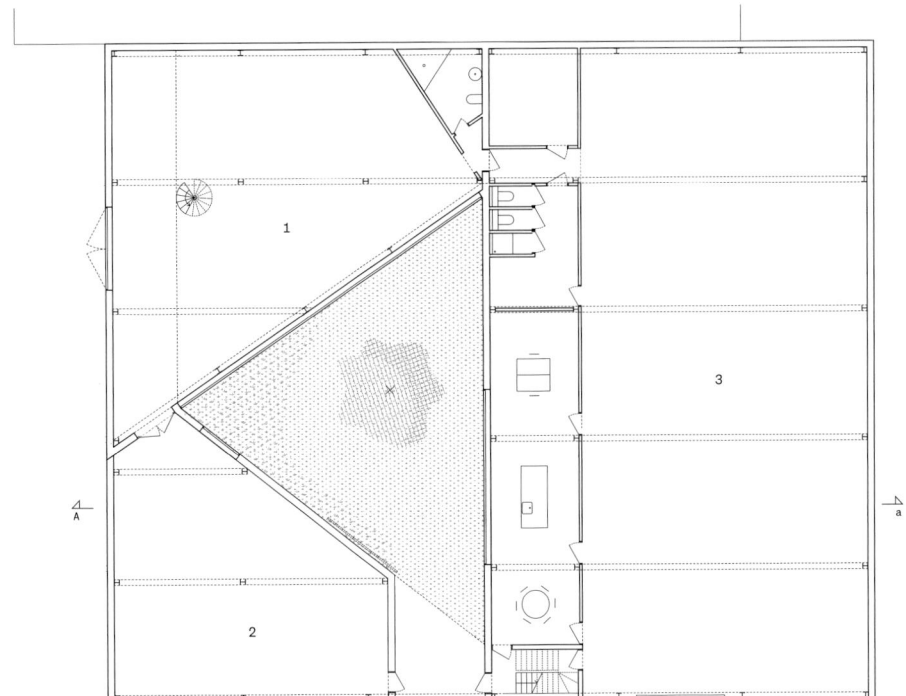

1. Coffee roastery
2. Coffee bean shop
3. Carpenter's workshop

Coffee roastery and carpenter's workshop

Coffee roastery and carpenter's workshop

Polderbos Crematorium, Ostend

OFFICE Kersten Geers David Van Severen and Richard Venlet

Ostend's new Polderbos Crematorium by OFFICE Kersten Geers David Van Severen and Richard Venlet lies just outside the city in a corner of a large polder field. Set back from the road, the landscape design around the building introduces some of its architectural features. Lines of trees form a system of parallel bands whose width follows the rhythm and orientation of the internal partitions that organize the building planimetrically. As visitors leave their vehicles in the car park, the building reveals itself through the shape of its roof, a large, tilted, flat surface pierced by three big, abstract volumes and supported by a regular system of concrete columns placed along its perimeter. Planimetrically, the roof is oriented parallel to the main road and slightly rotated compared to the bands of the landscape. For visitors approaching the crematorium for a ceremony, the roof's inclination, with the lower side facing the car park, renders the building as a welcoming domestic architecture. Unlike a contemporary temple, the crematorium seems to challenge some of the most common tropes about architecture and the celebration of death. Instead of monumental façades, elevations are defined by the alternation of abstract metal panelling – at times perforated, at others simply corrugated – and bare concrete surfaces. The different orientation between the roof and the internal spaces creates, on the outside, along the edges of the building, an irregular covered arcade that can be used to gather and shelter smaller groups of visitors.

After entering the building through a simple wooden door, visitors find themselves in a large, longitudinal space, the first of a series of parallel strips that organize the building plan. Open at the two shorter edges through large glass walls, this space lets visitors view the landscape from the inside while the perforated metal panels protect the interior from any exterior gaze. The two longer elevations of this lobby space – simple, concrete walls that reveal the pattern and colour of their timber formwork – are characterized by the rhythm of openings cut at regular intervals in the concrete surface. These are now used to place timber doors towards the two main celebration rooms or multiple service spaces, now filled with timber and wool-fabric panelling with an elegant built-in bench. While the elements in the main lobby are bright yellow, the two main celebration halls are a softer yet warm white. These two rooms, one larger and one smaller, are lit naturally through large skylights in the tilted roof and by the same large, glass opening towards the landscape. Furnished with beautiful plywood benches, each room is striking on account of its simplicity and warmth and the gentle way in which the architecture offers itself as a means to accompany the mourning and grieving of those attending the funeral functions. In each room, in front of the glass wall, a large, upholstered panel offers itself as a background for the speakers while defining at its back an intimate space for family members. Beyond these two rooms, a last strip contains all the crematorium's technical spaces.

While architecture has traditionally dramatized the condition of death and grief through heaviness and monumentality, the Polderbos Crematorium in Ostend reveals that death should rather be seen as a celebration of life for those that remain.

Martino Tattara

POLDERBOS CREMATORIUM

Office
OFFICE Kersten Geers David Van Severen and Richard Venlet
Website
www.officekgdvs.com
Address
Grintweg 120, Ostend
Client
Intercommunal Association for Crematorium Management in Ostend (OVCO)

Design
January 2014
Delivered
January 2021
Surface area
2,000 m²
Total building cost
€ 3,470,000 - excl. VAT
Total building cost per m²
€ 1,735 - excl. VAT
Main contractor
UTIL Struktuurstudies, Schaarbeek

Technology studies
Henk Pijpaert Engineering, Oudenaarde
Landscape design
Bureau Bas Smets, Brussels
Photographer
Bas Princen

Situation plan

Section Aa

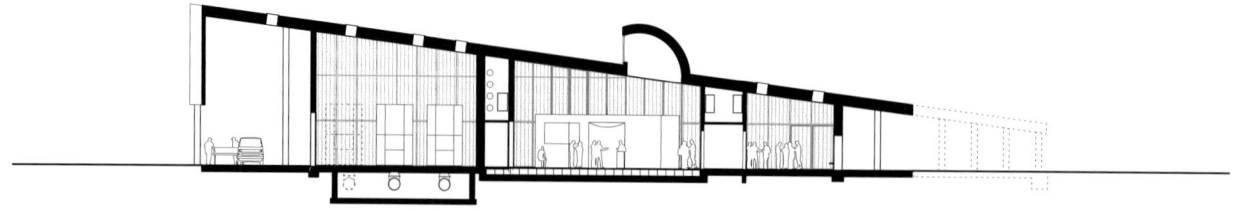

OFFICE Kersten Geers David Van Severen and Richard Venlet

Ground floor

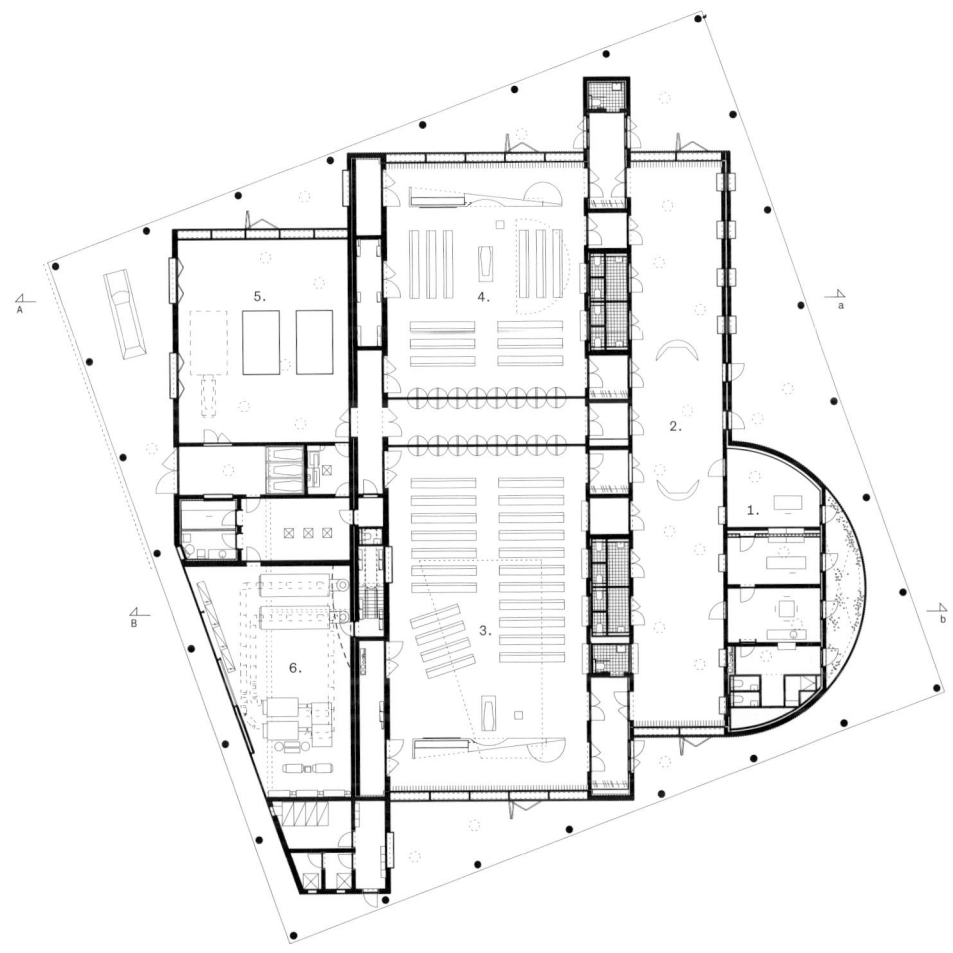

1. Staff rooms
2. Foyer
3. Main auditorium
4. Small auditorium
5. Furnace area
6. Technical area

Section Bb

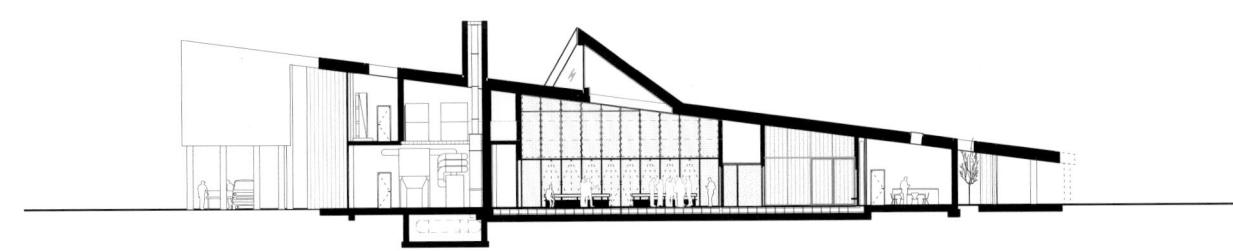

Polderbos Crematorium

OFFICE Kersten Geers David Van Severen and Richard Venlet

Infrabel Academy for railway infrastructure, Sint-Jans-Molenbeek

Atelier Kempe Thill architects and planners
and Canevas architectes et ingénieurs

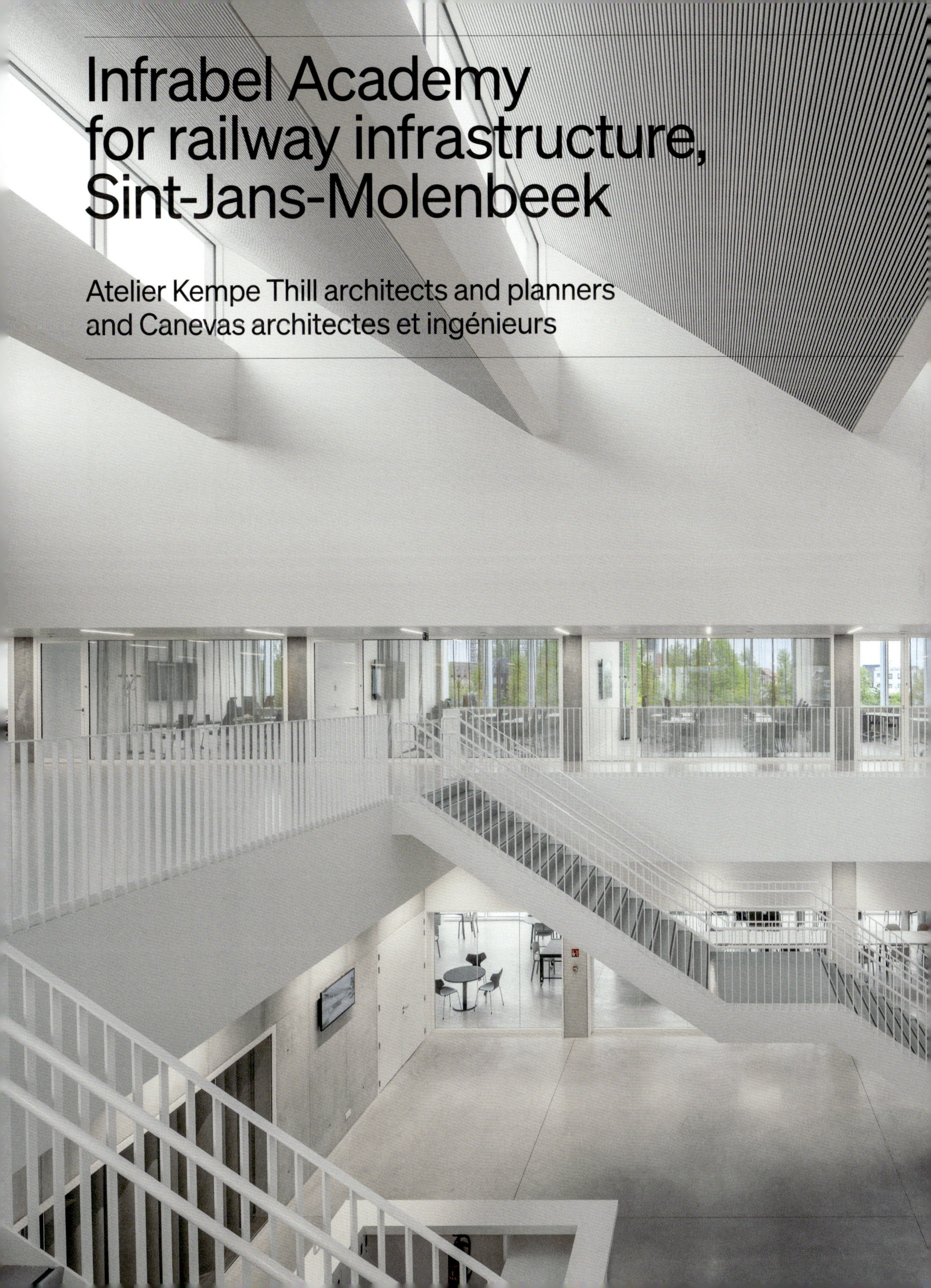

The Infrabel Academy is located in the Brussels municipality of Molenbeek, between the L28 railway tracks and the post-war housing blocks of De Roovere Machtens. The building is a training campus for the state-owned company Infrabel, the builder and maintainer of the Belgian rail network. As if to confirm the company's public-transport function, the new building can be accessed directly from the Brussels-West Station and offers only few spots for car parking. Infrabel staff come here from all over the country for training on how to maintain tracks, manage signals or solve the various crises that can occur on Belgium's dense rail network.

The project is part of Brussels Productive City, an aspiration of the Brussels Government Architect (BMA). Since 2008 Kristian Borret and his team have been reflecting on how to reintroduce (semi-)industry into the city. The aim is to offer a mix of uses in the urban context, creating blue-collar jobs and increasing economic activity. Following this ambition, the territorial development plan of Brussels-West includes activation of the abandoned zones along the train tracks. As a result of the competition organized by Infrabel and the BMA, Atelier Kempe Thill was commissioned to design the academy together with Canevas. Their design celebrates the site's industrial character by introducing corrugated metal sheets combined with aluminium slats over glazed surfaces which evoke the mechanical aesthetics of movement and speed.

The building sits on top of the metro line. The width of the volume is determined by the walls of the metro tunnel. These walls were also treated as load-bearing curtain walls and two rows of columns were added for structural stability. Since these new columns touch the bottom of the tunnel, they were constructed at night, when the metro was not in operation. Beams measuring 1.3 metres in height were placed on top of the metro tunnel's existing walls and the new rows of columns. This operation raised the ground level on the site, making it necessary to adapt the entrances of neighbouring buildings.

The building programme is divided in two: theory and practice. These two wings have their own entrances under the passage connecting the metro platform with the city. Entering both wings gives a similar feeling of spaciousness as the daylight entering from the skylights of the atriums welcomes Infrabel staff. The wide staircases and simply detailed circulation areas reflect a spatial quality that implies the company's respectful attitude towards its staff. The theory wing consists of an auditorium and cafeteria on the ground level and classrooms on the first floor, daylight entering from both the façade and the skylights through the glazed walls. The practice wing is longer than the theory wing and therefore contains two atriums, one at the entrance and the other between ateliers and classrooms. A series of visual connections have been created between the training spaces – vistas stretching from inside the building towards the atriums or towards the ateliers in the garden. The Infrabel Academy functions as a holistic learning space in which staff can see how to fix a railway track or solve a problem with signals while walking in and around the building.

Hülya Ertas

INFRABEL ACADEMY FOR RAILWAY INFRASTRUCTURE

Offices
Atelier Kempe Thill architects and planners and Canevas architectes et ingénieurs

Websites
www.atelierkempethill.com
www.canevas.be

Address
Rue Dubois-Thorn 105, Sint-Jans-Molenbeek

Client
Infrabel

Design
May 2016

Delivered
December 2020

Surface area
9,024 m²

Volume
48,455 m³

Total building cost
€ 23,600,000 – excl. VAT

Total building cost per m²
€ 1,800 – excl. VAT

Main contractor
BPC, Watermaal-Bosvoorde

Acoustics studies
ATS acoustique, Liège

Landscape design
LAND landschapsarchitect, Antwerp

Infrastructure studies
Greisch, Brussels

Photographer
Ulrich Schwarz

Situation plan

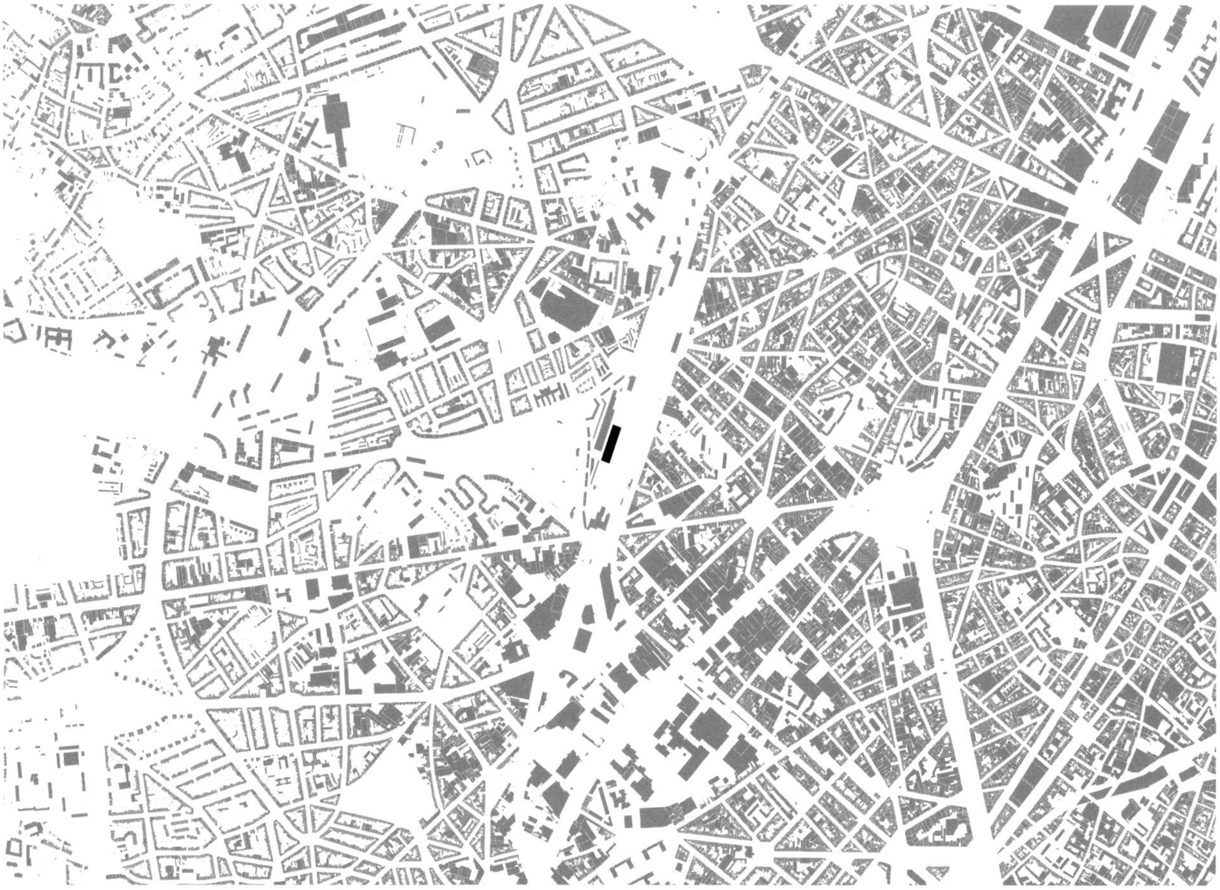

Section Aa

Section Bb

Atelier Kempe Thill architects and planners and Canevas architectes et ingénieurs

Level 2
Level 1
Ground floor

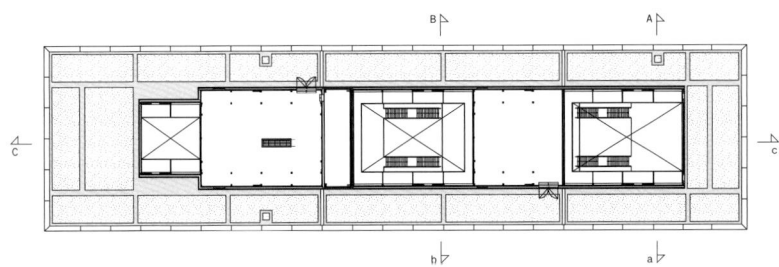

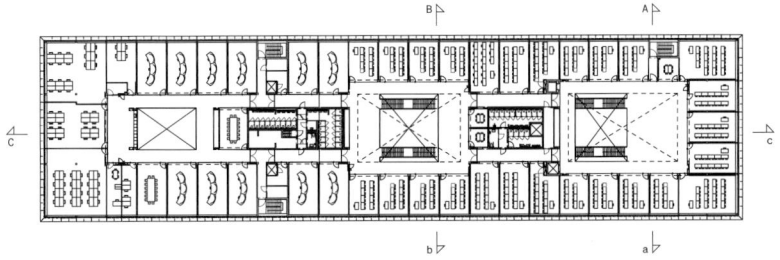

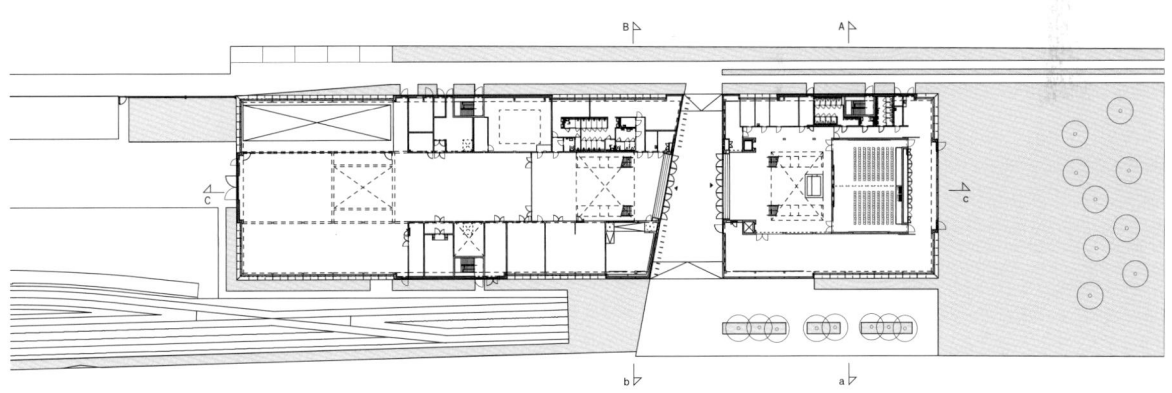

Section Cc

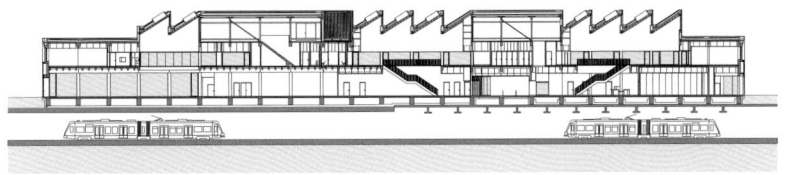

Infrabel Academy for railway infrastructure

Atelier Kempe Thill architects and planners and Canevas architectes et ingénieurs

Infrabel Academy for railway infrastructure

Gare Maritime, Brussels

Neutelings Riedijk Architecten

In light of today's climate crisis, one of the most sustainable options is to stop encroaching on undeveloped space. A new engagement for existing buildings is essential, and Gare Maritime is an inspiring example of the way forward. Neutelings Riedijk Architecten have placed twelve pavilions beneath the gigantic 140 by 280 metres canopies of the former freight depot constructed on the Thurn & Taxis site in the early twentieth century. The pavilions provide 40,000 m² of hospitality, retail and office space.

The ambition was to transform the art nouveau station into a city where it never rains. The pavilions are housed beneath the side canopies of the original building. They are accessible via lanes and small squares that open onto two 16 metres wide promenades. The architects allowed the central railway canopy to remain visible and have transformed it into a majestic boulevard. The green areas by Omgeving complete this composition and provide additional thermal buffering, alongside the natural ventilation. The balconies of the pavilions mean that there are 'eyes on the street', and the striking criss-cross stairways serve as a stage for an urban interplay of seeing and being seen.

The dimensions of the pavilions follow the rhythm and spans of the existing station canopies. Old and new fit harmoniously together, in terms of both dimensions and materialization. All the pavilions and stairways are constructed from prefabricated CLT elements (cross-laminated timber). The existing canopies created the ideal conditions for building the gigantic wooden structure as they kept the construction site dry. Furthermore, the decision to use this material allowed the existing foundations to be retained, and all interventions are reversible. The wood reappears in the original finish of the canopies, which were remarkably well preserved below the thick layer of soot deposited by the old steam trains.

The project is an expression of sustainability in several ways. Firstly, it ensures that the mercantile history of Thurn & Taxis remains visible. This cultural form of sustainability seems self-evident, given the exceptional architectural value of the station building. Nevertheless, before the developer Extensa joined forces with Neutelings Riedijk, it asked a number of architects from both Belgium and abroad for their vision of the repurposing. Certain proposals were more spectacular than others, and all of them broke through the logic of the existing volume. Neutelings Riedijk's relatively unassuming proposal does not just attest to the firm's respect for the site's history. The more modest proposal also provided an interesting business case for persuading the developer to restore the existing building – which is not a protected monument – where necessary.

In addition, every effort was made to apply the latest standards and techniques pertaining to energy, water and material usage to Gare Maritime, which is far from self-evident in a building that is more than a century old. Considerable quantities of bluestone and paved flooring were recovered and reused on site. For maximum sustainability, new technology was integrated into existing building elements where possible.

Finally, the project also aims to make a sustainable contribution to the development of Brussels. In a heavily built-up area with a relatively large number of young people and high unemployment, the project offers much-needed breathing space. The question is whether this social form of sustainability can be maintained once the dense residential development for the upper middle classes around Gare Maritime has been completed. In any case, the Brussels Government Architect ensured that several forms of manufacturing industry were retained on the Thurn & Taxis site in order to somewhat temper the area's already overly exclusive character and hopefully to offer employment to young people from the area.

Sofie De Caigny

GARE MARITIME

Office
Neutelings Riedijk Architecten
Website
www.neutelings-riedijk.com
Address
Picardstraat 7-11,
Brussels
Client
Extensa
Design
January 2017
Delivered
June 2020

Surface area
45,000 m²
Volume
450,000 m³
Total building cost
€ 100,000,000 - excl. VAT, incl. restoration
Total building cost per m²
€ 2,000 - excl. VAT, incl. restoration
Main contractor
MBG, Antwerp
Timber construction contractor
Züblin, Breda[NL]
Stability studies
Ney & Partners, Watermaal-Bosvoorde

Technology studies
Boydens engineering, Brussels
Landscape design
OMGEVING, Berchem
Acoustics studies
Venac, Brussels
Structural engineering design
Bureau Bouwtechniek, Antwerp
Restoration architect
Altstadt, Brussels
Artworks
Henri Jacobs, Brussels
Photographer
Filip Dujardin

Situation plan

0 33 165m

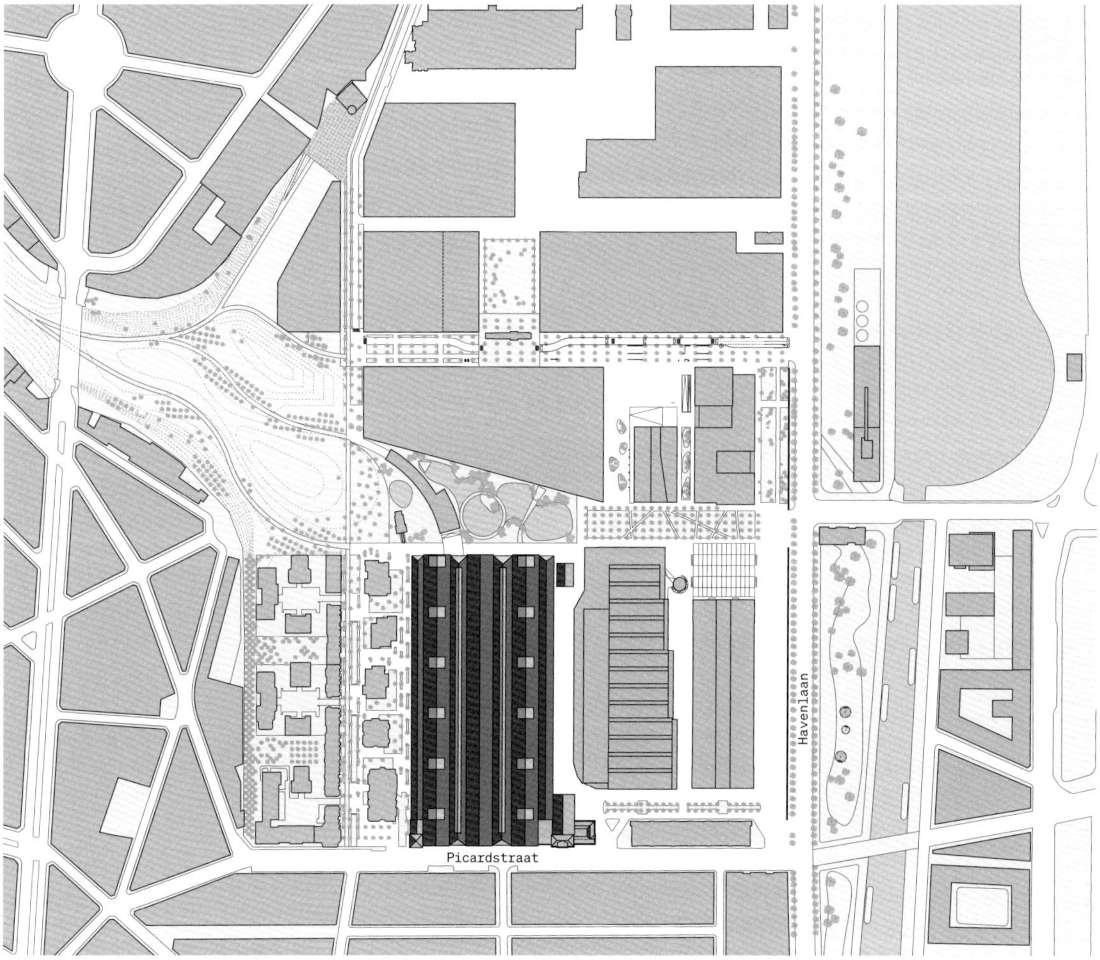

South façade

0 10 50m

Neutelings Riedijk Architecten 36

Ground floor

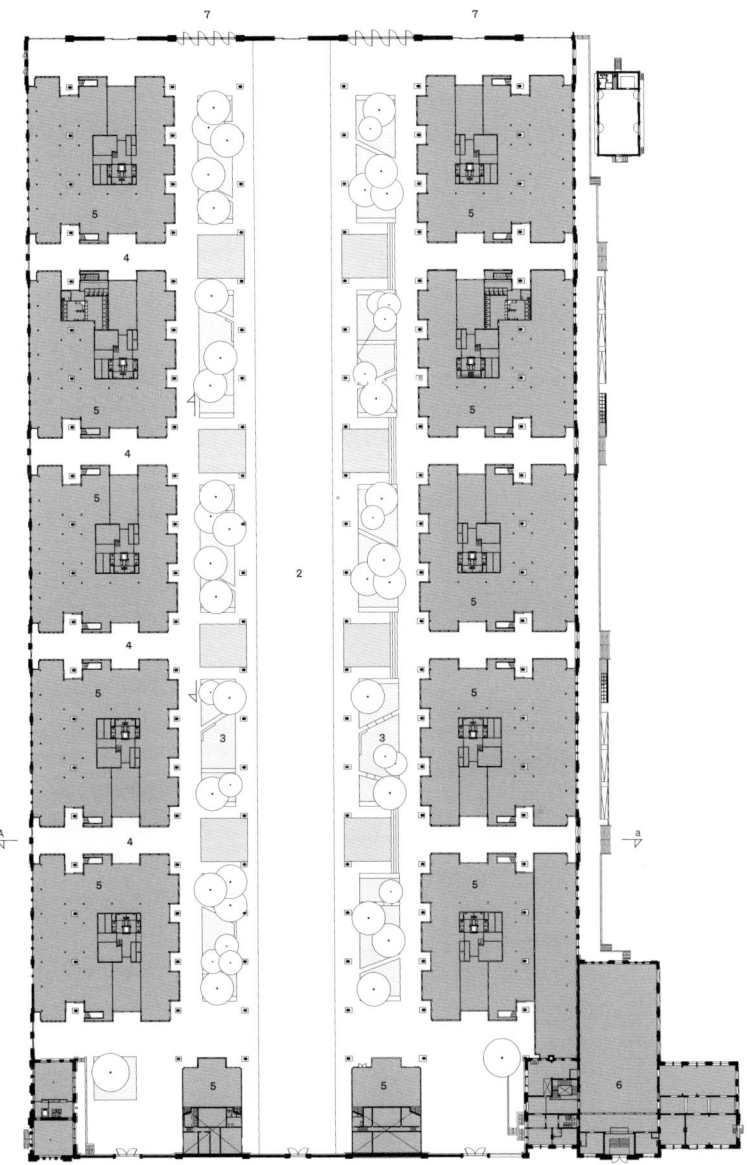

1. Picardstraat entrance
2. Public event space
3. Gardens
4. Inner streets
5. Pavilion for offices and retail
6. Maison de la poste
7. Park entrance

Section Aa

Gare Maritime

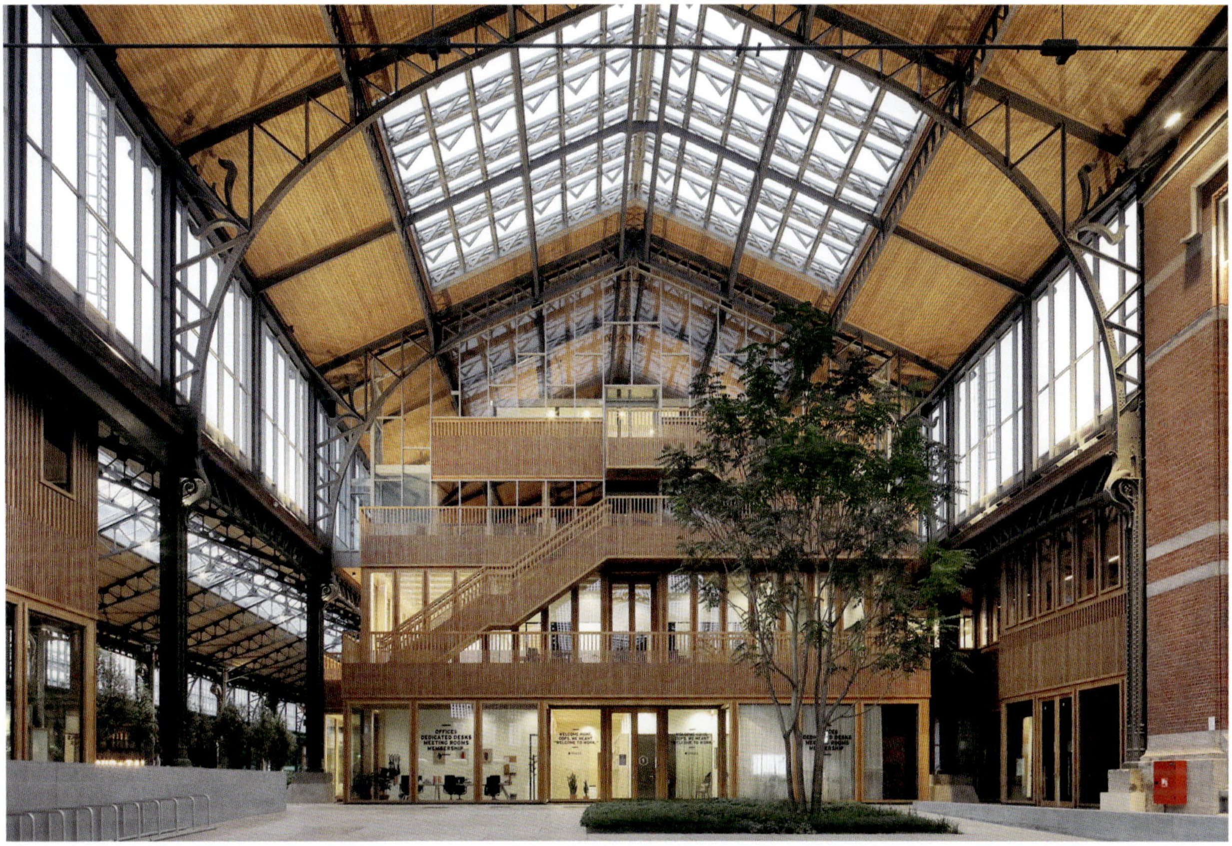

Gare Maritime

ZNA Cadix hospital, Antwerp

Robbrecht en Daem architecten and VK architects + engineers

This urban hospital was commissioned through a design and build procedure initiated in 2011 for which VK architects + engineers collaborated with Robbrecht en Daem architecten. It is intended to serve the metropolitan region and replace a series of existing facilities, including those of the nineteenth-century Stuivenberg hospital. A programme of 65,000 m² on a relatively small site – at Spoor Noord in the renewed Cadix harbour district of Antwerp – required its many medical and supporting departments to be organized vertically. The building volume accordingly consists of a substantial plinth, surmounted by an L-shaped configuration of higher blocks, culminating in a 'tower'. The mass of the whole is penetrated by several courtyards, a clear horizontal and vertical distribution system, and an extensive open public terrace at third-floor level that separates polyclinics, consultation rooms, study centres and medical technical services below from treatment and administrative areas above. The courtyards, each with a specific character, bring light into the deep interior – even into levels below ground – and significantly diminish the sense of the building's size. They are the dominant figures of a 'healing environment' shared by hospital staff, patients and visitors. The mass of the whole is further relieved on the exterior by the painterly deployment of pale-blue and pale-green ceramic cladding panels on alternating surfaces, and a regular distribution of identical windows projecting slightly from these surfaces, reflecting the light of the sky. Its repetitive patterns, at both large and small scale, produce a kind of monumentality. Yet an accumulation of apparently simple decisions renders the volume of the hospital less substantial – almost as if it were an image – and more light-hearted than any of the large structures in its vicinity.

A corresponding character of 'lightness' informs the public's contact with the hospital at street level. The ground floor is both clear and accessible: an inner street runs the length of the building, creating a truly public interior, with significant spaces directly connected to it that seem to tell the story of the whole complex. Among these is a deep courtyard that seems to incorporate and involve the entire structure, and a spiralling, monumental stair that leads to the public terrace on the third floor. Sheltered but otherwise open to the elements, this elevated 'plaza' serves as both a functional boundary and a visible interruption of the building's mass. It is also directly accessible from the city: at one corner, another external public staircase, visible upon approach from the city centre, brings the public here. It is a terrain that is at once ambiguous and free, a relief from the intensity of the hospital's working parts. From here, one senses the significance of the courtyards and one comes to understand that the hospital is a whole world and in so being is tied to its historical precedents, from monastic cloisters to the Hôtel-Dieu at Beaune.

As one rises through the structure to the patient rooms and the spaces that support them, and further still to the administrative areas atop the building, light abounds. Spaces are saturated with colour, predominantly pale mint green: a complete environment that has, miraculously, banished the fact that one is in the midst of a densely configured machine that sustains the life and operations of the complex. Such machines typically reduce the patient to a subject without identity or agency, but here, as is evident in the design of the patient rooms, surroundings have been designed with empathy, attention to intimacy, and something like tenderness. As one lies in bed, the window, which from the street below appeared as an abstract and formal device, has become at once a generous frame through which one can see the city and its territory, and a place where one's friends or loved ones might sit – where, if feeling able to, one might look out at the world as if it were one's own.

Mark Pimlott

ZNA CADIX HOSPITAL

Offices
Robbrecht en Daem architecten and VK architects + engineers
Websites
www.robbrechtendaem.com
www.vkgroup.be
Address
Kempenstraat - Noorderlaan, Antwerp
Client
K.EUR Development for the Hospital Network Antwerp (ZNA)
Design
2012

Delivered
October 2021
Surface area
65,000 m² + 42,000 m² underground parking
Volume
280,000 m³
Total building cost
€ 187,000,000 - excl. VAT
Total building cost per m²
€ 1,750 - excl. VAT
Main contractor
THV Ziekenhuis Noord (BAM Interbuild - MBG, temporary association)
Stability engineer and technology
VK architects + engineers, Merelbeke
Landscape architect (patios)
Robbrecht en Daem architecten, Ghent

Urban planning and construction
VK architects + engineers, Merelbeke
OMGEVING, Berchem
Robbrecht en Daem architecten, Ghent
Acoustics engineer
VK architects + engineers, Roeselare
Transport & mobility
OMGEVING, Berchem
Project manager
VK architects + engineers, Merelbeke
Budget control
Interbuild - MBG, Antwerp
VK architects + engineers, Merelbeke
Photographer
Filip Dujardin

Situation plan

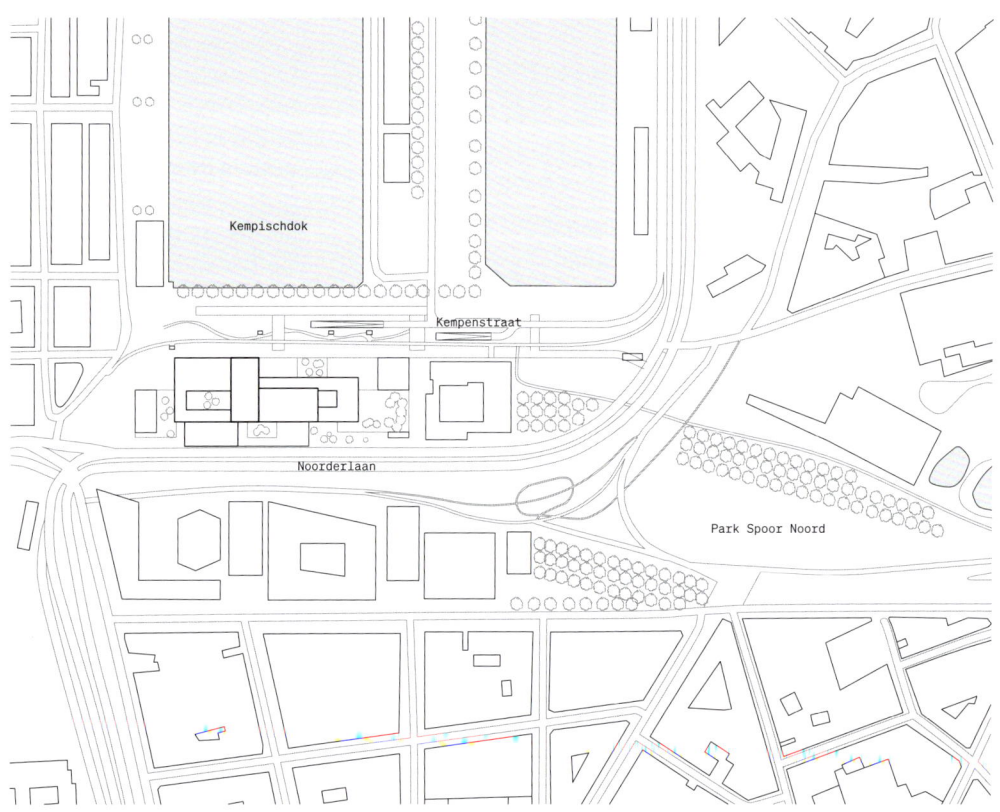

Section Aa

Section Bb

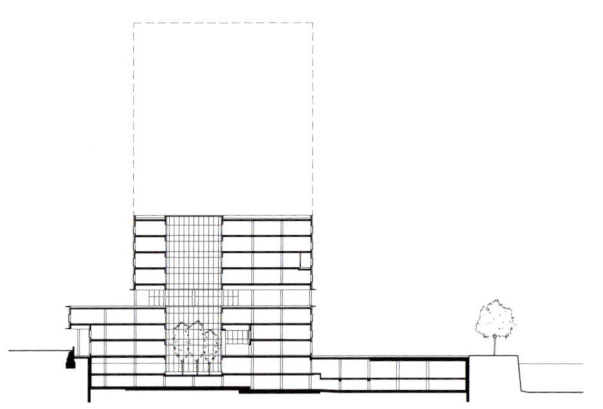

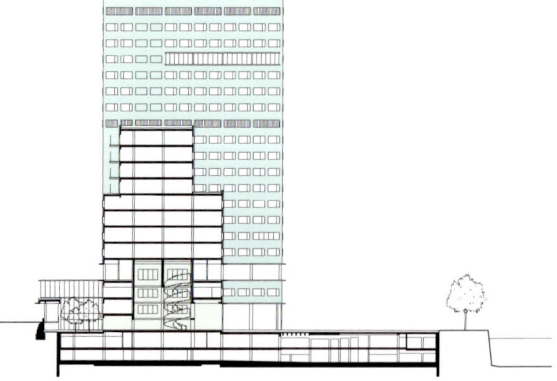

Robbrecht en Daem architecten and VK architects + engineers

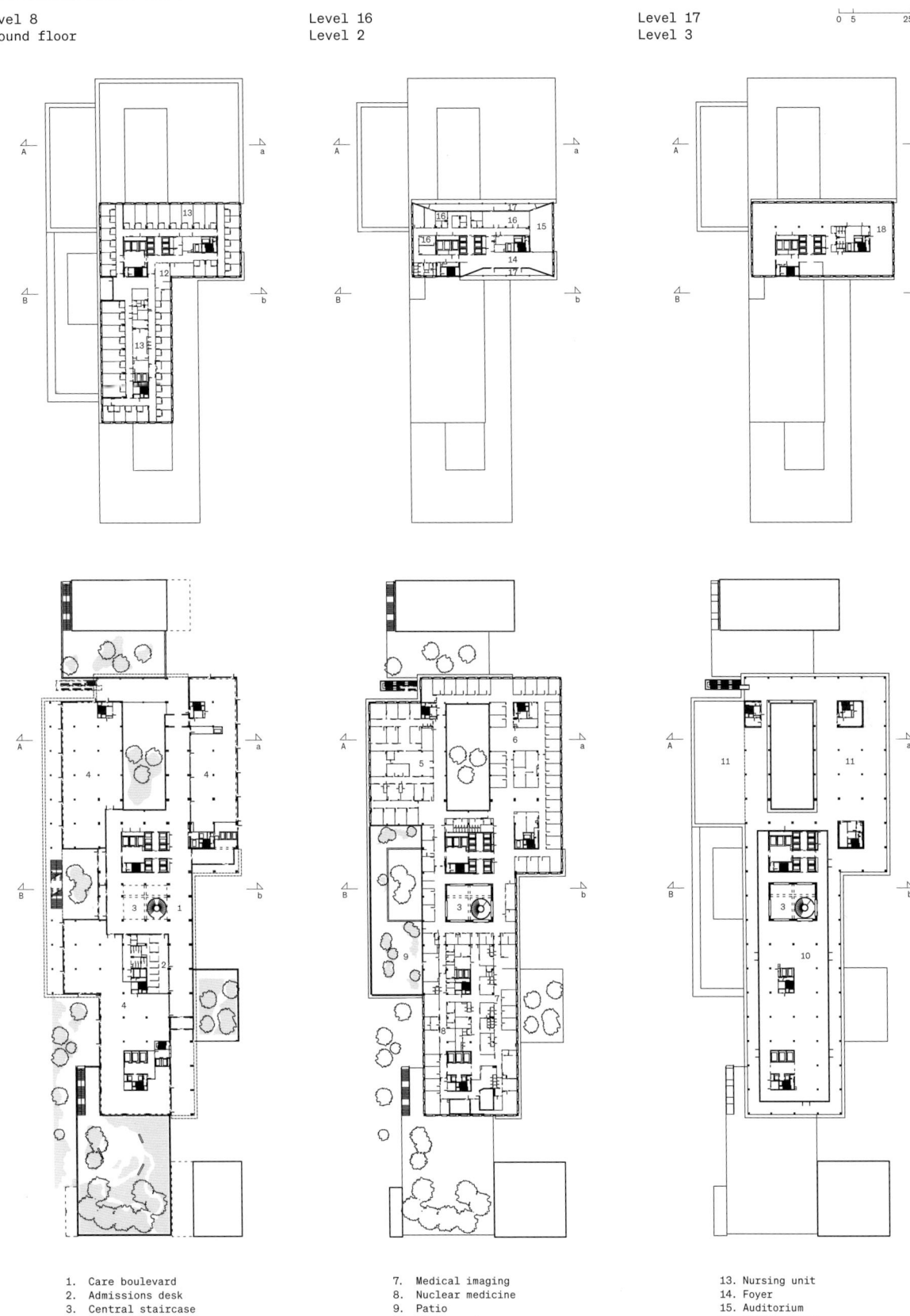

Level 8
Ground floor

Level 16
Level 2

Level 17
Level 3

1. Care boulevard
2. Admissions desk
3. Central staircase
4. Commercial space
5. Day hospital
6. Consultations
7. Medical imaging
8. Nuclear medicine
9. Patio
10. Restaurant
11. Panoramic terrace
12. Central nursing station
13. Nursing unit
14. Foyer
15. Auditorium
16. Meeting room
17. Terrace
18. Open-plan office

ZNA Cadix hospital

Robbrecht en Daem architecten and VK architects + engineers

ZNA Cadix hospital

Nekkersput social housing, Ghent

DBLV architecten (Dierendonck–Blancke–Lust–Van De Ginste)

For many years, the high-rises that characterize the landscape of many Flemish cities were identified as the relics of a bygone past. Generally built in the 1960s and 1970s, this large housing stock today faces a process of material decay. For a long time, the only possible solution appeared to be their demolition and reconstruction. But in recent years this approach has increasingly been challenged. Perhaps following some exemplary experiences of retrofitting of large-scale modern housing in countries such as France and the Netherlands, and because of the growing environmental concerns about the incredible amount of waste that demolishing such housing stock would generate, some social housing agencies have started exploring alternative paths.

A first such experiment in the retrofitting of a social housing slab in Flanders is represented by the Nekkersput block by Dierendonckblancke architecten and L.U.S.T. architecten in Ghent. The firms recently completed a pilot project in the retrofitting of modern housing. Completed at the start of the 1970s and located in the north-east of the city just beyond the ring road, the block was an eight-storey building, typologically characterized by two vertical circulation cores, each giving access to four single-facing apartments on each floor. This meant that, given the building's orientation, each apartment's windows faced either east or west. In engaging with the existing building, the architects removed all secondary partitions and retained the main concrete structure made of transversal load-bearing walls and horizontal slabs, which were thought to still have a long lifespan. By stripping down the buildings, the architects managed to grasp the potential of the existing concrete framework to accommodate a much richer set of living types made of larger duplex units and smaller studios. Instead of a building typified by the repetition of identical apartments, by reducing horizontal circulation to only three of the eight floors, the architects were able to save space and thereby obtain within the same volume a richer set of duplex units, each characterized by windows on both elevations and incorporating within the space of an apartment some of the qualities normally found in family houses. Besides the capacity of these different types to accommodate the demographic conditions of today's social housing inhabitants – with the growing need for social housing agencies to accommodate either small or large households – the new units offer more privacy, better lighting conditions and more flexible plans within which to organize everyday activities. Each of the larger units in plan is characterized by a living room spanning the two elevations, with the kitchen positioned in the middle. Instead of being isolated within the plan of the apartment, this space acquires a central role within the familiar organization of daily activities. In addition to typological reinvention, the intervention also comprises the recladding of the building with a new, light-colour brick façade, the addition on the western elevation of a light balcony structure offering all units an external space, and the construction of two new volumes with extra living units.

These simple yet radical operations go beyond mere renovation and the upgrading of a decaying block to contemporary standards. They form some of the possible exemplary tools that would support intervention in other similar instances of modern housing heritage, revealing that large-scale modern housing architecture is not something of the past but rather an unfinished project seeking to be reinvented.

Martino Tattara

NEKKERSPUT SOCIAL HOUSING

Office
DBLV architecten
(Dierendonck-Blancke-Lust-Van De Ginste)
Website
www.dlbvarchitecten.eu
Address
Nekkersputstraat 61/187, Ghent
Client
De Ghentse Haard
(social housing association)

Design
April 2014
Delivered
May 2020
Surface area
8,230 m² above ground
650 m² underground
Volume
22,488 m³
Total building cost
€ 8,827,009 - excl. VAT
Total building cost per m²
€ 995 - excl. VAT

Main contractor
BBC Bekaert Building Company, Waregem
Stability studies
Sileghem & Partners, Zwevegem
Technology studies
Tech 3, Ghent
Landscape design
Lieve Van De Ginste
EPB and ventilation studies, safety coordination
V.E.T.O. & Partner, Oosterzele
Photographer
Filip Dujardin

Situation plan

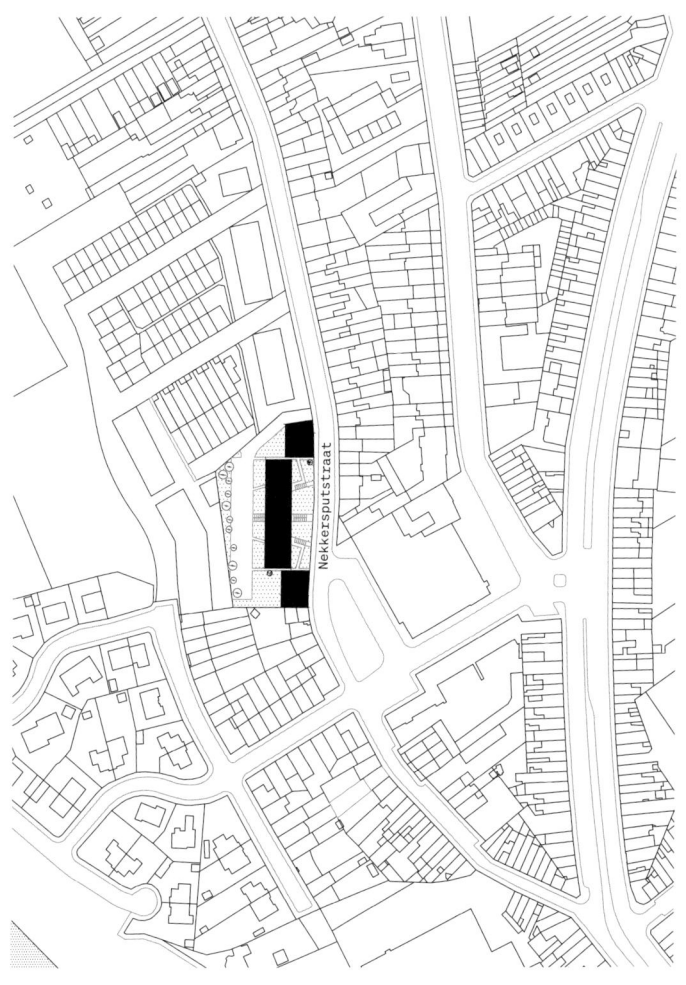

Section Aa

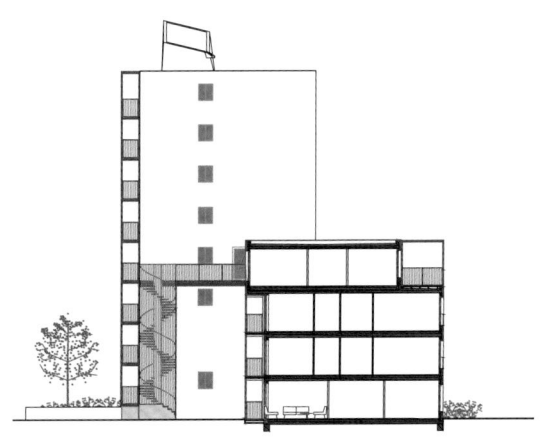

Section Bb

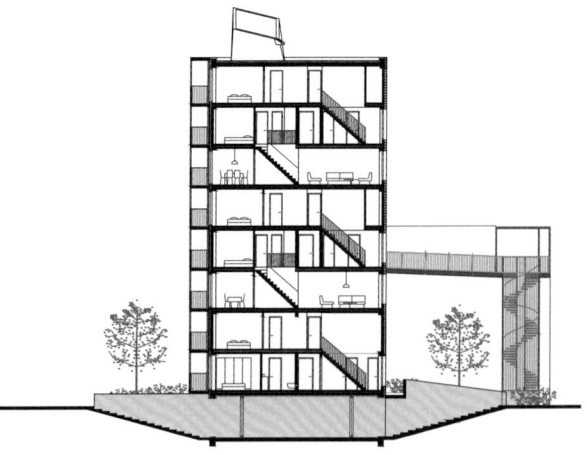

DBLV architecten (Dierendonck-Blancke-Lust-Van De Ginste)

Level 3
Level 2
Level 1
Ground floor

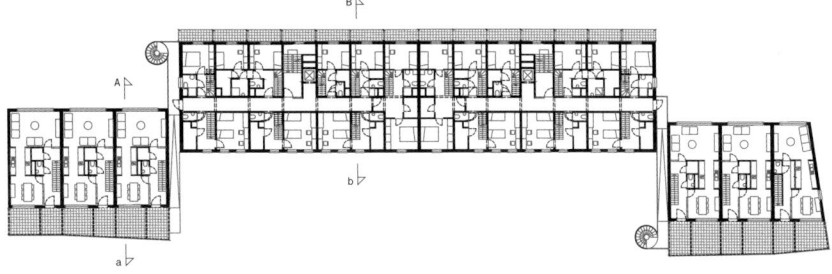

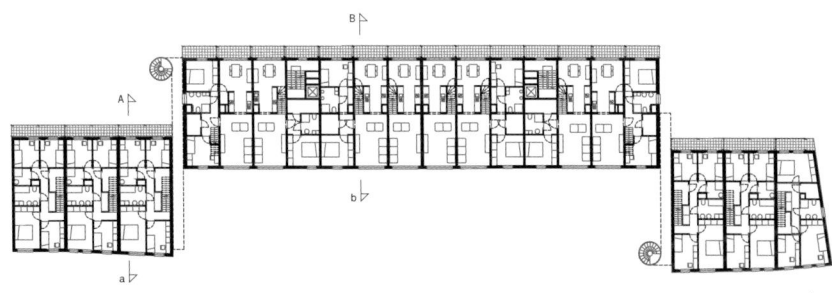

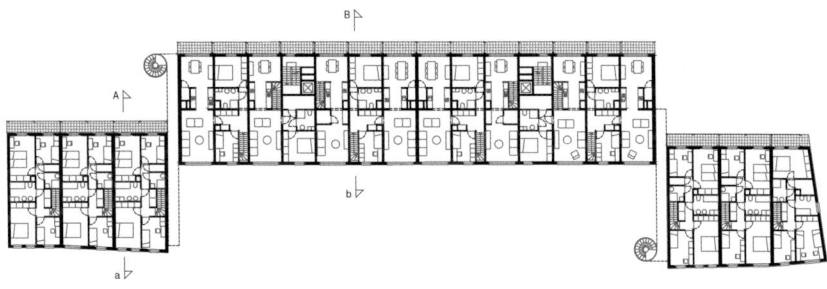

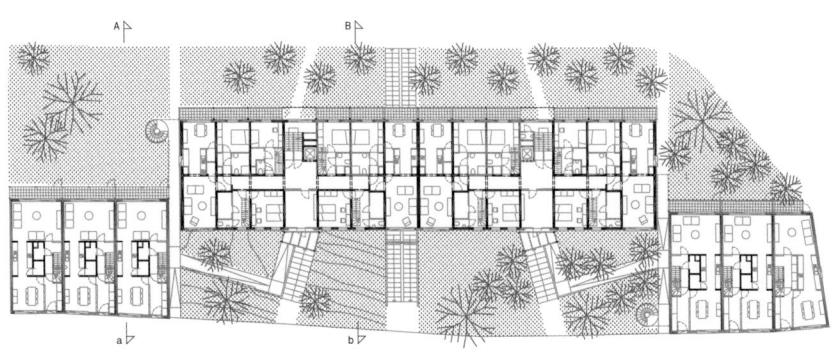

Nekkersput social housing

DBLV architecten (Dierendonck–Blancke–Lust–Van De Ginste)

Malibran youth centre, Elsene

Carton123 architecten

Building youth infrastructure is a balancing act. Municipal authorities want to retain oversight, perhaps even control, of what local youngsters are up to while the teenagers themselves need a bolthole that they can call their own. Things are no different in the Brussels municipality of Elsene, where Carton123 architecten has tackled this balancing act in the Malibran youth centre. Given that the area lacked a history of youth work, the architectural commission was closely interwoven with the aim of the organization: this included studying similar associations in Brussels (like JES) and winning the trust of the local youths, residents, administration and government. The design for Malibran thus involved helping to identify the elements that weigh heavily in this exercise, over and above the already difficult balancing act of building youth infrastructure.

Carton123 succeeds in this task with a succession of carefully crafted junctures. The public face of the project is the entrance in an existing corner house, with large windows on the ground floor that allow local residents (and officials) to see within. Once inside, the visitor encounters the supervisor's office in a key position: between the entrance hall and the corridor which subtly turns away, out of sight of the street and towards the rest of the youth centre. At the heart of the floor plan, the corridor runs diagonally through the kitchen to the hall in the new rear building. This consists of two parts, separated by a central concrete element that, upon closer inspection, turns out to be the chimney of the barbecue in the newly opened-up inner courtyard beside the kitchen. The rear wall is largely comprised of glass doors, some of which are screened on the outside by perforated metal panels on rails.

It is only on the other side of these windows and panels that the true face of Malibran is revealed. The rear building actually borders a unique open space in the dense urban fabric. Indeed, the corner where the entrance is situated is formed by Korte Malibranstraat, a modest cobbled street that winds up the hill in the enclosed interior of a nineteenth-century city block, passing a small square, a play area and the graffitied garden walls of the neighbouring town houses. With its robust materials, Malibran's new volume nestles in this island of 'improper' use, making it appear to lay definitive claim to the outdoor space on behalf of the young people. Once the windows and doors are thrown open, this seemingly forgotten park becomes the youth centre's de facto rear garden.

The door of a storeroom for outdoor furniture is marked with broad blue and whites stripes, a nod to coastal beach huts and a theme that is taken up in the front door of the old corner dwelling at the front. Furthermore, the dark-red facing bricks seem oversized, as do the perforations in the white sliding panels. These recall the same robust playfulness as the interior elements such as the barbecue chimney and the two T-shaped metal structures that (appear to) support the roof. In this robust playfulness, Malibran achieves a balance between control and freedom. Today, the chimney's exposed concrete is considerably less visible. A wooden bench, tailor-made to fit an idiosyncratic corner in the floor plan, wanders through the building. It is a wonderful idea for a centre that encourages young people to relax and do their own thing, both in- and outdoors.

Petrus Kemme

MALIBRAN YOUTH CENTRE		
Office Carton123 architecten	**Delivered** July 2020	**Stability studies** Lambda-max, Aalst
Website www.carton123.be	**Surface area** 310 m² (incl. terrace and patio)	**Technology studies** Tech3, Ghent
Address Petite Rue Malibran 14-16, Elsene	**Volume** 607 m³	**EPB reporting** EMS, Deinze
Client Municipality of Elsene	**Total building cost** € 560,000 – excl. VAT	**Safety coordination** 2bSafe, Glabbeek
Design May 2016	**Total building cost per m²** € 1,806 – excl. VAT	**Photographer** Olmo Peeters
	Main contractor Phénicks, Charleroi	

Ground floor

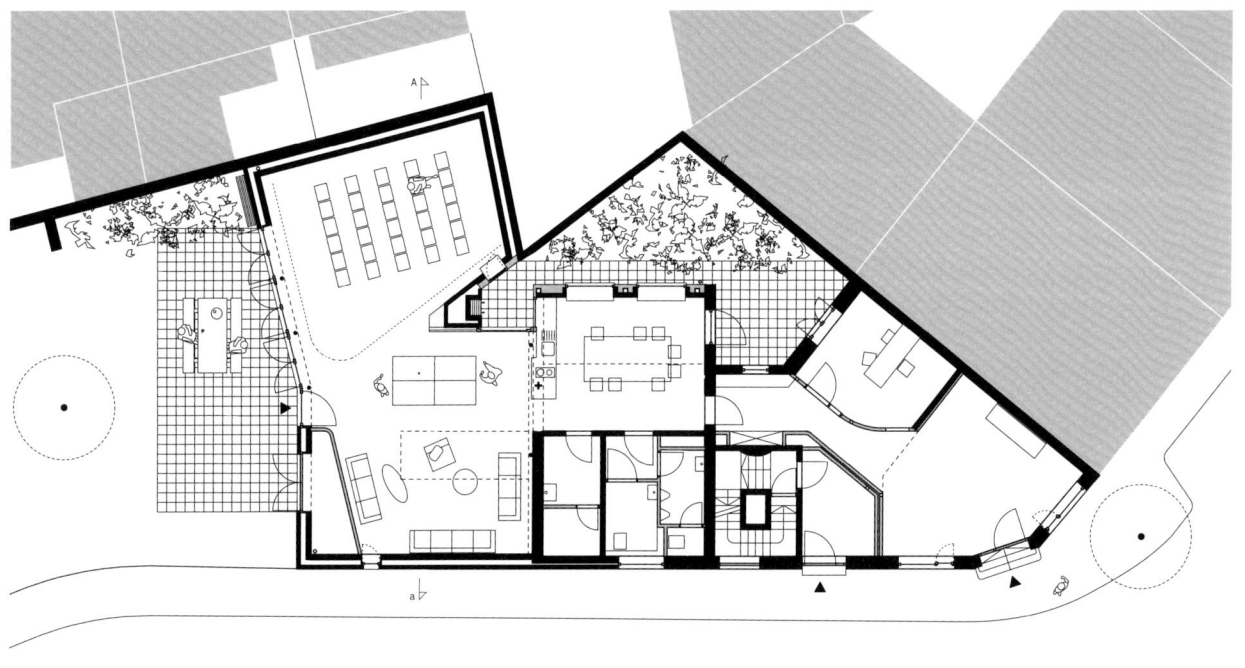

Section Aa

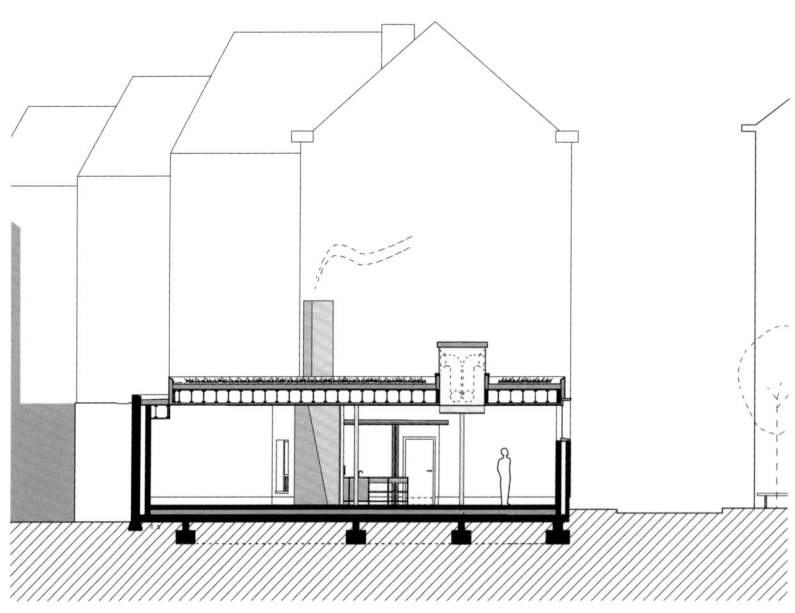

Carton123 architecten

Malibran youth centre

Park School, Melle

Petillon Ceuppens architecten and
Schenk Hattori Architecture Atelier

In a spacious block in Melle, among a grey mass of individual dwellings constructed between two train tracks, Petillon Ceuppens architecten and Schenk Hattori Architecture Atelier have built a new kindergarten and primary school. This was intended to replace the old school in the historic village centre (on the other side of the tracks) while introducing green space into the homogeneous residential fabric. The assigned site is roughly in the shape of a cross and is bordered by batteries of individual lots.

The compact new school building is positioned centrally, leaving as much free space as possible for a park that is visually and physically accessible to local residents. This position also allows the school to screen off two playgrounds in the dead-end arms of the cross (aside from one informal path between two residential lots). In another arm, which reaches all the way to the street, a sports hall has been built parallel to the path. The hall chimes with the communal vision of sharing the school infrastructure (and the investment) with out-of-hours activities and local clubs and societies.

The impact of the compact yet sturdy buildings on the site is nuanced by their stepped layout and visible structure. These offer points of contact for the human scale and split the visual impact of the volumes into discrete parts. A walkway on the first floor introduces an indentation around the entire school. It meticulously follows the staggered contours of the building, widening out on a single occasion into the dimensions of an outdoor classroom. It creates a direct connection with the surrounding park via two staircases.

Inside too, the offsetting of the spaces from one another interrupts the regular sightlines. Given their dimensions, flexible usage and outdoor circulation possibilities, the spaces between the classrooms resolutely distance themselves from the idea of the classic school corridor. On the upper floor, spacious halls divide the primary school into three clusters from where the pupils can be led directly outside via the walkway and the staircases. Downstairs, we see a twofold division: on one side the central hall of the kindergarten, on the other the canteen and the reception area, flanked by the staff rooms. On both floors, the intervening spaces criss-cross the entire building, from the park side to the playground side, beneath the well-considered corner that is ingrained in the structure. But in terms of circulation and usage, their role varies on each floor in accordance with the surrounding spaces, both in- and outdoors.

The school and the sports hall are constructed with a limited yet carefully chosen palette of materials. The rough concrete block walls, the robust woodwork in shades of red and the steel balustrades feel solid but have been carefully designed and assembled. The fibre-cement corrugated roof and zinc gutters of the sports hall seem to be a subtle nod to the undulating roof and brass gutters of the school building.

The limited number of construction elements places the emphasis firmly on the children and the usage. In terms of composition, each of the buildings has its own character, yet they all strike a careful balance between robustness and elegance. They look as if they will remain in place a long time, while it would actually be relatively easy to dismantle the entire construction.

Petrus Kemme

PARK SCHOOL

Offices
Petillon Ceuppens architecten and
Schenk Hattori Architecture Atelier
Websites
www.petillonceuppens.be
www.schenkhattori.com
Address
Beekstraat 34, Melle
Client
Municipality of Melle
Design
2017

Delivered
August 2021
Surface area
3,750 m²
Volume
15,000 m³
Total building cost
€ 7,000,000 - excl. VAT
Total building cost per m²
€ 1,670 - excl. VAT
Main contractor
STRABAG Belgium,
Antwerp

Subcontractors
Bourdeaud'hui, Geraardsbergen
De Mulder, Maarkedal
Geramat, Halle
LW-construct, Ieper
Steurbaut, Gavere
Tectum Dekkers, Genk
Stability studies
Tandem Ingenieurs, Kessel-Lo
Technology, EPB and acoustics studies
NVTS, Ghent
Photographer
Franziska Krieck

Situation plan

Sports hall Ground floor
Sports hall Section Aa

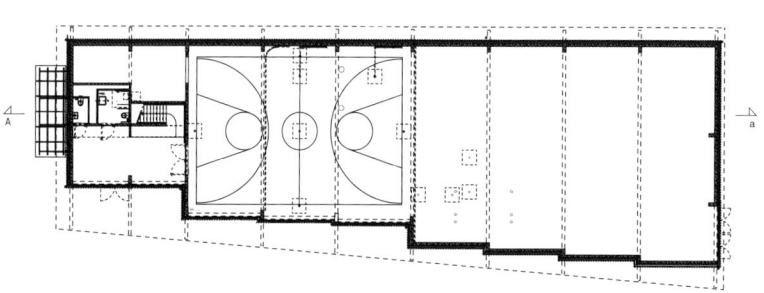

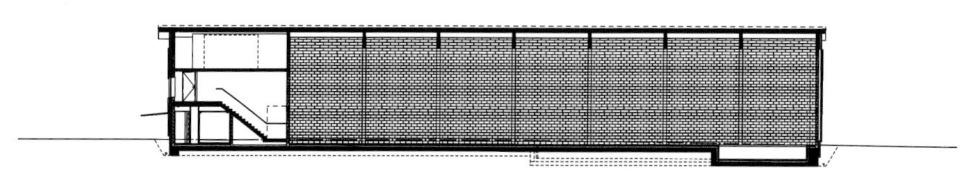

Petillon Ceuppens architecten and Schenk Hattori Architecture Atelier

School building Level 1
School building Ground floor

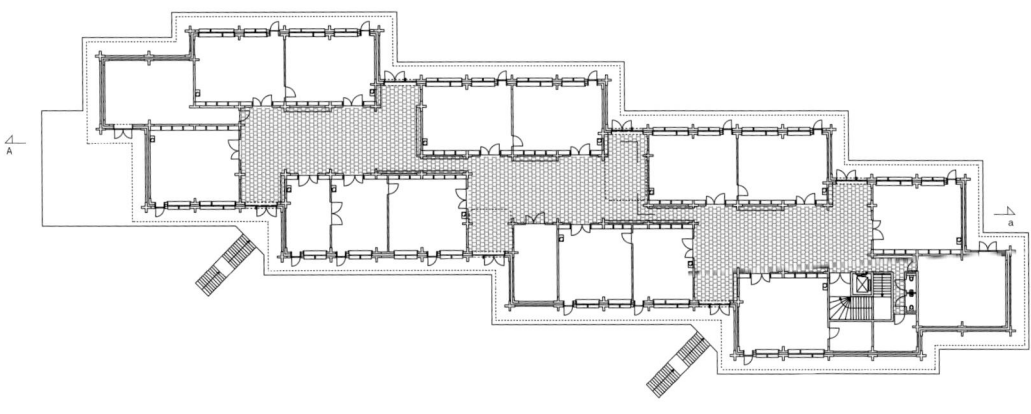

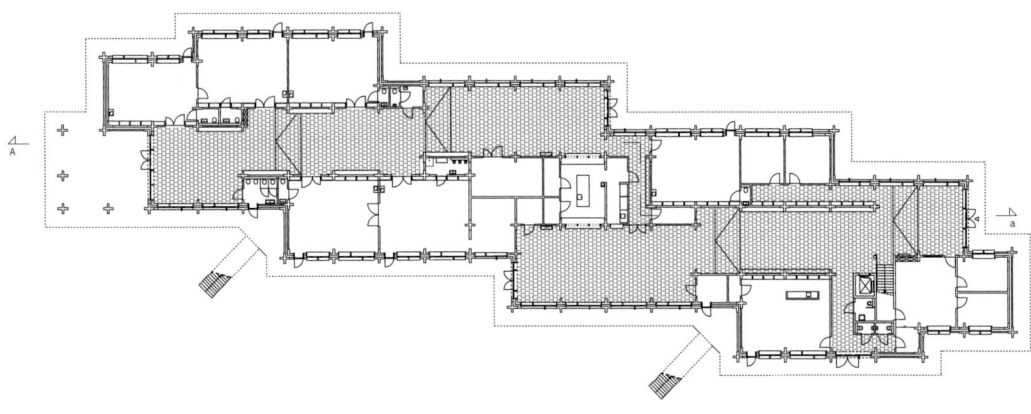

School building Section Aa

Park School

Petillon Ceuppens architecten and Schenk Hattori Architecture Atelier

Redevelopment of the Academie site, Ghent

Robbrecht en Daem architecten, Marie-José Van Hee architecten, architecten Els Claessens Tania Vandenbussche, Dierendonckblancke architecten, Callebaut Architecten

Having the chance to repurpose an entire city block – especially in the context of Flemish cities, where property is traditionally fragmented – is a rare occasion. The transformation of the urban block at Academiestraat in Ghent is one such case, a perfect opportunity to integrate urban design and architecture. The block, located in the historical city centre, was long the seat of the Royal Academy of Fine Arts and of the city's fire station, until their recent move to new premises in other parts of the city. While most of the buildings within the perimeter of the block could be razed, the three historical buildings along Academiestraat – the nineteenth-century building of the academy, the red-brick building of 1870–71 of the fire station, and the Gatehouse of 1871 – were marked for historic preservation.

The recently completed project is the result of a sale procedure initiated a decade ago by sogent and Hogeschool Gent with the aim of selecting a team composed of architects and a real-estate company willing to buy up the entire area to develop a high-quality residential project with added value for the neighbourhood. Selected from among fifteen submissions, the winning proposal was that of the Ghent-based offices of Robbrecht en Daem architecten, architecten Els Claessens and Tania Vandenbussche, Marie-José Van Hee architecten and Dierendonckblancke architecten supported by 3D Real Estate.

In terms of urban planning, the proposal is based on the development of an inner pedestrian street on areas previously occupied by some of the secondary volumes of the academy and of the fire station. Starting at the Gatehouse along Academiestraat, this inner road cuts through the entire block in a north-south direction before reaching Brandweerstraat on the opposite side. The road becomes a sort of 'urban spine' from which residential buildings can be entered either directly or through a series of inner gardens, courtyards and alleys that fan out from this central space. In terms of architecture, each office was responsible for developing a part of the complex. Despite the multiplicity of authors, they all deployed a common, sober and coherent architectural idiom capable of accommodating differences as regards details, finishing and construction budgets, but without transforming the complex into a cacophony of architectural styles. Close attention was paid to the relation with the architectural heritage of the two main historic buildings, where the architects showed great care in preserving both the typological and structural integrity of the old architecture, in the deployment of traditional materials and in the use of old construction techniques, without all this becoming a paralysing impasse for architectural invention.

Whether the project will fulfil all of its original promises remains to be seen. Some have certainly been met: the overall architectural quality, the care with regard to the past heritage of the site, the typologically varied housing offer. Yet the closing of the inner road by an entrance gate might limit the possibility to cross the urban block – an exceptional experience in Flemish cities – to residents alone. Also, detaching the social housing block at the crossing of Brandweerstraat and Sint-Margrietstraat from the rest of the complex seems controversial. These might be necessary compromises in projects run by a private developer, but they show us once again how architectural quality often depends on an array of different and often opposing interests and intentions.

Martino Tattara

REDEVELOPMENT OF THE ACADEMIE SITE

Offices
Robbrecht en Daem architecten,
Marie-José Van Hee architecten,
architecten Els Claessens
Tania Vandenbussche,
Dierendonckblancke architecten,
Callebaut Architecten
Websites
www.robbrechtendaem.com
www.mjvanhee.be
www.ectv.be
www.dierendonckblancke.eu
www.callebaut-architecten.be

Address
Academiestraat, Molenaarsstraat,
Brandweerstraat and
Sint-Margrietstraat, Ghent
Client
Academie Vastgoedontwikkeling
Design
2012-16
Delivered
2021-22
Surface areas
12,772 m² residential,
3,774 m² offices/retail,
6,400 m² parking,
4,600 m² private and
communal outdoor space

Total building cost
€ 42,500,000 - excl. VAT
Main contractors
Denys, Wondelgem academy
Dherte, Namur (fire station)
Willemen construct, Mechelen (new build)
Master plan
Robbrecht en Daem architecten, Ghent
Restoration
Callebaut Architecten, Ghent
Stability and technology studies
VK architects + engineers, Merelbeke
Landscaping
Robbrecht en Daem architecten, Ghent
Photographer
Filip Dujardin

Situation plan

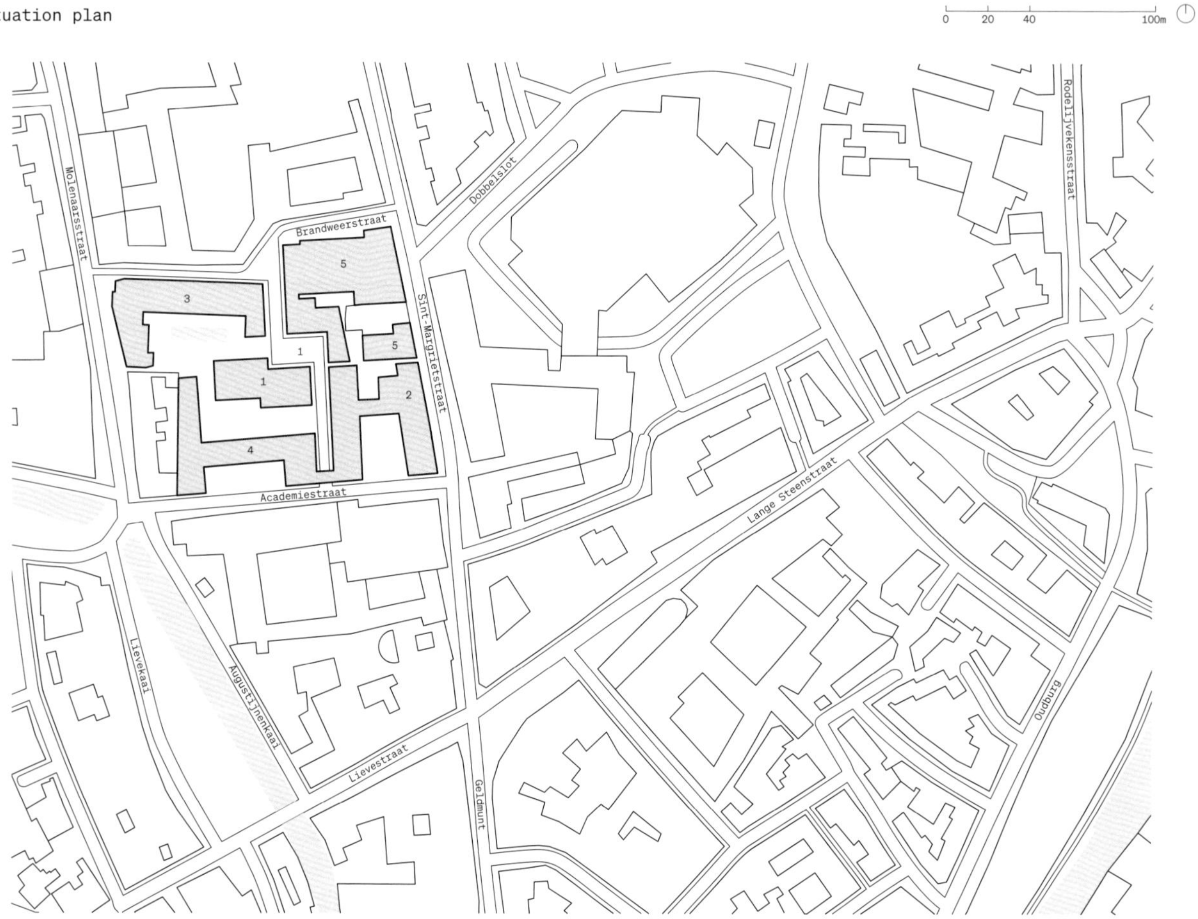

1. Robbrecht en Daem architecten
2. Robbrecht en Daem architecten and Callebaut Architecten
3. Marie-José Van Hee architecten
4. Architecten Els Claessens Tania Vandenbussche
5. Dierendonckblancke architecten

Section Aa

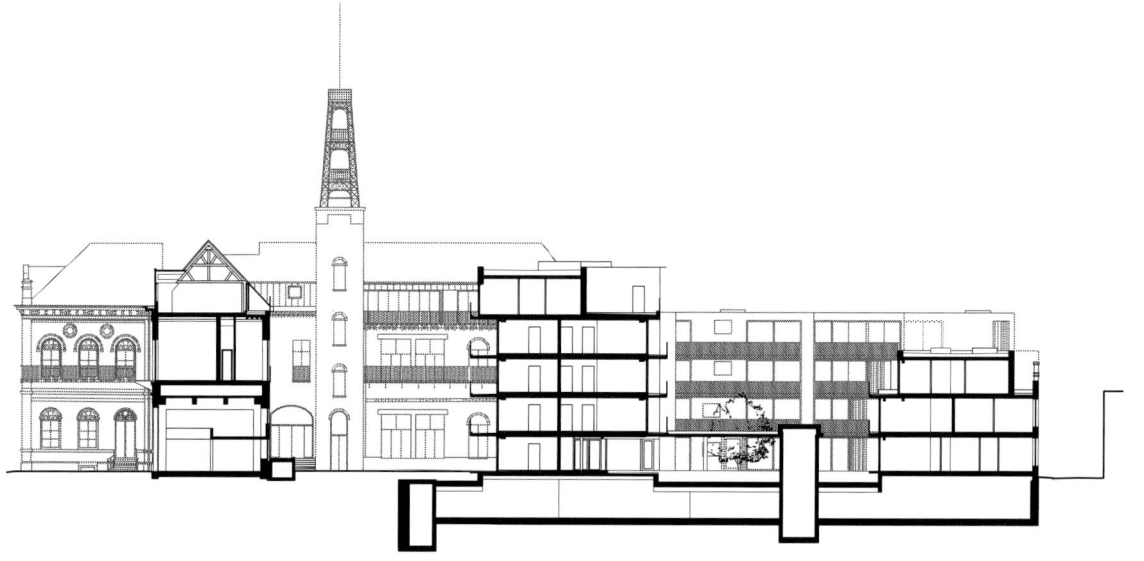

Robbrecht en Daem architecten, Marie-José Van Hee architecten, architecten Els Claessens Tania Vandenbussche, Dierendonckblancke architecten, Callebaut Architecten

Ground floor

Redevelopment of the Academie site

Robbrecht en Daem architecten, Marie-José Van Hee architecten, architecten Els Claessens Tania Vandenbussche, Dierendonckblancke architecten, Callebaut Architecten

Redevelopment of the Academie site

Cadix school campus, Antwerp

Korteknie Stuhlmacher Architecten

The Cadix municipal school complex is sited in the former port district Het Eilandje, which is rapidly transforming into a prized waterside residential area. The school campus comprises three buildings, each with its own characteristics and challenges. First there is a new-build block for an arts and technical secondary school with workshops, workspaces, staff rooms and head teachers' offices, classrooms and art studios. The second building, designed by former city architect Emiel Van Averbeke, consists of the restoration and renovation of three (out of four) warehouses that served from 1940 as recruitment buildings for port workers. The project's final building comprises the actualization of Van Averbeke's existing school from 1927. Typologically, this is a corridor-based school that was constructed somewhat punctiliously around three patios. The listed monument had slowly deteriorated in recent decades while continuing to function as a school building.

The core task was to create a single school campus from three buildings with highly divergent typologies. This posed specific design challenges. Korteknie Stuhlmacher Architecten went back to a set of starting points that the firm invariably applies to its projects. Mechthild Stuhlmacher detailed these points in *The Persistence of Questioning* (Archined, 2022). First, she talks about rigour. Here, the focus is on the artistic and practical precision of both designer and contractor; on having the skill to read spaces and a context; and, with these as a base point, on setting a series of rules as a designer and adhering to them consistently. Second, a sense of connectedness with a place and continuity are essential elements in Korteknie Stuhlmacher's design approach. As the third starting point, Stuhlmacher cites appropriation: the architecture's capacity to allow itself to be lived in, both in the present and by future users with as yet unknown needs.

In the Cadix campus, these principles translated into a restrained, almost industrial materialization for the new build, which chimes with the history of Het Eilandje. The façade of the new school building, constructed in ochre yellow bricks with glazed masonry, recalls the original 'yellow' identity of this former quarter of dock workers, warehouses and industry. The roofs of the new construction are the same shape as those designed by Van Averbeke for the dock workers' warehouses. The industrial strength of these warehouses is also reflected in the new construction, built with a concrete column structure that has been left visible. Future appropriation with classroom adaptability is written into the building's DNA. Green terraces and large windows in the new build look out onto the former port quarter and the dock beyond. In a rapidly gentrifying area, these breathtaking panoramas are a generous gesture towards the pupils following an arts and technical education.

The warehouses were perforated twice: once to create a patio and draw light and air into the block, once to create a cut-through to the restored school building from 1927. The surgical precision of the incisions, combined with the restoration of the original rafters, also assured the project's approval by the Flanders Monuments Watch Agency. The school designed by Van Averbeke himself was treated with respect and restraint. Technical spaces and bicycle storage were housed in two pavilions in the inner courtyards. In the interior, the designers visibly step back to allow the existing attributes to speak for themselves. They found colours that proved a warm gift, staircases of rare craftsmanship, and attics with unexpectedly high-quality studios. The campus was transformed from a dark, tightly dimensioned school into a traversable space, a creative oasis at the heart of an up-and-coming residential area.

Sofie De Caigny

CADIX SCHOOL CAMPUS

Office
Korteknie Stuhlmacher Architecten
Website
www.ksa.nl
Address
Kempischdok-Westkaai, Antwerp
Client
AG Real Estate / DBFM Scholen Van Morgen
(Printing school 'Het KOT' was tendered separately and commissioned by City Education in Antwerp, or AGSO)
Design
December 2014 ('Het KOT': February 2017)

Delivered
December 2020 ('Het KOT': March 2020)
Surface Area
24,000 m² ('Het KOT': 1,490 m²)
Total building cost
€ 40,184,585 - excl. VAT
('Het KOT': € 1,854,709 - excl. VAT)
Totale building cost per m²
€ 1,674 - excl. VAT
('Het KOT': € 1,245 - excl. VAT)
Main contractor
Strabag (DBFM), Antwerp
('Het KOT': Monument, Ingelmunster)
Stability studies
ABT, Antwerp ('Het KOT': H4D Raadgevend ingenieurs, Dongen[NL])

Technology studies
RCR, Herent ('Het KOT': Adviesbureau VanderWeele, Groningen[NL])
Specifications
Bureau Bouwtechniek, Antwerp
('Het KOT': Korteknie Stuhlmacher Architecten, Rotterdam[NL])
Advisor restoration
Callebaut Architecten, Ghent
Garden design
Atelier Arne Deruyter, Roeselare
Photographer
Luuk Kramer except
p. 84: Maurice Tjon a Tham
and p. 87 top: Karin Borghouts

Situation plan

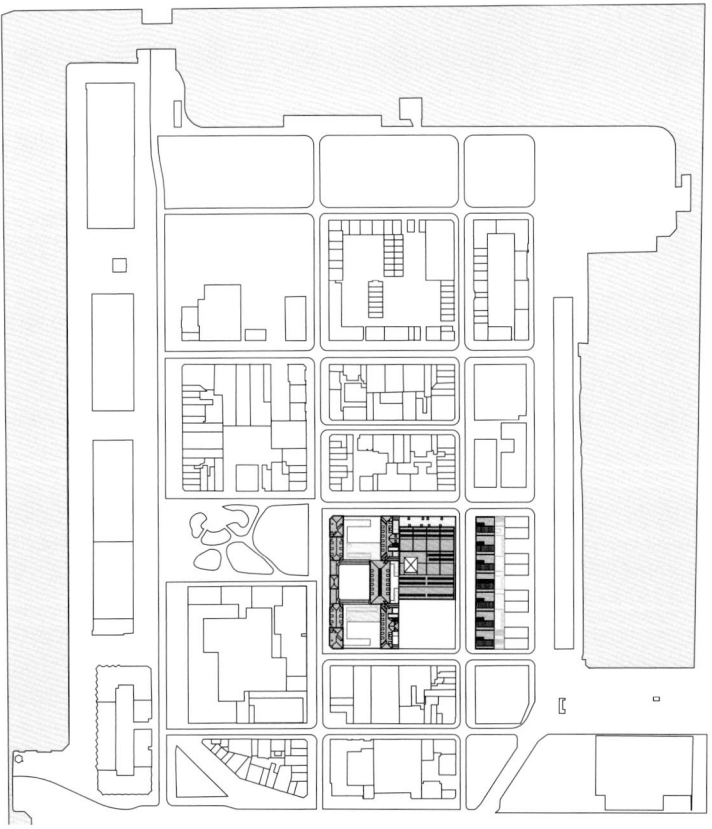

Section Aa
Section Bb

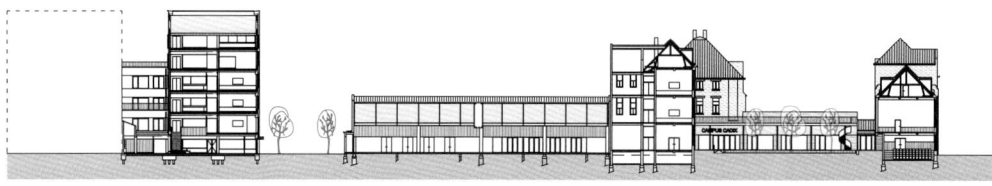

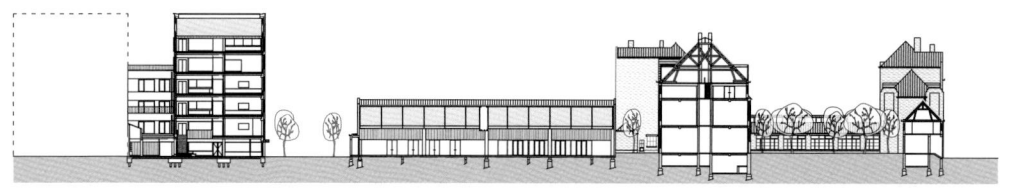

Korteknie Stuhlmacher Architecten

Level 2
Ground floor

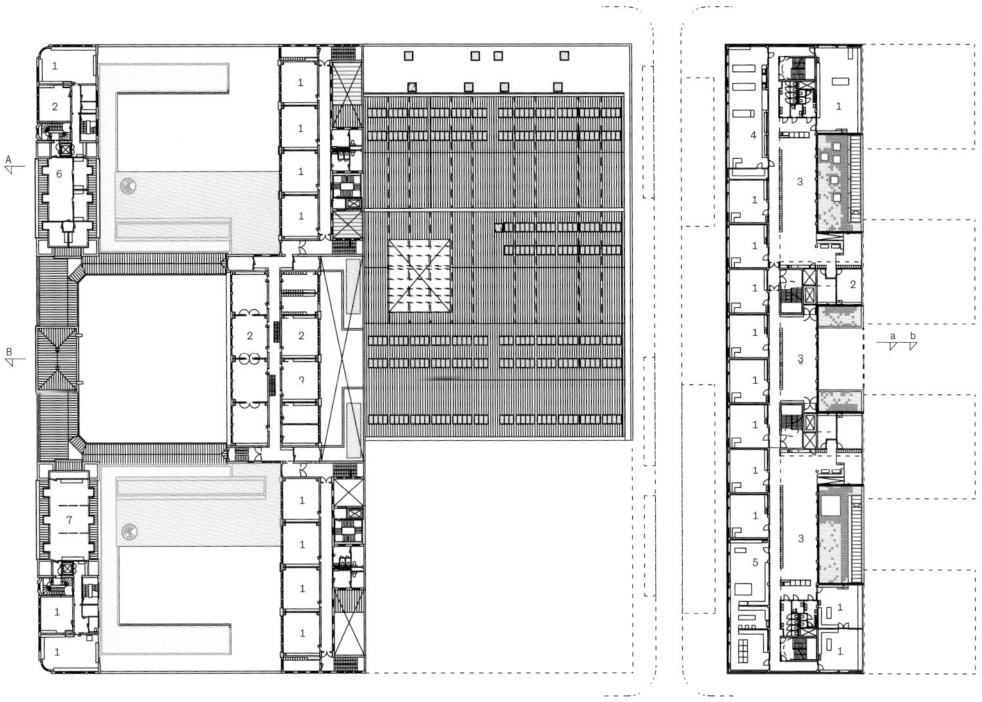

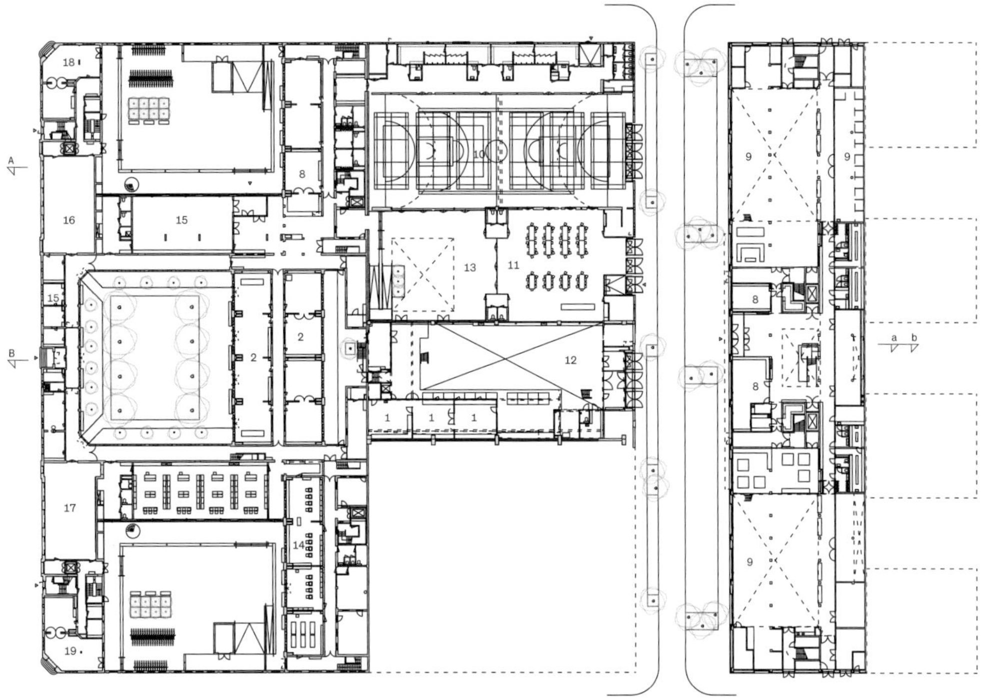

1. Classroom
2. Staff room
3. Open workspace
4. Pharmacy
5. Building Sciences
6. Editing studio
7. Photo studio
8. Reception and administration
9. Workshop
10. Gymnasium
11. Cafeteria
12. Printing school
13. Covered outdoor space
14. Hair salon
15. Multipurpose hall
16. Auditorium
17. Dance studio
18. Music room
19. Expression room

Cadix school campus

Korteknie Stuhlmacher Architecten

Cadix school campus

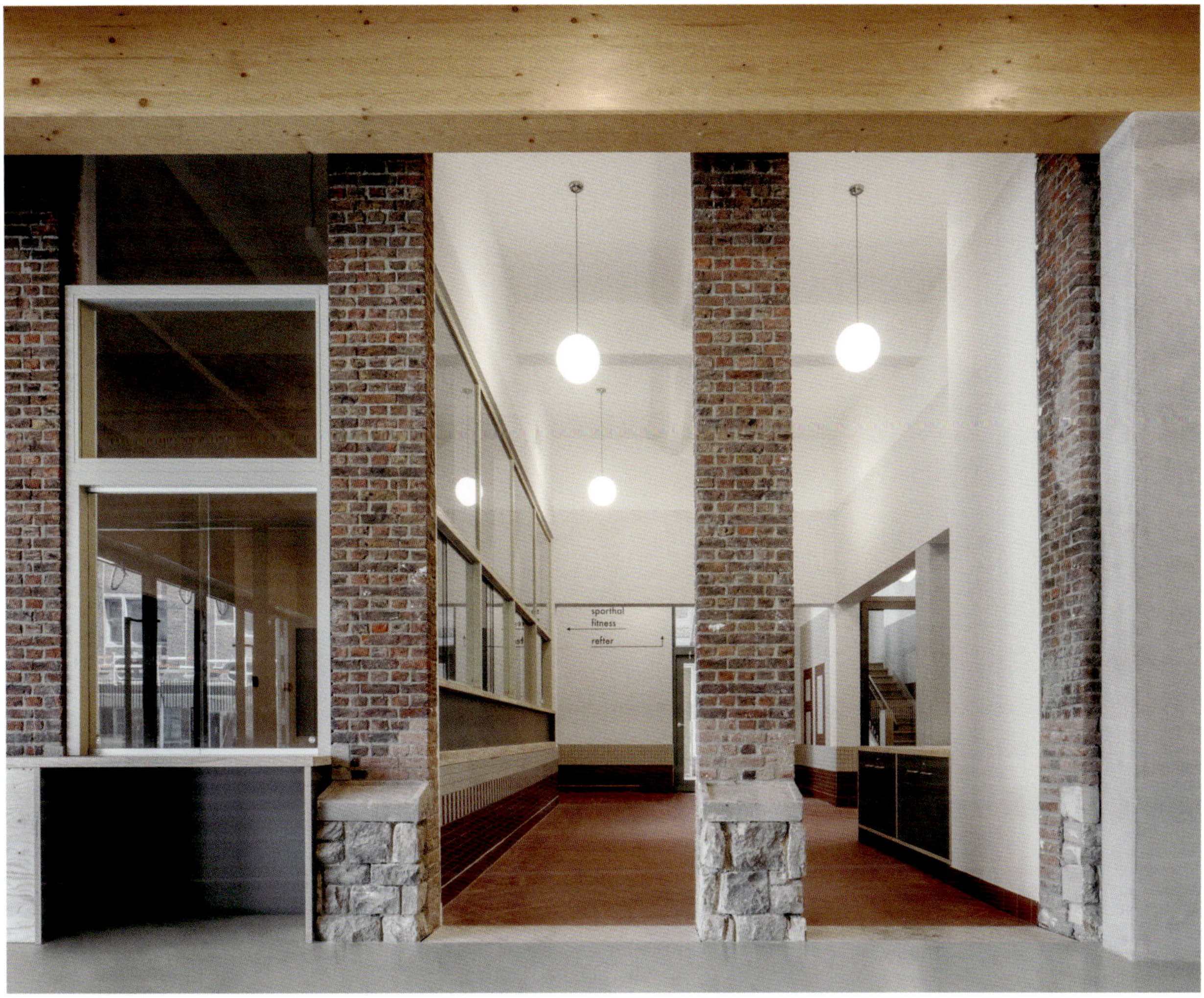
sporthal
fitness
refter

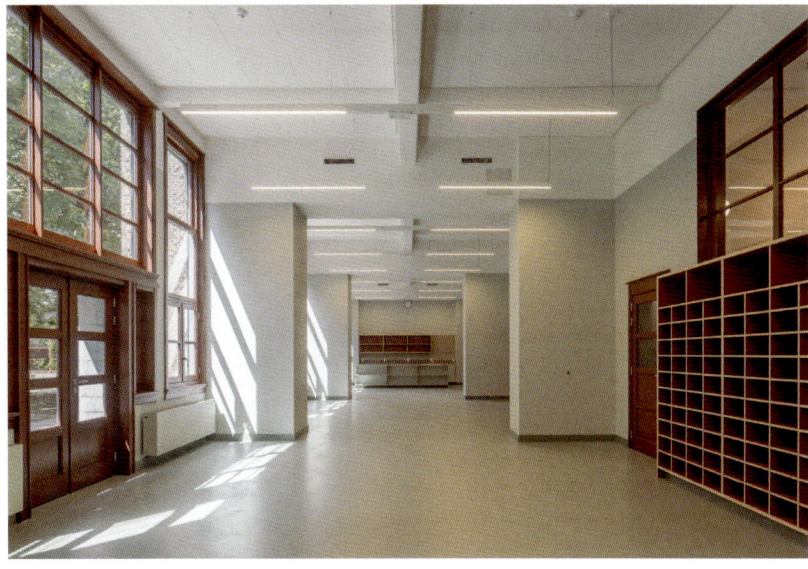

Timber construction workshop, Ghent

GAFPA

On a new industrial estate in the north of Ghent, GAFPA has built a workshop for a contractor who specializes in timber frameworks and solid wood constructions. The contractor prefabricates large building elements (if not entire buildings) that can be quickly assembled on site. With just under twenty employees, the operation has the intimate scale of an extended family business, while working with wood expresses a clear ambition to build sustainably. It would hardly come as a surprise, therefore, if the contractor had directed his specialist knowledge at this project and constructed – and perhaps even designed – his own wooden building.

GAFPA's design originates, remarkably enough, from a concrete structure. A stretched U-shaped wall embraces the entire project and creates an architecturally and structurally robust shelter, with the highest fire-safety standards, in which the wood structures can be fabricated. On its most closed side, the building abuts the plot boundary. It steps aside, as it were, to let visitors in. A row of concrete columns creates rhythm down the long façade: the opening of the U-shape in the ground plan. Within it, a careful composition of wood and glass panels and generous openings stages the sidelong entry of light, materials and people.

An unmissable opening leads visitors to a generous covered outdoor area. Daylight penetrates the core of the building thanks to the omission of several roof panels along the line of the concrete rear walls. The outline of the roof opening is reflected on the floor level as the boundary of a garden that is carefully lit from above. From the garden, varicoloured climbing plants cover the concrete back wall. The remainder of the space is paved and doubles up as a manoeuvring area and collective outdoor space. The transverse wood and glass façades diffuse the light and allow the atmosphere of the indoor-outdoor area to filter through the rest of the building. In this way, the outdoor space will always be the tangible heart of both the site and the business. The fact that this has been achieved through omission – of parts of the façade, roof and floor – makes GAFPA's design seem deceptively effortless. But it also invites visitors to step straight into the heart of the company.

The exterior area further divides the building into customized workspaces: at the front, two compact floors (plus attic) containing a reception area and meeting rooms, offices and sanitary facilities; at the rear, the workshop. The concrete columns and wooden infill of the long outer wall are hidden behind the stock of building materials in the workshop. Up above, daylight streams in through the windows that run the entire length of the shed. The roof, which seems to have been raised specifically for this purpose, is supported by impressive wooden trusses. Resting on the concrete structure, the trusses appear to have been installed almost in reverse, as though originally intended for a lightly pitched gable roof, so as to reconcile the roof pitch and the horizontal upper limit of the free working height. Below, a crane runs down the length of the studio, its rails supported by the brackets of the concrete structure. The wooden trusses lend the building a distinctive profile, also in the covered outdoor area and in the offices. A metal canopy refines the clearance height and emphasizes the character of a seemingly straightforward but extremely precise and thoughtful building.

Petrus Kemme

TIMBER CONSTRUCTION WORKSHOP

Office
GAFPA
Website
www.gafpa.net
Address
Logboekstraat 10, Ghent
Client
Lab15

Design
2018
Delivered
May 2020
Surface area
1,700 m²
Volume
14,490 m³
Total building cost
€ 716,000 - excl. VAT

Total building cost per m²
€ 421 - excl. VAT
Main contractor
Lab15, Ghent
Contractors
Beeuwsaert, Ledegem
Lab15, Ghent
Energy
Proheat, Erpe-Mere
Photographer
GAFPA

Situation plan

Ground floor

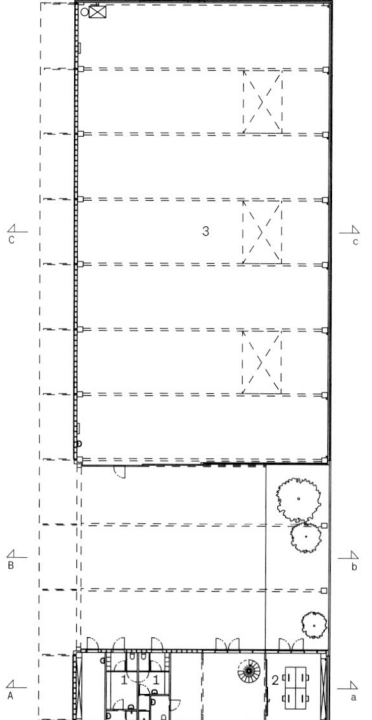

1. Sanitary facilities
2. Offices
3. Workshop

Section Cc
Section Bb
Section Aa

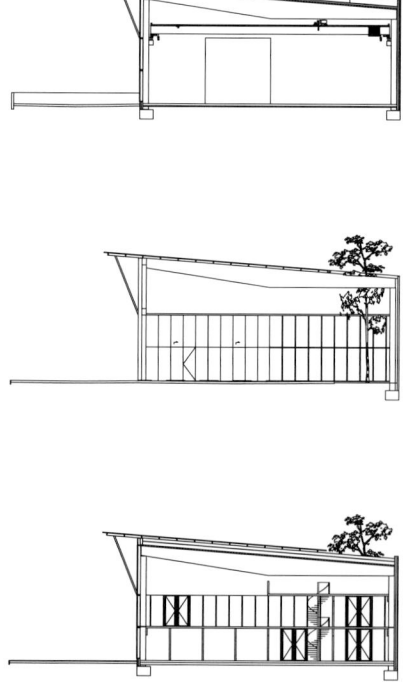

GAFPA

92

Timber construction workshop

De Boekentoren
University Library, Ghent

Robbrecht en Daem architecten with BARO, SumProject and Barbara Van der Wee architects

In 2007 Robbrecht en Daem architecten, in a team including Barbara Van der Wee architects, won an Open Call from the Flemish Government Architect to restore De Boekentoren University Library and transform it into a research and heritage library fit for the twenty-first century. The designers were confronted with the challenges posed by modern heritage, the high climate standards required for the conservation of the cultural heritage collection, and the needs of today's library users. They found answers to these challenges in the existing building.

De Boekentoren, Henry van de Velde's magnum opus, was designed in 1933–35 and built between 1936 and 1945. In the volume effect, restrained ornamentation, proportions and compositions, Van de Velde sought an appropriate monumentality for the programme. He strived for a 'logical beauty' in which efficiency and aesthetics reinforced each other. By the time it was listed as a monument in 1992, the building had lost much of its original strength, having already started to decay during the Second World War. The post-war period reads like a saga of ad hoc interventions that included patching up the façades, replacing the joinery and adapting the interiors. The ambition to restore the tower's artistic integrity was only revived through the unexpected interaction between an enthusiastic head librarian and a private investor who had acquired the archival plans for De Boekentoren.

During the restoration campaign, the tower's skin was scraped off and the building was clad in a new layer of concrete. The external transformation is so imperceptible as to only be noticeable to specialists. This subtlety continues in the renewal of the interior. The architects found so many starting points in Van de Velde's building for creating new architecture – and for updating the existing building to meet the needs of contemporary library users – that old and new are almost indistinguishable. Robbrecht en Daem's design, like Van de Velde's own, is the result of a rigorous quest for pure and abstract linear ornaments, a balanced colour scheme, and a generous spatiality in which light plays the leading role. Robbrecht en Daem make Van de Velde's design their own, as it were, by getting under the skin of the master in order to complete the original building. In places, this occurs aesthetically, as in the case of the proportions of the columns in the belvedere, which they enhanced by removing the cross-beams. Elsewhere the improvement is spatial, for example by combining two smaller rooms into one large volume, so that the Special Collections reading room is more in balance with the generous proportions of its previous space, the latter having been renamed 'Study Landscape'. A new underground depot provides much-needed additional space for the collection and creates new connections to the existing cellars, which hugely increases their potential for use.

This approach can only succeed from embedded knowledge of the original design, which goes far beyond a purely scientific approach to architectural and building history. Robbrecht en Daem's interventions bear witness to a deep understanding of the expressiveness, materiality, tactility, composition and spatial experience of the library, so that these aspects also become guiding principles in the contemporary transformation of the building. The new is so deeply grounded in the old that exciting transgressions occur between restoration and design. The original is more itself than it ever was.

Sofie De Caigny

DE BOEKENTOREN UNIVERSITY LIBRARY

Offices
Robbrecht en Daem architecten
with BARO, SumProject and
Barbara Van der Wee architects
Websites
www.robbrechtendaem.com
www.baro-architectuur.be
www.sum.be
Address
Rozier 9, Ghent
Client
Ghent University

Design
March 2007
Delivered
April 2021
Surface area
20,000 m²
Total building cost
€ 34,000,000 - excl. VAT
Main contractors
Furnibo, Ghent (phase 1)
BAM-Renotec, Geel (phase 2)
Artes Depret - Roegiers -
Woudenberg, Kruibeke (phase 3)

Stability studies
Bureau d'Etudes Greisch, Liège
Technology studies
VK architects + engineers, Merelbeke
Building physics engineer
Daidalos Peutz, Leuven
Photographer
Kristien Daem
except p. 101 and p. 102:
Stijn Bollaert

Situation plan

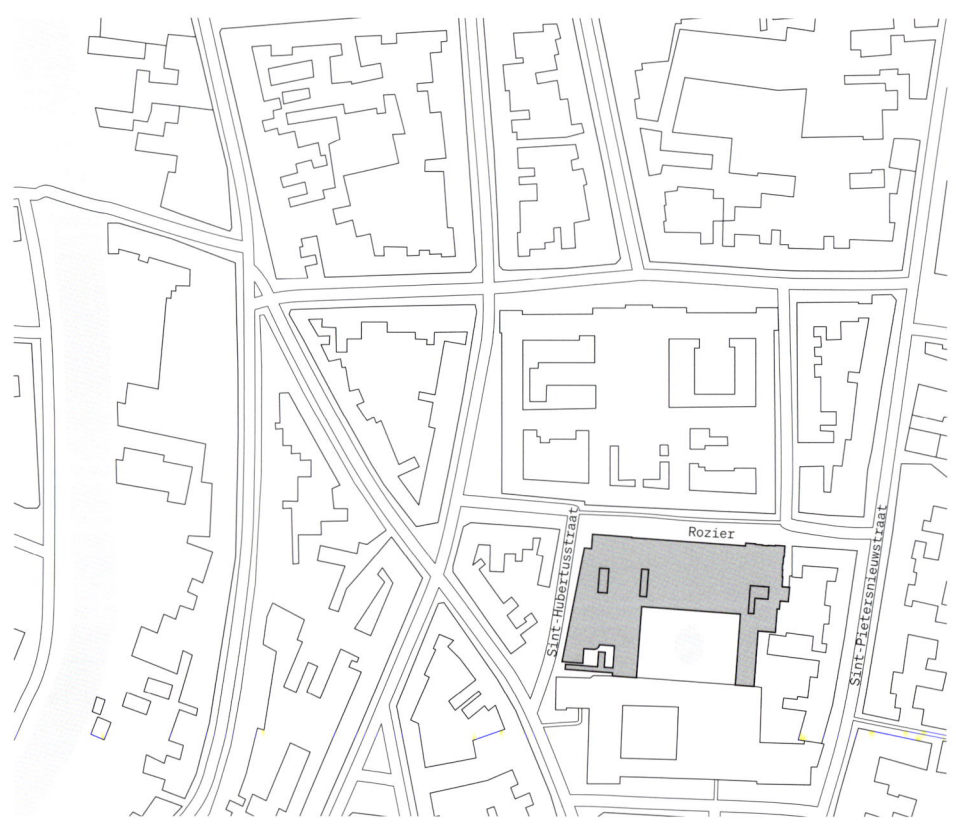

Section Aa

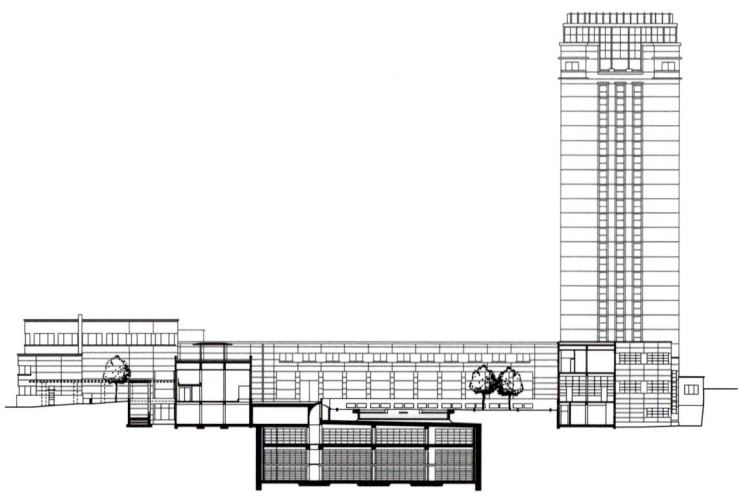

Robbrecht en Daem architecten with BARO, SumProject and Barbara Van der Wee architects

Ground floor
Level -1

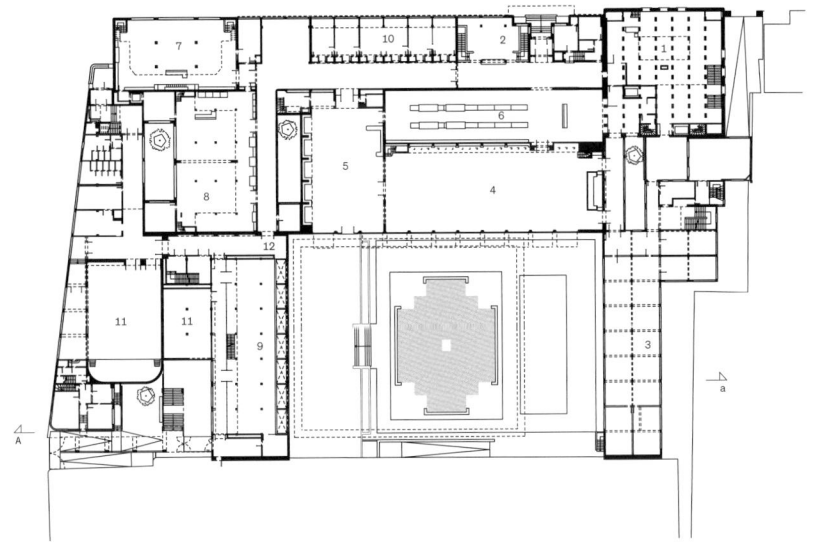

1. Reception
2. Cloakroom
3. Staff room
4. Main reading room
5. Periodicals reading room
6. Library computers
7. Special collections reading room
8. Manuscript reading room
9. IT study room
10. Meeting room
11. Auditorium
12. New internal passage

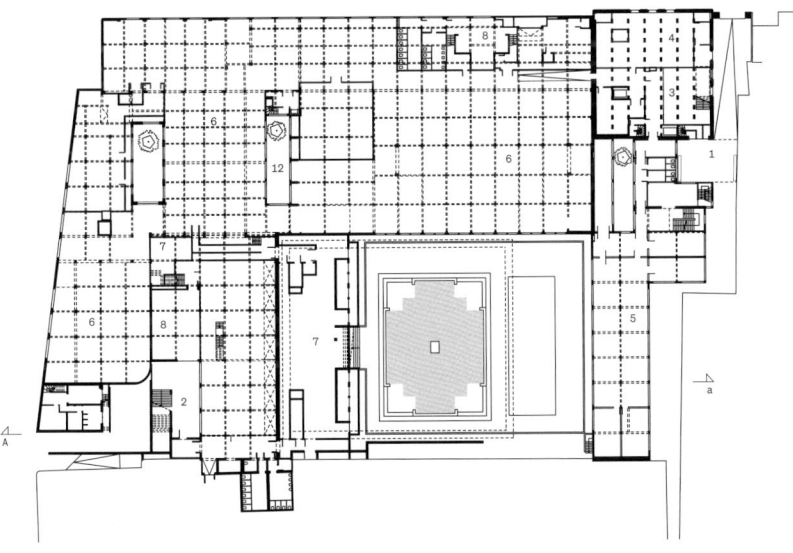

1. New access to belvedere
2. New workspace access
3. Public foyer and cloakroom
4. Quarantine and book restoration
5. Staff room
6. Depot
7. Workspace
8. Auditorium

Type plan, Level 20 and Level 21

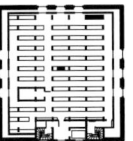 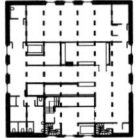 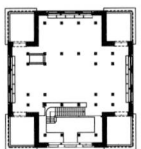

De Boekentoren University Library

Robbrecht en Daem architecten with BARO, SumProject and Barbara Van der Wee architects

De Boekentoren University Library

Steiner School, Ghent

Perneel Osten architecten and BACK architectenbureau

On the east side of Ghent city centre, wedged between Kasteellaan and Visserijvaart, lies an oversized housing block. Long rows of mainly nineteenth-century houses form a virtually impenetrable screen that shields a vast inner area. The Steiner School (crèche to secondary) occupies just half this site. The school, which started out in a stately building on Kasteellaan, has expanded in various stages since the late twentieth century. In the side streets, gaps in the rows of houses provide access to the school grounds, along winding paths flanked by stacks of bicycles. To bring a degree of order to the inner area, a master plan was drawn up in 2020 by the architectural firms Compagnie-O, Perneel Osten architecten and BACK architectuurbureau. The latter two firms also designed the first building to be constructed on the site, which is home to the secondary-school classrooms.

Against the backdrop of divergent architectural styles, the new school building excels in an appropriate kind of unobtrusiveness. The first impression is that of an oversized house, one featuring familiar elements such as brick walls, a main pitched roof and a flat canopy 'at the back'. In this way, the building strikes a balance between the architecture found in the surrounding residential area and that of the school buildings in the block. At the same time, it acquires a character of its own through the detailing, with open joints between the bricks; a subtle slope through which the roof connects the various parts of the new building; and a carefully executed wooden structure in the canopy (with a well-placed opening for daylight in the core of the ground floor and a green roof on top).

In the way its spaces are connected, the building effectively punctures the traditional educational order. It comprises two volumes: a three-storey stack of classrooms and a two-storey battery of studios. The volumes are turned at a subtle angle to each other. In-between, a generous external staircase leads to the various levels. A gallery gives access to the upper studios and ends in a more informal staircase at the side wall. Walking to and from the classrooms, one passes a variety of clever intersections of views and light. For example, the canopy at the front has been raised to just above gallery level to create a descending perspective. The building is thus not only arranged most conveniently, but also invites informal connections.

In the elongated wing, the ground-floor studios are directly connected to the playground, where activities can unfold beneath the canopy. At the back, tilted skylights add to the luminosity and create a vaguely 1970s atmosphere. The rooms above are double height and filled with indirect light thanks to the large windows on the north side. On the other hand, the joinery can be opened to provide natural ventilation, although the door to the gallery remains open on a regular basis anyway. In the other volume of stacked classrooms, only the fire escape is made of concrete, as would be expected. The rest of the structure is made of CLT (cross-laminated timber) panels, which brings an essential visual, tactile and acoustic calmness to the rooms. In addition, the architects succeeded in preserving the surrounding trees (even those barely a metre from the new building). As a result, an ascent in the building creates a corresponding rise in the canopy. This, in turn, contributes to the pleasant atmosphere of a light shelter in which the building bathes.

Petrus Kemme

STEINER SCHOOL

Offices
Perneel Osten architecten and BACK architectenbureau
Websites
www.perneelosten.be
www.back-ar.be
Address
Kasteellaan 54, Ghent
Client
Steiner secondary schools in Flanders (MSV)
Design
March 2016
Delivered
August 2021

Surface area
2,244 m²
Volume
8,235 m³
Total building cost
€ 3,663,784 – excl. VAT
Total building cost per m²
€ 1,568 – excl. VAT
Main contractor
Alheembouw, Staden
Timber construction contractor
LTS Laminated Timber Solutions, Moorslede
HVAC contractor
Zaman, Ghent
Electrical contractor
Van Vooren, Bruges

Exterior joinery contractor
Detrac, Anzegem
Interior joinery contractor
Drafab, Poperinge
Stability studies
Mouton, Ghent
Technology studies
Tech3, Ghent
EPB studies
EA+, Ghent
Safety coordination
Macobo Vekmo, Ghent
3D model
Corneel Cannaerts, Ghent
Photographer
Filip Dujardin

Situation plan

1. Steiner secondary school, phase 1
2. Steiner secondary school, phase 2
3. Steiner kindergarten
4. Steiner primary school

Section Aa

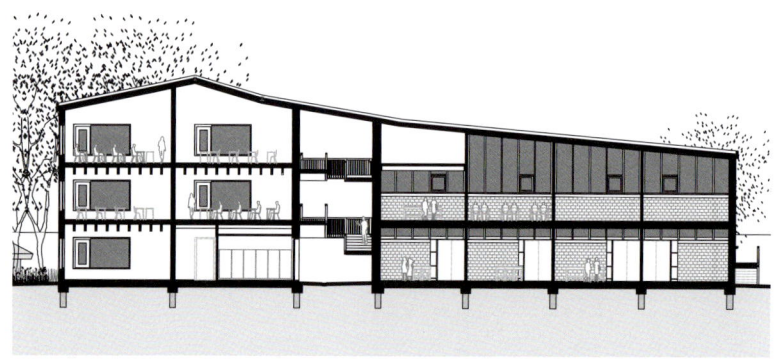

Perneel Osten architecten and BACK architectenbureau

Level 2
Level 1
Ground floor

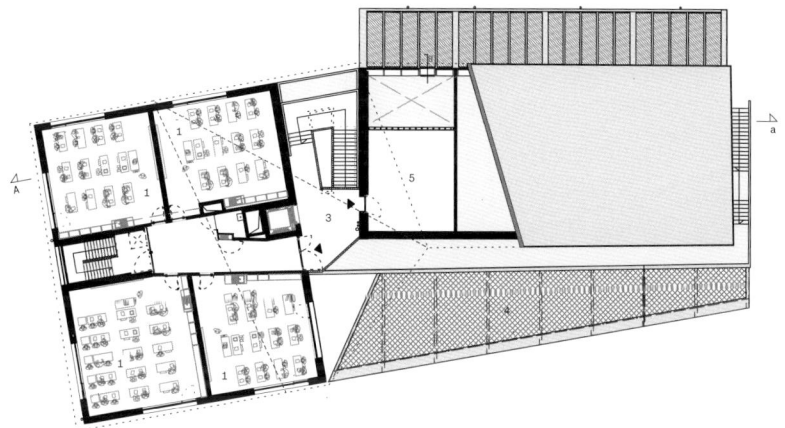

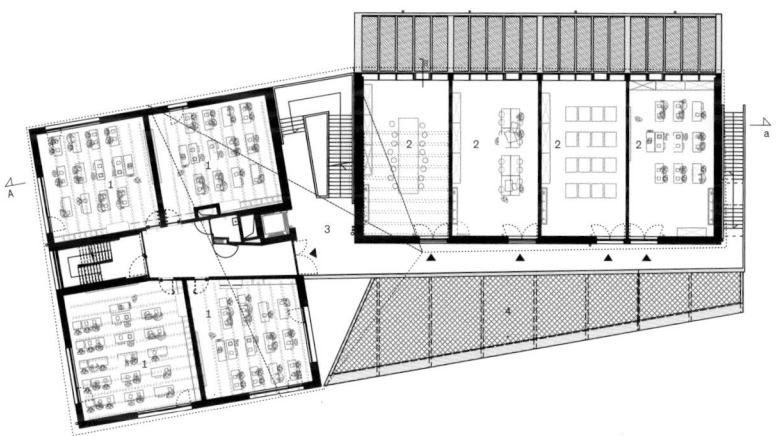

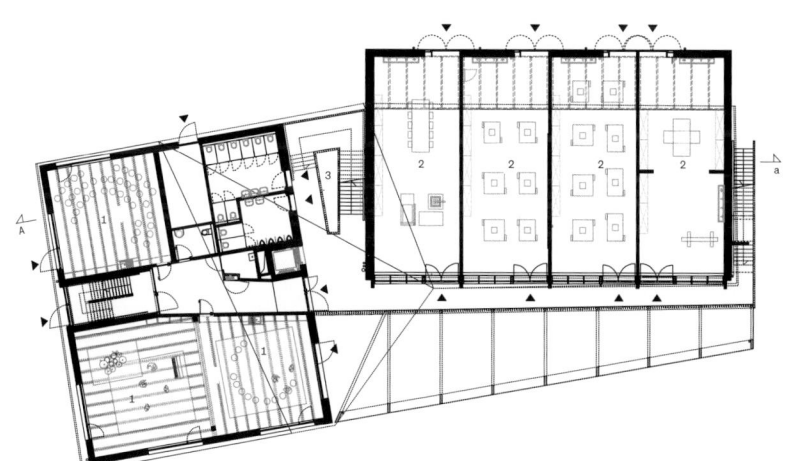

1. Classroom
2. Workshop
3. External stairs
4. Canopy planted with herbs
5. Storage and technical space

Perneel Osten architecten and BACK architectenbureau

Omer Vander Ghinste brewery, Bellegem

Architecten- en ingenieursbureau D'hondt Beyens Goesaert
and Claeys/Haelvoet Architecten

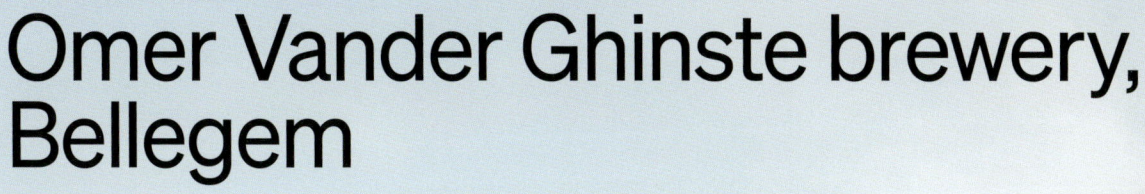

A brewery has existed in the centre of Bellegem, a rural municipality of Kortrijk with about 3,700 inhabitants, since 1892. It is literally a stone's throw from the church. The Vander Ghinste family, who own the business, are determined to keep brewing in Bellegem. This makes Vander Ghinste an exception to the rule in Flanders. Most local breweries vacated the villages after World War II. They found it difficult to comply with the increasingly stringent regulations, contravened the regional urban planning guidelines, or were taken over by larger breweries. The very opposite happened in Bellegem: production is steadily increasing and the brewery, which is akin to the beating heart of the village, is a source of life and identity.

To scale up production, the family commissioned Architecten- en ingenieursbureau D'hondt Beyens Goesaert and Claeys/Haelvoet architecten to build a new brewing hall. The hall is situated opposite the existing art deco building that has been the flagship premises of the family business since 1929. The site is home to buildings from many different eras, all analogous to the successive generations of the Vander Ghinste family. The latest addition by D'hondt Beyens Goesaert and Claeys/Haelvoet consists of a lower and upper room enabling the company to double production. The new brewing hall endeavours to occupy a position between its imposing art deco neighbour and the village houses at the back. Its curved shape leaves little space around the silos and brewing vats while also embracing visitors, who can explore the building in one fluid movement. The façade in different types of weathered brick lends the building the materiality of an oversized villa, despite its closed volume. In this way, the industrial building connects with the detached houses nearby. The compact nature of the partially sunken volume corresponds with the logic of the village. In contrast to this, the tower – which houses five silos 22 metres high – has an undeniably industrial feel. The field of tension between the two volumes externalizes the quest to find the ideal way of keeping a growing company embedded in the village, on both a spatial and functional level.

The street between the existing buildings and the new brewing hall has been pedestrianized. It appears to be part of the Omer Vander Ghinste brewery yard because the new brewing hall seeks out the boundaries of the whimsical plot. This yard is now a favourite with walkers and cyclists. Opening onto it is the sculpturally designed entrance to the new brewery hall. In the contemporary building, only the upper room is included in the brewery's visitor circuit. Ingredients are shown in fixed wooden furniture. The wood is mirrored in the cladding of the walls and a decorative ceiling with a round skylight that lets all-important daylight into the space. The architecture, with its attention to finish and tactility, radiates craftsmanship and underscores the Vander Ghinste family's commitment to traditional brewing methods. Even the lower room, which is inaccessible to visitors, has been executed with great attention to detail, thus reflecting the knowledge and skills that have accrued from one generation to the next.

The Vander Ghinste family is deeply sensitive to the connection between the buildings, the activities carried out in them and the image of the final product. The story of Omer – told through stained-glass windows that have adorned the windows of bars in Flanders, Brussels and northern France for more than a century – teaches us that material things are part of a collective biography that can in fact be given a twist. The new brewery hall is the embodiment of the Vander Ghinste family's cultural capital and craftsmanship. It is the signboard of a client who builds not for himself, but for posterity.

Sofie De Caigny

OMER VANDER GHINSTE BREWERY

Offices
Architecten- en ingenieursbureau D'hondt Beyens Goesaert and Claeys/Haelvoet Architecten
Websites
www.bureaudbg.be
www.claeys-haelvoet.be
Address
Brouwtorenstraat 5, Bellegem
Client
Omer Vander Ghinste brewery

Design
January 2016
Delivered
June 2019
Surface area
1,463 m²
Volume
11,318 m³
Total building cost
€ 3,500,000 - excl. VAT
Total building cost per m²
€ 2,420 - excl. VAT

Main contractor
Verstraete Bouw, Roeselare
Stability studies
BM engineering, Kortrijk (overall stability)
Ney & Partners, Watermaal-Bosvoorde (roof structure stability)
Technology studies
Boydens engineering, Zedelgem
Photographer
Klaas Verdru

Situation plan

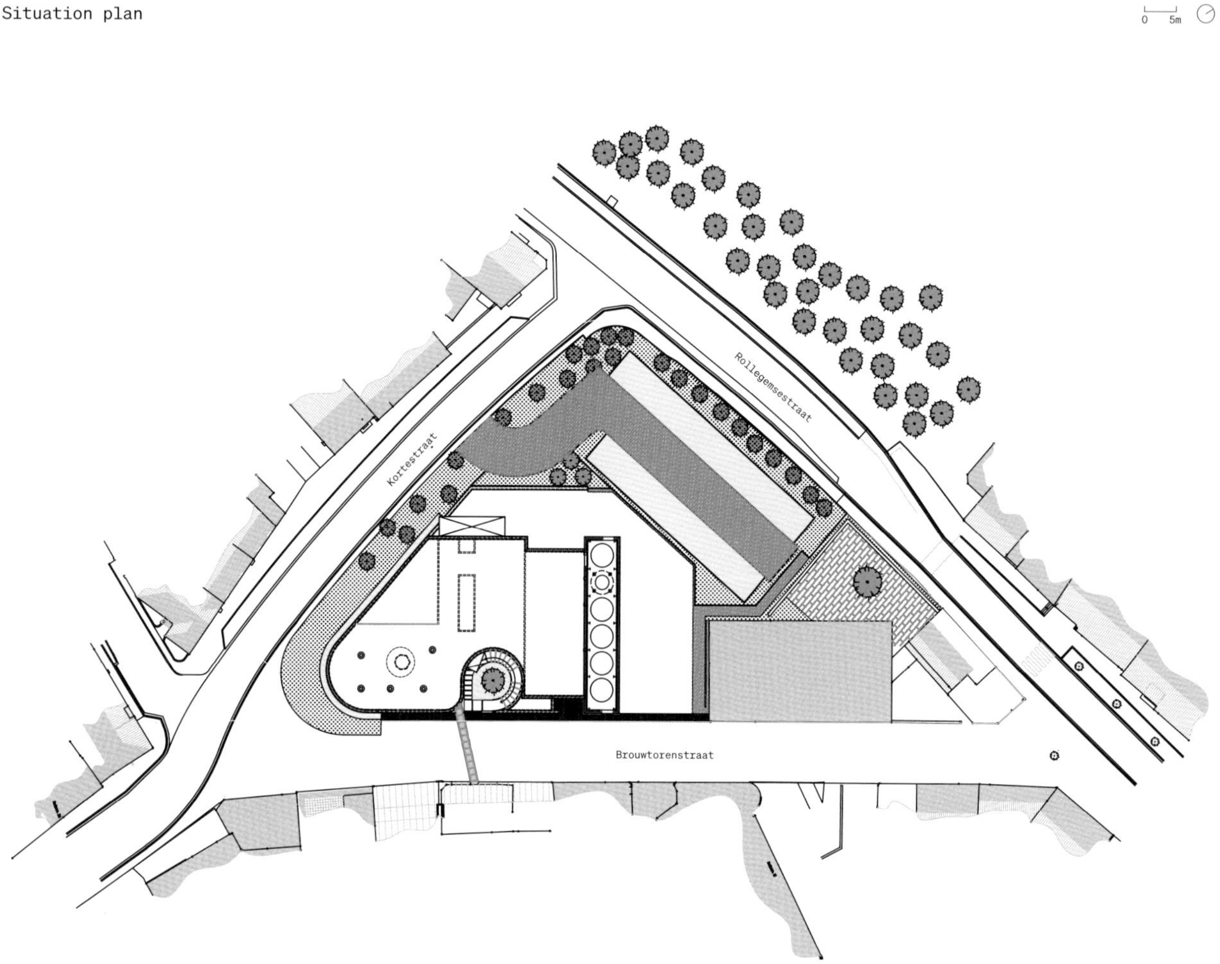

Section Aa

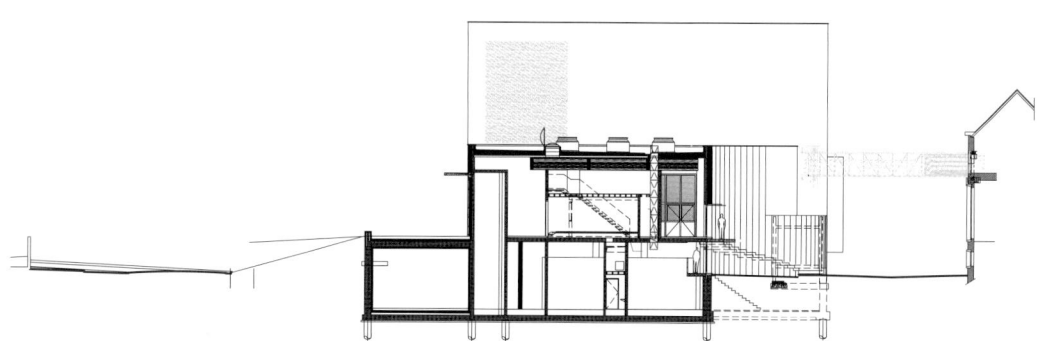

Architecten- en ingenieursbureau D'hondt Beyens Goesaert and Claeys/Haelvoet Architecten

Level 1
Ground floor
Level -1

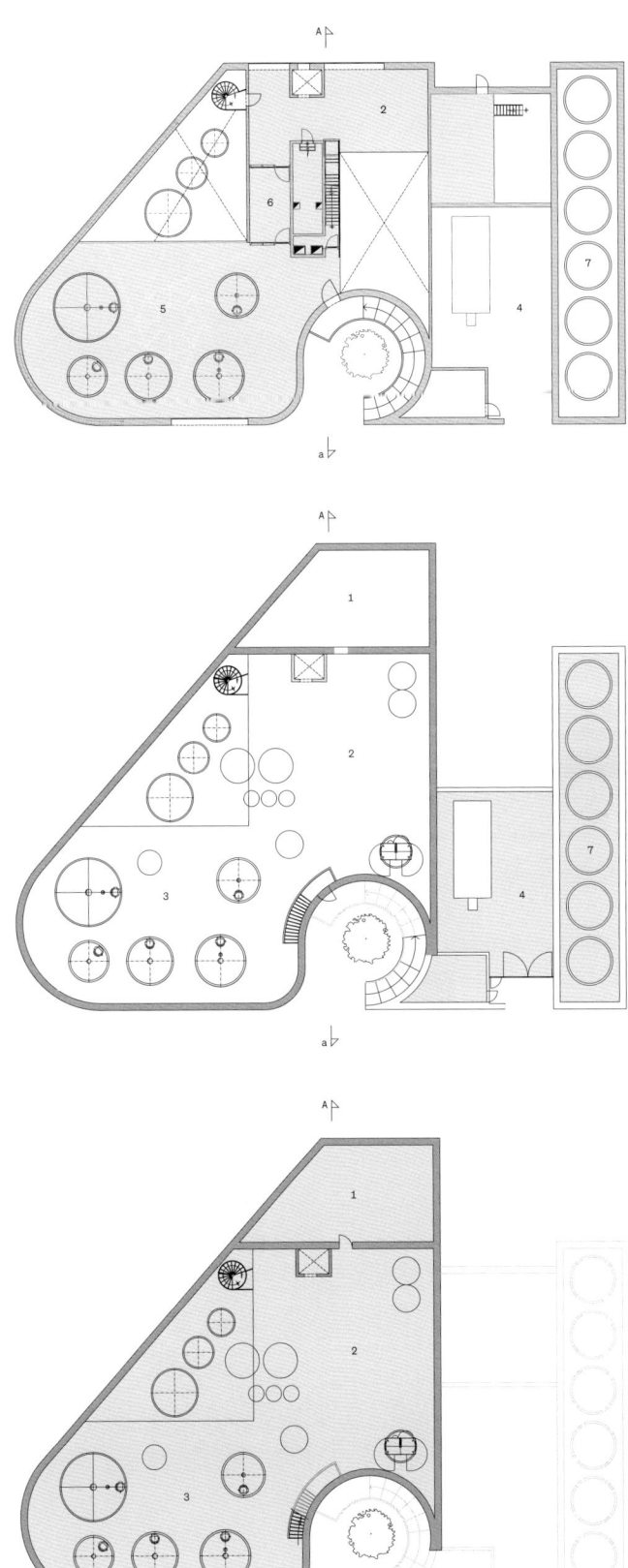

1. Hop cellar
2. Processing area, raw ingredients
3. Lower brewery hall
4. Boiling kettles
5. Upper brewery hall
6. Operators
7. Silos

Omer Vander Ghinste brewery

Architecten- en ingenieursbureau D'hondt Beyens Goesaert and Claeys/Haelvoet Architecten

Omer Vander Ghinste brewery

Agrotopia rooftop greenhouse, Roeselare

META architectuurbureau and van Bergen Kolpa Architecten

On the outskirts of Roeselare, META architectuurbureau developed the Agrotopia rooftop greenhouse with van Bergen Kolpa Architecten. This was prompted by the 2013 Pilot Projects Productive Landscape, initiated by the Flemish Government Architect with the aim to reconcile different sectors and, in so doing, make more efficient use of rural land in Flanders. This begs the question of how residual urban space can be activated for agricultural purposes in order to allow for higher-quality open space. Inagro, the Flemish research centre for agriculture and horticulture in West Flanders, was tasked with realizing the new testing facility.

A (sub)urban rooftop greenhouse of 9,500 m² provides space for research into urban food production. As a transparent crown atop an existing auction house for vegetables and fruit, Agrotopia literally nests on top of the network it wants to serve. From this position, it offers panoramic views of the city and the surrounding landscape. The 'agrotopian' greenhouse is more than a purely functional structure. Above all, it is a showcase for Inagro's pioneering work. The greenhouse rests upon the existing warehouse, five new concrete water silos and a row of added columns.

In two carefully chosen places, the standard flat greenhouse façade in diffused glass makes way for a more expressive and transparent variant. On the south side, the serrated roof surface folds over the concrete base. A dynamic frontage of upright bay windows is thus created, marked by the regal concrete staircase that leads from ground level to the entrance plaza. Moreover, the zig-zag pattern allows for targeted sun protection while retaining views of the wider environment. On the west side – above the water silos beside the city ring road – the typical roof construction of the greenhouse again lies on its side. Behind it, a double-height greenhouse offers facilities for experiments in vertical horticulture. The horizontally articulated façade plays with the movement of the traffic but avoids any undesirable reflections. Moreover, it optimizes the angle of the sunlight for vertical agriculture.

Sustainability plays a key role in Inagro's project, in both operational and housing terms. The intensive usage of the available space around a city and working with circular provisions for cultivation follow on from this. Rainwater (collected via the roof) is stored in silos and subsequently used to irrigate the crops. Agrotopia utilizes the residual heat from the waste incinerator Mirom when solar gain fails to deliver the desired temperature. A box-in-box principle creates four different climate zones, making it possible to grow a variety of vegetables simultaneously. This allows for heating that is both targeted and economical. An educational route beyond the climate zones gives visitors the opportunity to learn about these horticultural experiments.

Agrotopia is the symbiosis between the forward-thinking ambition of the Pilot Projects Productive Landscape, Inagro's progressive research, and the quest for an architecture that is at once functional, sustainable, economical and representative. Research, agriculture, distribution and the city are closely intertwined in this initiative. It is an excellent example of densification for urbanized areas.

Fabian De Vriendt

AGROTOPIA ROOFTOP GREENHOUSE

Offices
META architectuurbureau and van Bergen Kolpa Architecten
Websites
www.meta.be
www.vanbergenkolpa.nl
Address
Oostnieuwkerksesteenweg 122, Roeselare
Client
Inagro, REO Veiling

Design
January 2015
Delivered
September 2021
Surface area
9,500 m²
Total building cost
€ 10,559,711 - excl. VAT
Total building cost per m²
€ 1,112 - excl. VAT
Main contractor
Persyn, Zwevegem

Stability studies
Tractebel Engineering, Antwerp
Technology studies
Wageningen UR Glastuinbouw, Blieswijk[NL]
Greenhouse studies
Smiemans Projecten, Kwintsheul[NL]
Photographer
Filip Dujardin

Situation plan

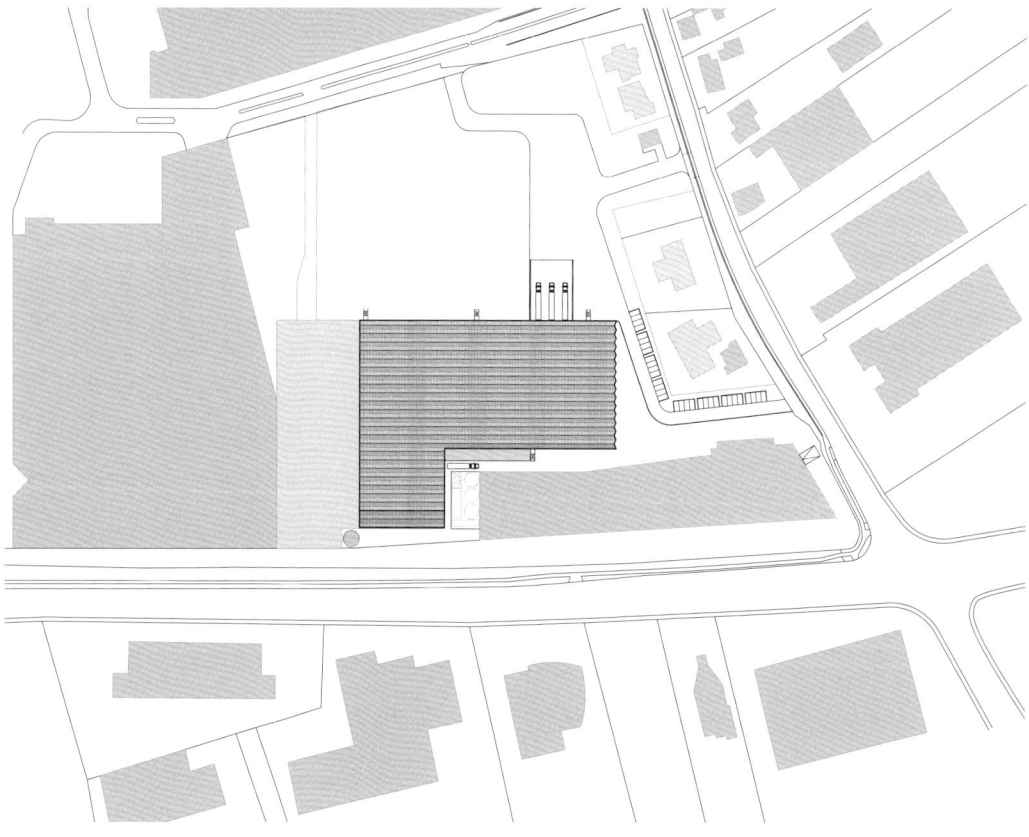

Axonometric projection

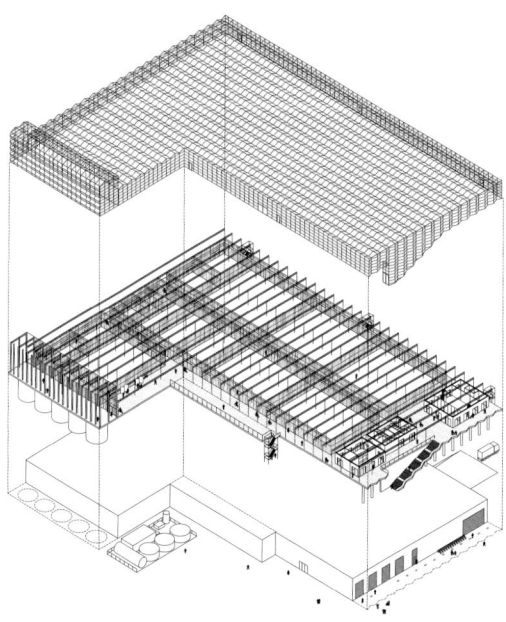

META architectuurbureau and van Bergen Kolpa Architecten

Level 1

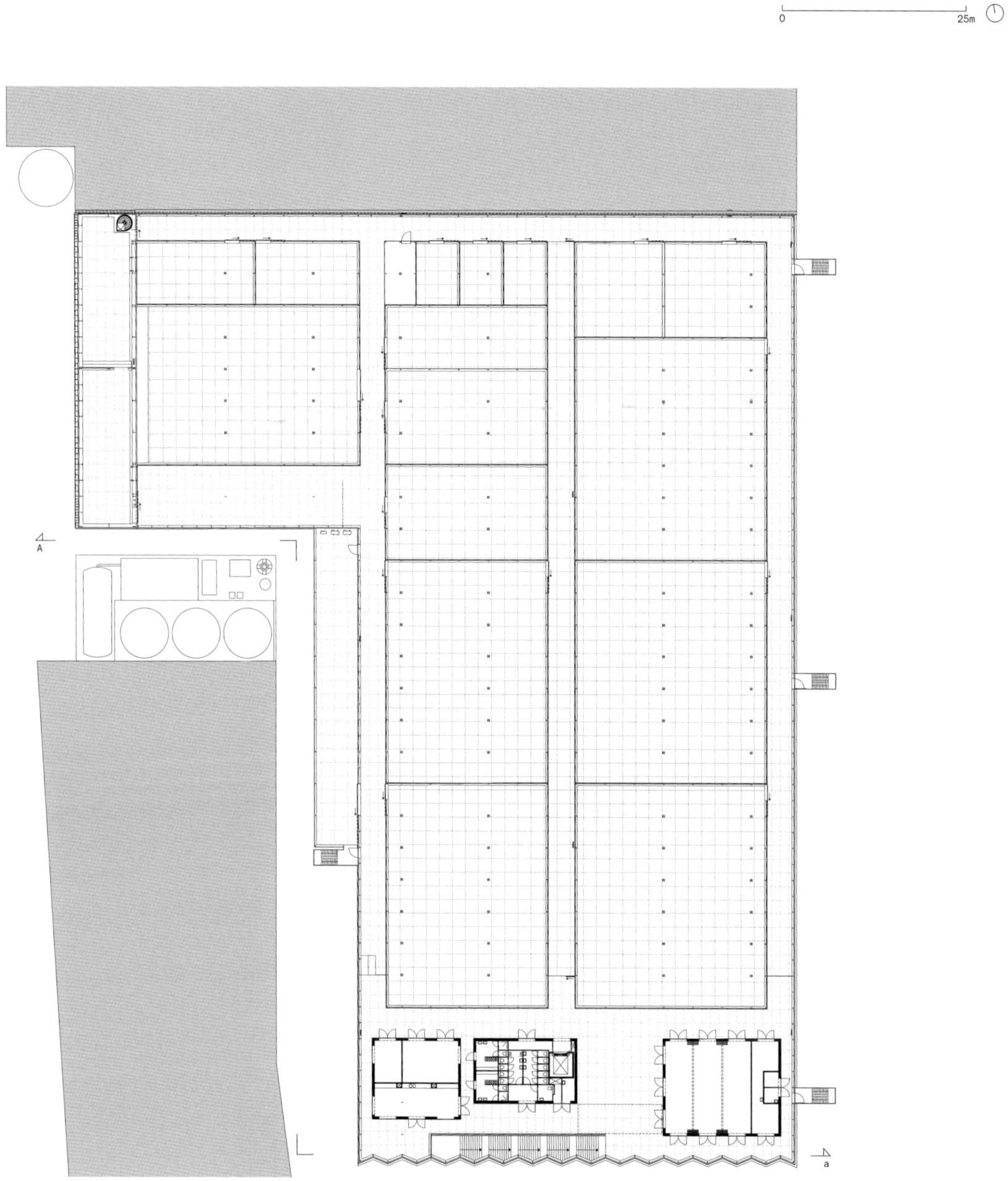

Section Aa

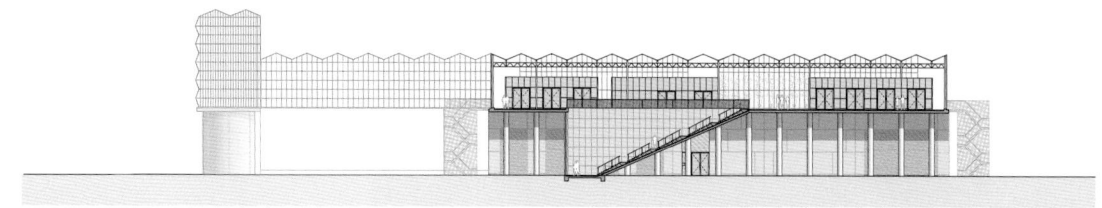

Agrotopia rooftop greenhouse

META architectuurbureau and van Bergen Kolpa Architecten

Park + Ride buildings, Antwerp

HUB

HUB has designed three new park-and-ride buildings on the Linkeroever (Left Bank), in Luchtbal and in Merksem as a modest contribution towards alleviating the colossal and seemingly intractable mobility issues in and around Antwerp. Each building is located close to public transport links to the city centre in the hope that visitors will be persuaded to leave their cars and travel on public transport, thereby relieving congestion. As an incentive, the cost of a day's parking is negligible compared to the parking fees in the centre. But the convenience should actually speak for itself: P+R Linkeroever offers spaces for cars arriving from Waasland, Ghent and West Flanders (to name but a few regions) and is located just a few tram stops from Groenplaats. It is the ideal solution for visitors wanting to avoid the almost permanent traffic jam from Kruibeke, through the Kennedy tunnel, and onto the Ring Road.

Nevertheless, the threshold for the first operational year of parking buildings is still relatively high and more encouragement is needed. Further increasing the difference in parking costs seems obvious. The infrastructure will not be the problem. HUB's park-and-ride buildings are a refreshing interpretation of well-known issues. The objective was not simply to cram as many vehicles as possible into a given space, but rather to organize their density in such a way that a high-quality spatial experience is created for pedestrians. In addition to a clever three-dimensional puzzle involving two different user flows, the primary aim here is to create an atypically open and light atmosphere.

This is achieved through the use of laminated timber trusses, which transfer the load from the floor slabs to the columns, both of which are made of concrete. Timber requires more height for the same structural load. The architects thus had to raise the ceiling far above the minimum height that defines most car parks. The structure therefore allows one to envisage alternative infill options for a less car-dependent future. In addition, the wood adds a measure of warmth to an otherwise grey palette of materials. It also led to a number of secondary design aspects that inject character into the building, such as the slightly curving horizontal lines and the detailing of the building nodes. Moreover, the floor slabs are always a little wider than the distance between the columns. Although structurally advantageous, this makes the space 'outside' the columns read like a pedestrian zone, if only because of the spatial proportions and the absence of a coat of paint.

The three park-and-ride buildings present a close structural affinity but are all individual in terms of organization. In the P+R Linkeroever, spacious patios let plenty of light and air into the vast horizontal parking levels. The lift shafts and stairwells take clever advantage of this, turning the walk to and from the cars into something other than a slalom course between vehicles. In Luchtbal, a central patio divides the building into two manageable sections. The monotony of the parking structure is further interrupted by the slight difference in the orientation of the two halves, a feature gladly carried over from the plot boundary. On the narrow parcel in Merksem, patios are not an issue and the parking levels are steadily sloped, so that users engage with a combination of climbing, descending and parking. In this way, each of the buildings uses the same constructive logic in its own unique way, tailored to the specific location.

Petrus Kemme

PARK + RIDE BUILDINGS

Office
HUB
Website
www.hub.eu
Addresses
Blancefloerlaan 501, Antwerp (Linkeroever)
Noorderlaan 502, Antwerp (Luchtbal)
Bredabaan 4 772, Merksem (Merksem)
Client
Lantis
Designs
January 2016 (Linkeroever)
January 2016 (Luchtbal)
September 2016 (Merksem)

Delivered
October 2021 (Linkeroever)
November 2021 (Luchtbal)
September 2021 (Merksem)
Surface areas
45,000 m² (Linkeroever)
51,000 m² (Luchtbal)
19,989 m² (Merksem)
Volumes
248,578 m³ (Linkeroever)
286,800 m³ (Luchtbal)
80,955 m³ (Merksem)
Total building costs
€ 25,000,000 - excl. VAT (Linkeroever)
€ 37,200,000 - excl. VAT (Luchtbal)
€ 12,500,000 - excl. VAT (Merksem)

Total building costs per m²
€ 556 - excl. VAT (Linkeroever)
€ 729 - excl. VAT (Luchtbal)
€ 625 - excl. VAT (Merksem)
Main contractors
RINK (Artes-CitBlaiton-Mobilis) (Linkeroever)
AB Eiffiage, Antwerp (Luchtbal)
Franki, Veerle (Merksem)
Stability and electrical studies
Sweco, Brussels
Photographer
Jeroen Verrecht

Section Aa Linkeroever

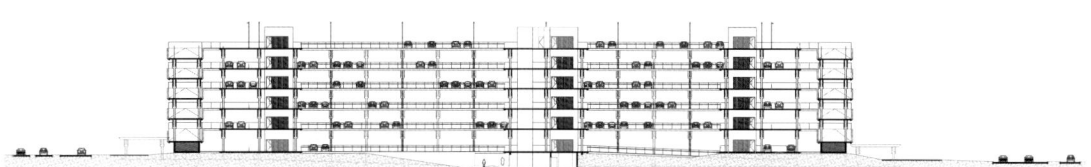

Section Bb Luchtbal

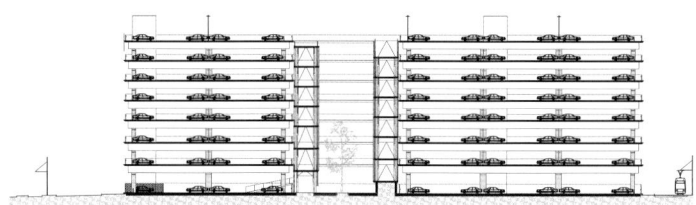

North façade Merksem

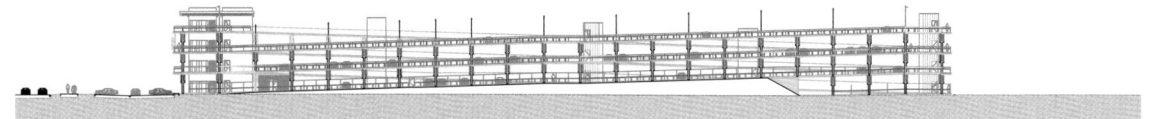

Type plan Linkeroever

Type plan Luchtbal

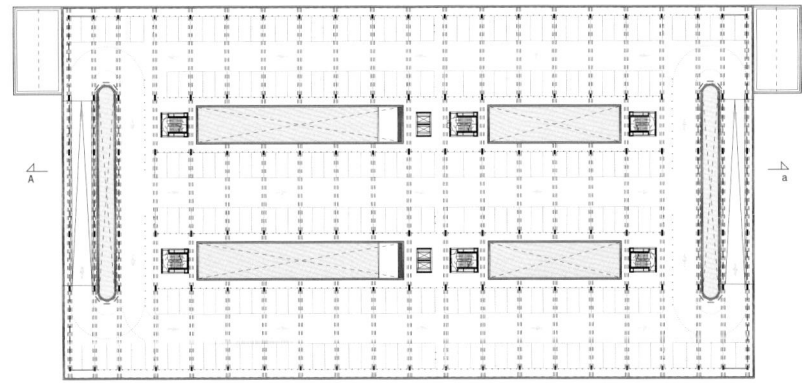

Type plan Merksem

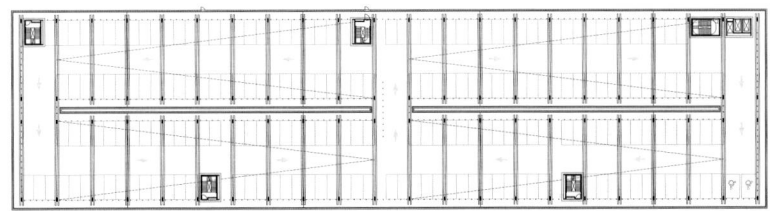

Park + Ride buildings

Park + Ride buildings

Collective housing, Borgerhout

Architecten Broekx–Schiepers

Just before the intersection of Turnhoutsebaan and the Singel ring road, Borgerhout's nineteenth-century urban fabric, comprising blocks of houses and streets, is falling apart. Where once the end walls of two blocks neatly enclosed the road on both sides, there now lies a vague grassy area, car parks and a dog paddock. The recently completed collective housing project by Architecten Broekx-Schiepers is a first step towards restoring the blocks that were damaged in the 1970s. It thus fits within the approach taken by AG Vespa (the Autonomous Municipal Agency for Real Estate and Urban Projects in Antwerp) for tackling urban blight. In so doing, it stimulates urban renewal in the surrounding neighbourhoods.

Four terraced houses in Gijselsstraat and six flats in Gravinstraat complete the street walls of narrow workers' houses. In-between lies the project's collective programme: a garden with toilet and storage shed, plus a generous bicycle rack with canopy that provides a shelter for the residents' outdoor activities. The ground-floor patios of the terraced houses, the access to the indoor but open staircase to the flats, and the two exits from the underground garage all seem designed to encourage spontaneous encounters along the perimeter of the garden. Because the dog paddock and car park on Turnhoutsebaan are temporarily being retained, the project will present blind, provisionally finished side walls until the block is completed.

The flexible floor plans for the houses, which are sold as empty shells, form an interesting architectural response to the question of designing a housing project that can accommodate the many varied lifestyles within a superdiverse society. The terraced houses contain seven or eight equally spacious rooms, linked in twos or threes, which are connected to the party walls by an open staircase. Two terraced houses contain a four-storey stack of two interconnecting rooms; the other two terraced houses comprise a single storey with three rooms and two storeys with two rooms. The living spaces can be permanently or flexibly divided with lightweight walls (to be added later). In the show home along the front façade, for instance, the ground-floor room has been separated into an entrance hall, toilet and kitchen. The first floor contains two small children's rooms. The adjoining room at the rear offers additional space for a study or playroom while also functioning as the circulation area for the staircase.

The flats have a similar structure. The front and back are separated by an intermediate strip containing a bathroom and, in the show flat, a kitchen and hallway. In the strips along the façades, columns suggest rooms. The four bright spaces, each with two windows, are equally spacious, meaning their purpose is interchangeable and their surfaces divisible. In addition, the apartment is reached by stairs at the back and by a lift at the front: entering from the street side or the garden side is equivalent. The show flat has glazed doors (both sliding and revolving) that either turn away from, or slide into, the thickness of the walls. This creates long views between the front and rear rooms.

The different façade heights as well as the sense of rhythm, the mouldings, cornices and door accents all reflect the narrow middle-class and workers' houses of varying heights in Antwerp's nineteenth-century belt, thus ensuring a familiar streetscape.

Marleen Goethals

COLLECTIVE HOUSING

Office
Architecten Broekx-Schiepers
Website
www.broekx-schiepers.be
Addresses
Gravinstraat 31-33-35, Gijselsstraat 162-164-166-168, Borgerhout
Client
AG Vespa
Design
August 2016

Delivered
June 2021
Surface area
2,259 m² (incl. private outdoor space, excl. communal outdoor space)
Volume
6,770 m³
Total building cost
€ 2,694,911 - excl. VAT
Total building cost per m²
€ 1,192 - excl. VAT
Main contractor
dhulst', Lier

Stability studies
AB Associates, Hasselt
Technology studies
AE+, Sint-Truiden
Acoustics studies
PS-Acoustics, Sint-Truiden
EPB reporting
Buro Conform, Bilzen
Safety coordination
Vekmo, Tessenderlo
Photographer
Tim Vande Velde

Situation plan

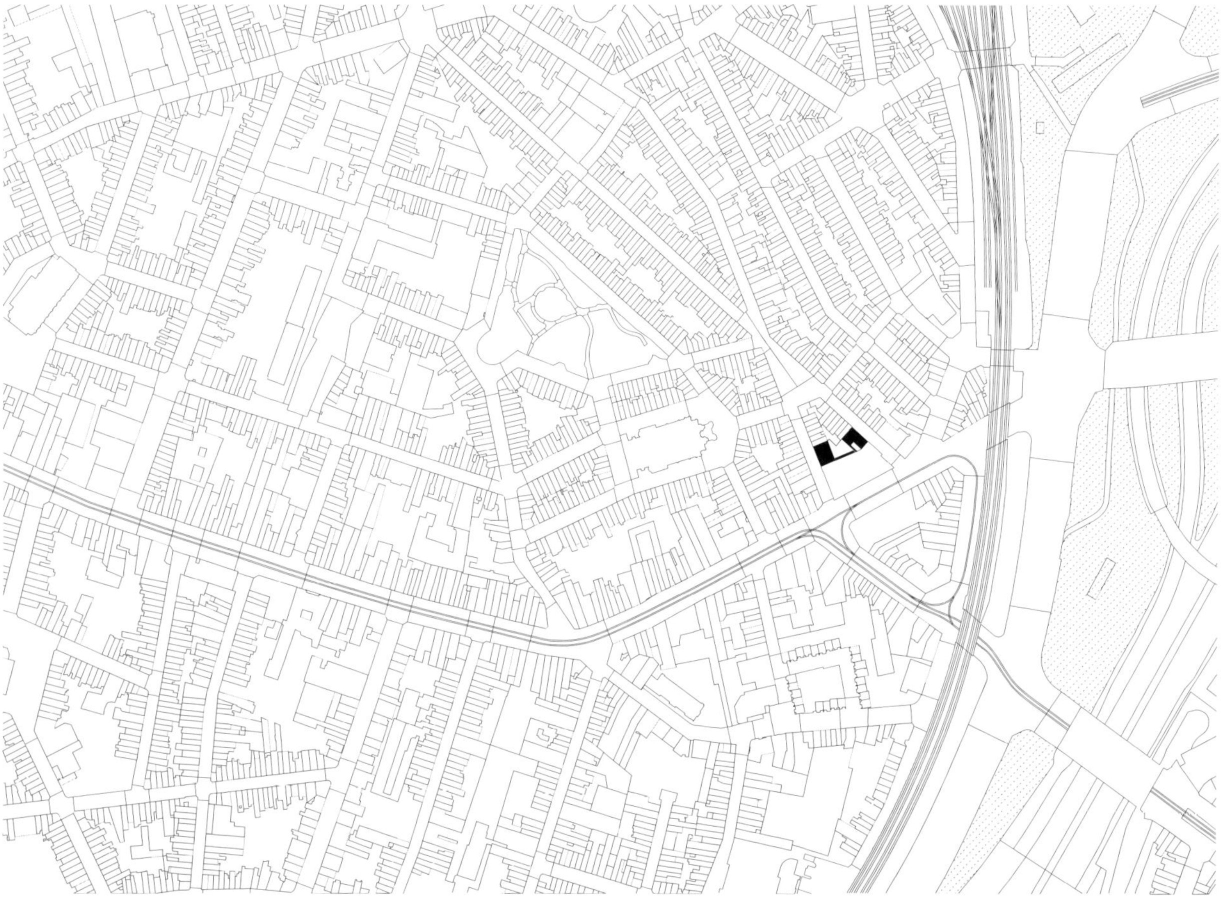

Section Aa

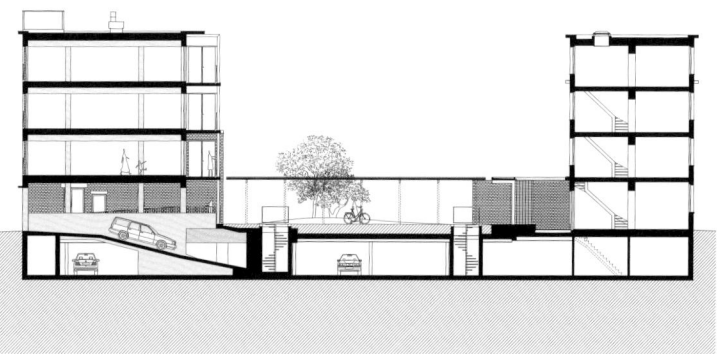

Level 2
Ground floor

Level 3
Level 1

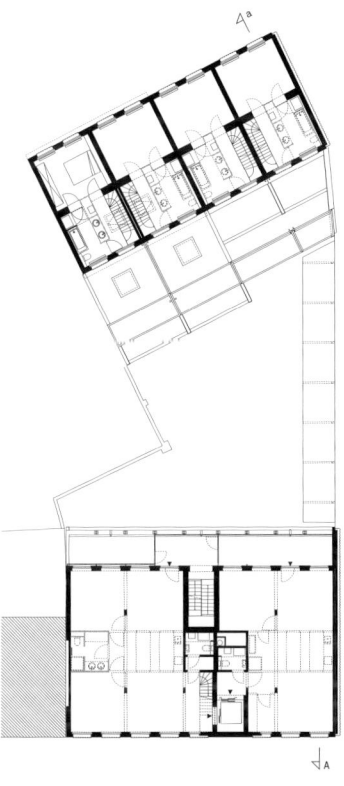
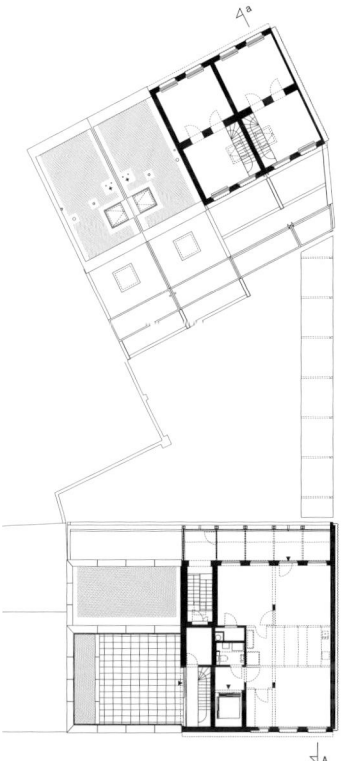
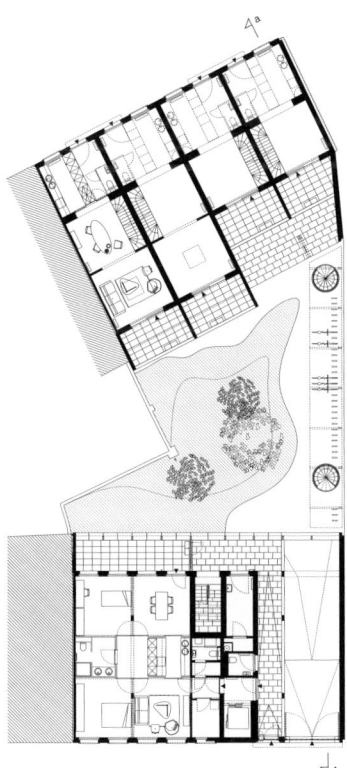
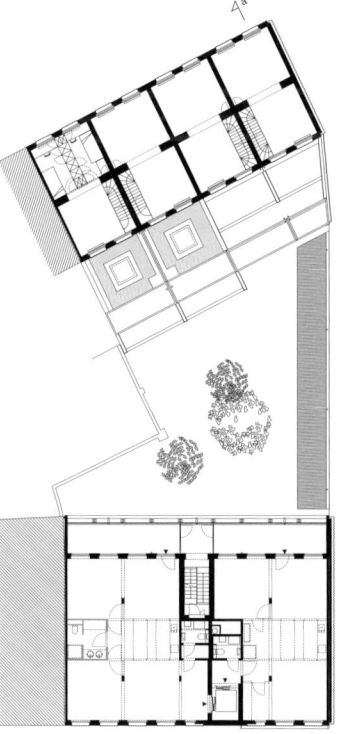

Collective housing

Collective housing

De Bijloke concert hall, Ghent

DRDH Architects and Julian Harrap Architects

In Ghent, by the river Leie, a group of buildings from the thirteenth to the twentieth century stand next to each other, generating a patchwork of different materials and styles from the Gothic to the baroque. The Bijloke site comprises the STAM Ghent City Museum, the KASK School of Arts, an art library and a ballet studio. One can read the site as a museum quarter like we see in other cities, such as Vienna and Amsterdam. The site also includes the Bijloke Music Centre, which houses a concert hall, a café and multipurpose rooms with varying capacities and possibilities for performances and meetings. The master plan of De Bijloke was designed by DRDH Architects and Julian Harrap Architects in collaboration with Arup Venue and Acoustics, ABT and RCR, which won the invited competition in 2017. As part of the master plan, the first phase was the refurbishment of the café situated next to the entrance and designed by Studio Helder and Onbetaalbaar. Following the entrance and café, one reaches an interstitial space between two buildings with a covered roof. The threshold between these two historical buildings introduces a pause and entering the concert hall provides a feeling of grandiosity that is not rooted in monumentality but in being ancient, while time and scent give a hidden dimension to the space, especially with the oak roof truss.

The Bijloke concert hall is located inside one of the oldest structures of the complex of buildings, an infirmary erected in 1228 with its rose windows and high pitch roof. After the infirmary moved to another location in Ghent in 1982, the first classical music concert was held in the abandoned building in 1988, while a decade later the city of Ghent set up an organization to recognize it as a concert venue. Under the heavy weight of the roof structure, the ancient load-bearing walls have been pushed outwards. This aggravated the acoustic characteristics of the structure, which was not initially erected to function as a music venue. The primary motivation behind the latest renovation was to ensure that the acoustics of the hall were of the highest quality. The architects' answer was to add a sunken ship to the listed building.

The building floor was dug 1.2 metres underground to provide the space for the sunken ship. It works almost as a mirror of the ancient roof structure, making you feel like you are looking inside a ship structure from below. In the short section, the sequence of timber wall panelling along the long side of the hall, elevated seats, central seating, elevated seats and wall panelling corresponds to the geometry of the roof structure. Another symmetry occurs on the long section, in which the higher seats in the back rows are mirrored by the rear seating behind the orchestra, which can also serve for a choir, depending on the performance. This rear seating, a feature generally found in major concert venues like the Berliner Philharmonie, gains new and intimate meaning in this relatively modest hall with 830 seats.

The newly added wall panels, stage and flooring are all made of thin plates of fumed oak timber in reference to the solid oak roof truss. This generates a continuity between the sunken ship and the building it is situated in. All these design decisions – mirroring, choice of materials, location of the stage – ensure that the audience enjoys a comfortable and distinctive listening experience. The acoustics in the concert hall are so peculiar that as you talk, you feel like the space is correcting your tone and frequency.

Hülya Ertas

DE BIJLOKE CONCERT HALL

Offices
DRDH Architects and
Julian Harrap Architects
Websites
www.drdharchitects.co.uk
www.julianharraparchitects.co.uk
Address
Bijlokekaai 7, Ghent
Client
Muziekcentrum de Bijloke
Design
June 2017
Delivered
September 2020

Surface areas
Master plan: 2,700 m²
Concert hall and chapel: 1,150m²
Total building cost
€ 4,604,000 – excl. VAT
Main contractor
Denys, Ghent
Stage technology contractor
DTS-2, Groningen[NL]
A/V contractor
Amptec, Diepenbeek
Seating contractor
Poltrona Frau, Tolentino[IT]
Stability studies
ABT, Antwerp

Technology studies
RCR, Herent
Acoustics and theatre technology studies
Arup, London[UK]
Client project management
A-RES, Ghent
Safety coordination
Vekmo, Tessenderlo
Photographer
Karin Borghouts
except p. 147 top:
Michiel De Cleene

Ground floor

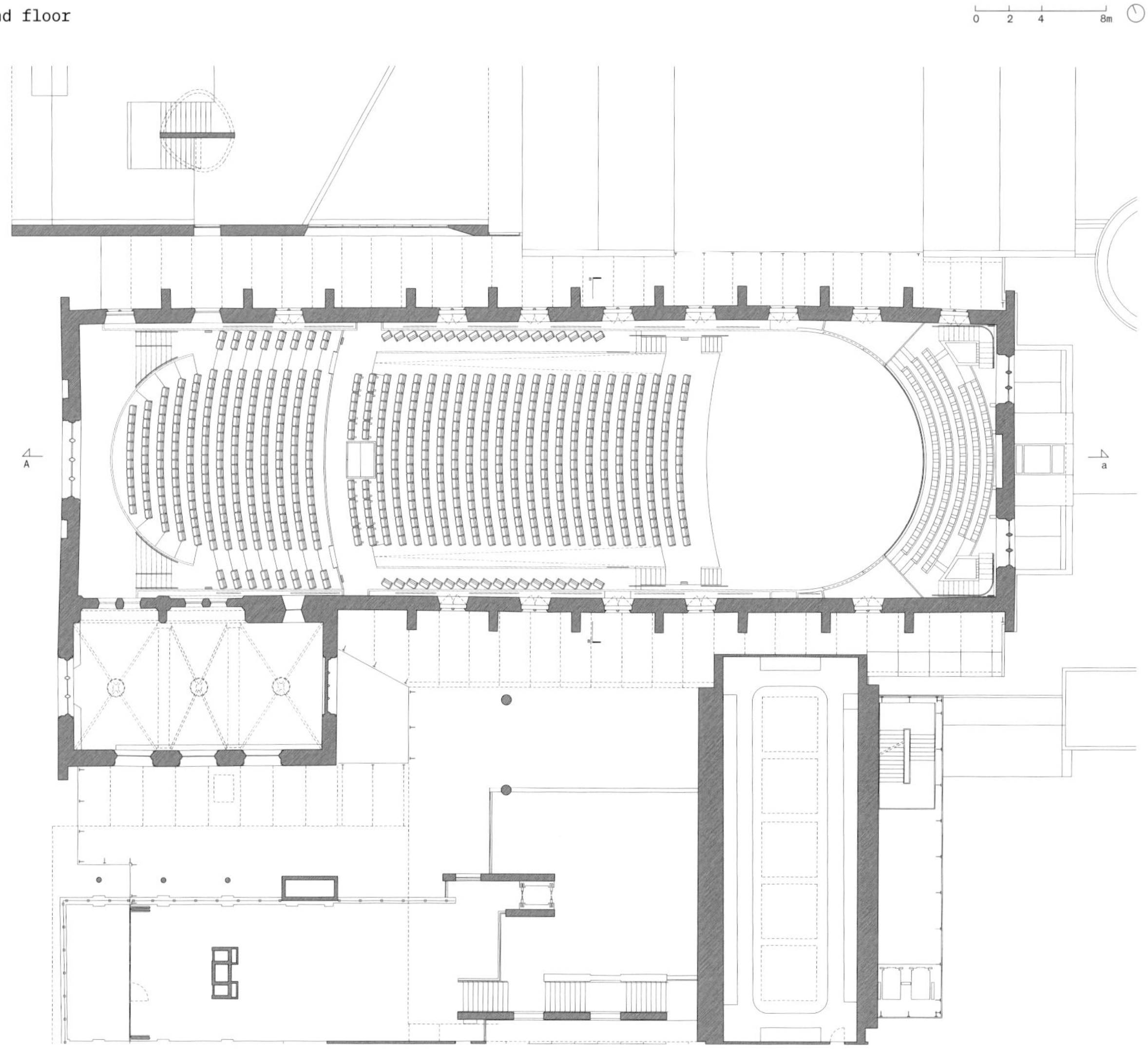

Section Aa

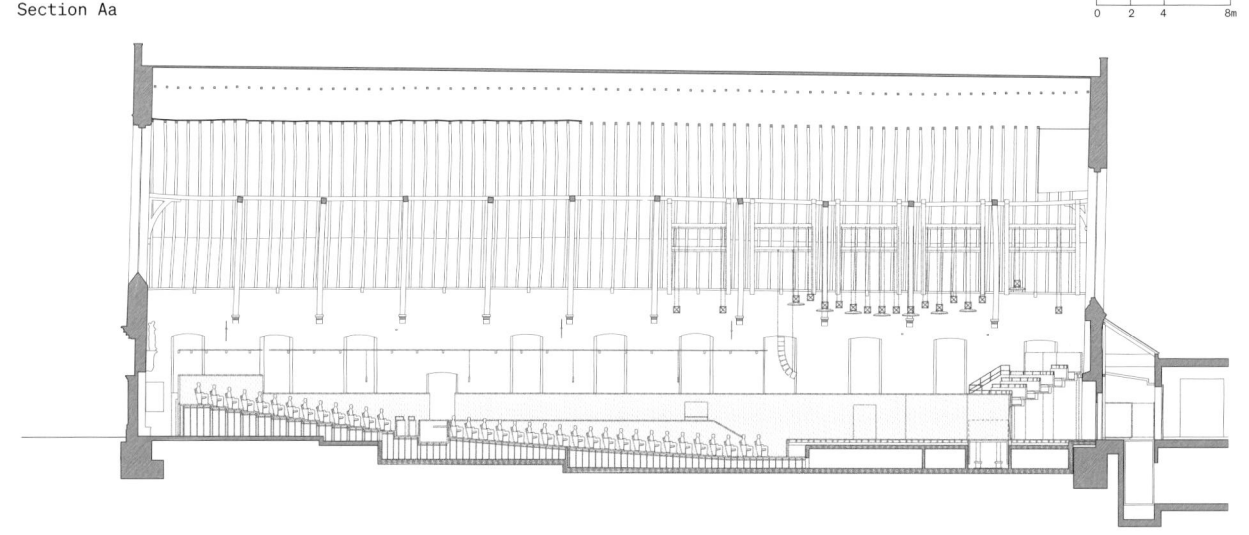

DRDH Architects and Julian Harrap Architects

De Bijloke concert hall

Rivierenhof provincial school campus, Deurne

architectuuratelier ambiorix

A thin plate draws a new abstract line in the Rivierenhof landscape. The existing site is characterized by stately classical school buildings surrounded by greenery. Multiple renovations and extensions to the original main volume by architect Pol Berger had completely severed the link between street and park. This building, once a pavilion in the open, has been liberated from all the weighty additions and has regained its original freshness. The new project is a recalibration, one that opens up the landscape and also provides a novel view of the park.

The intervention is twofold: an L-shaped building block completes the monastic typology of the original school with the classrooms for the theory lessons; the new building project consists of a low, detached volume that accommodates the studio spaces.

The detached building is both abstract and ambiguous. The radical nature of the project is reminiscent of Superstudio's work, the architects who dreamed of new and better worlds. Here too, the approach is utterly democratic. A single open square in which everything and everyone coalesces, both school and surroundings. The roof makes the transition between street and park, and also functions as an entrance. A white, open space – defined by a number of well-placed patios and skylights – forms a contemporary belvedere overlooking the park. The skylight grid suggests a densely occupied subterranean world. It piques your curiosity. The practical aspect of the school programme is embedded here in a semi-underground level, hidden from the eyes of visitors. A new world is secreted beneath the rooftop square. Creativity can flourish here in peace and quiet. Studio rooms are usually arranged as large neutral spaces, with closed walls and one-sided daylight. Here, in this project, all the studios are connected visually and physically. No walls, but glass partitions. The divisions are wafer-thin. The classrooms are lined up like shop windows, you can look through them, which means that all the attention goes to the students and their creations. Because of this reciprocal openness, all hierarchy is eliminated: classrooms, storage spaces, technical facilities, they all have equal value. One large studio floor connects all the classrooms. Conventional corridors are avoided as much as possible. The overall feeling is extremely intense, in terms of both use and sensory perception. The visual and physical impact is powerful and creates a unique experience.

The central zone between the classrooms is an outdoor area that forges the connection to the old building. Giant boulders reinforce the alienating effect and provide a link to the world above. The abstraction of the above-ground intervention is given an innately human and warm continuation in the subterranean level. This duality – in terms of both concept and experience – makes for an extremely pleasant and palpable experience.

Kiki Verbeeck

RIVIERENHOF PROVINCIAL SCHOOL CAMPUS

Office
architectuuratelier ambiorix
Website
www.aaa.studio
Address
Turnhoutsebaan 250, Deurne
Client
Province of Antwerp,
Logistics Department (DAV)

Design
December 2014
Delivered
December 2020
Surface area
7,800 m²
Volume
29,600 m³
Total building cost
€ 12,153,840 - excl. VAT
Total building cost per m²
€ 1,558 - excl. VAT

Main contractor
Strabag Belgium, Antwerp
Stability studies
Ney & Partners, Watermaal-Bosvoorde
Special technology studies
Boydens Engineering, Brussels
Acoustics studies
Blasco, Knokke-Heist
Photographer
Michiel De Cleene
except p. 154 and p. 155
bottom: Frans Parthesius

Situation plan

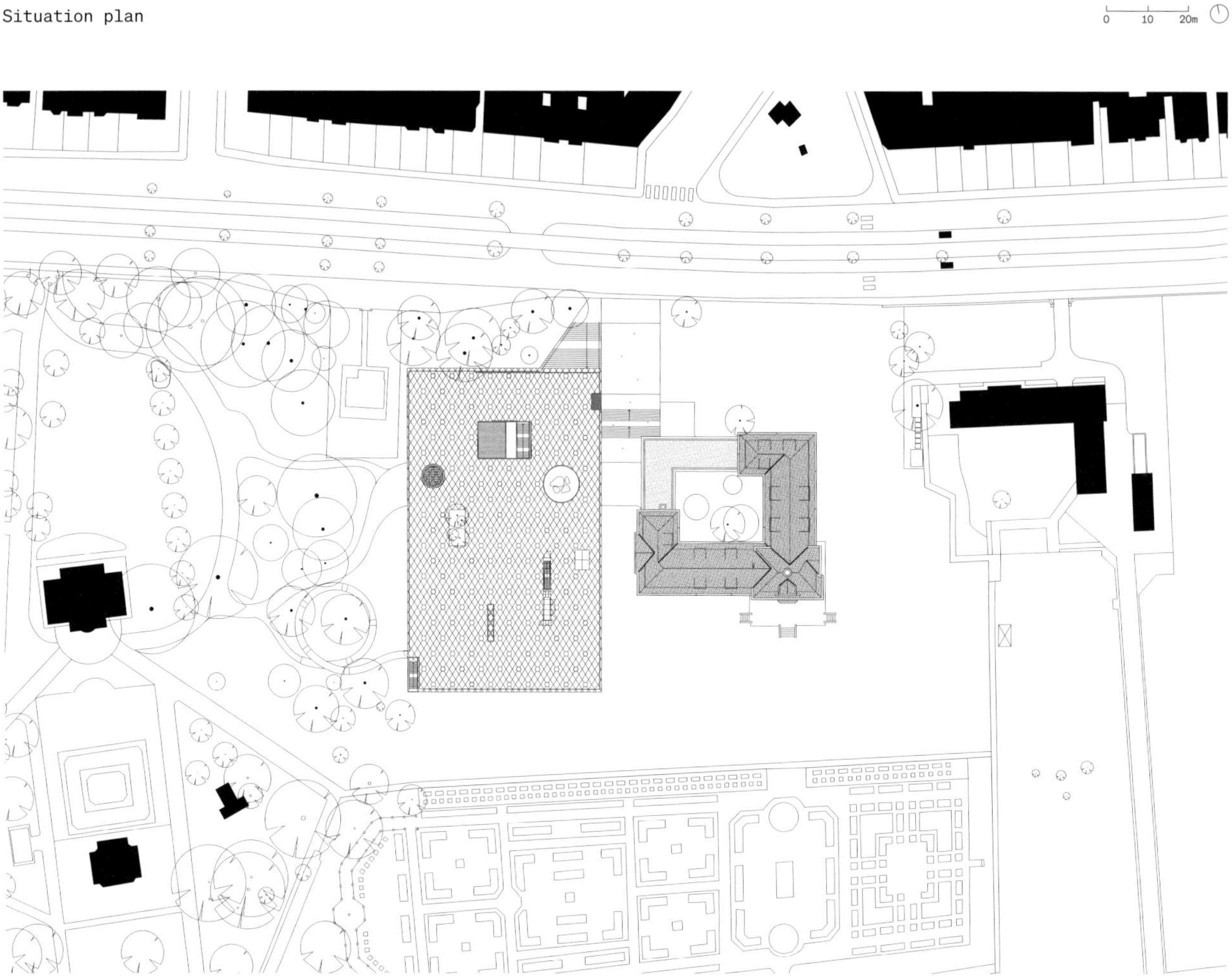

South façade

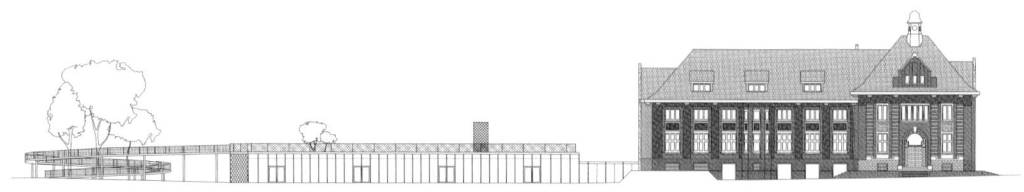

architectuuratelier ambiorix

Level 1
Ground floor

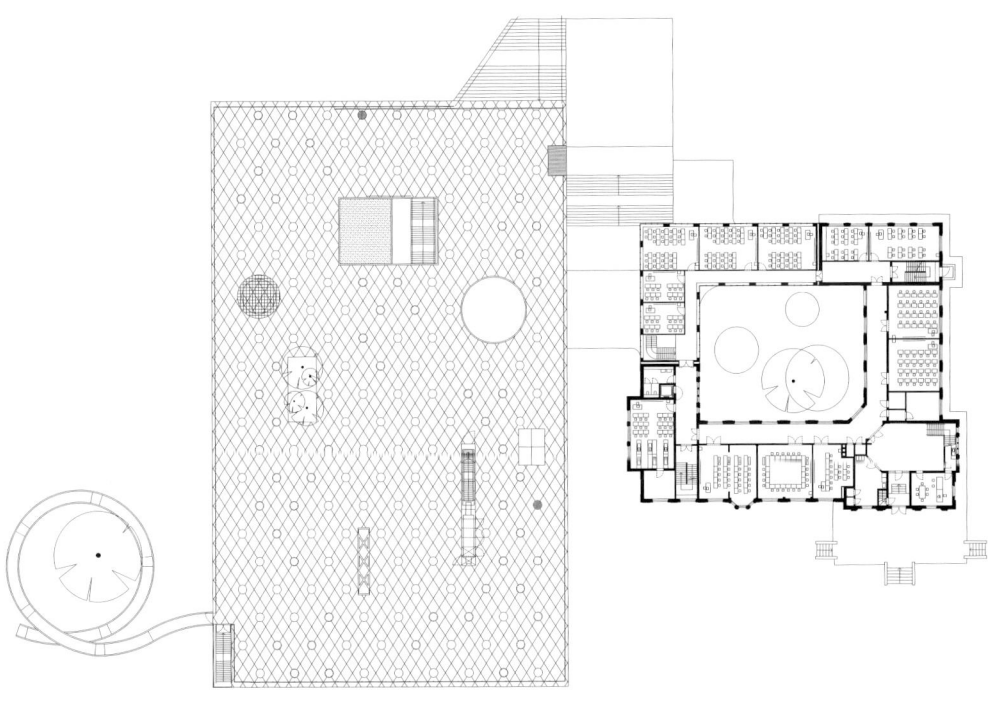

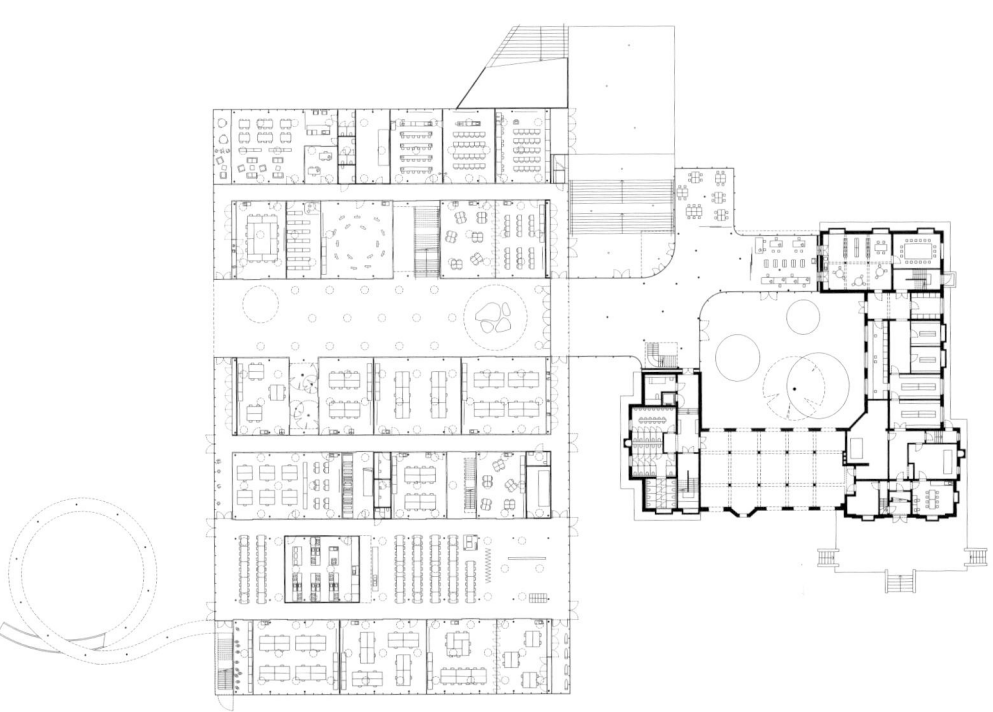

Rivierenhof provincial school campus

architectuuratelier ambiorix

Rivierenhof provincial school campus

Melopee municipal building, Ghent

Xaveer De Geyter Architects

The most striking building along the Oude Dokken is a large, abstract climbing frame. Between the various residential volumes lined up by OMA's master plan, this open structure incorporates both indoor and outdoor spaces in a single gesture.

Just as Le Corbusier had his 'machine for living in', Xaveer De Geyter Architects in Ghent presents a 'machine for education' or, better still, a 'machine for playing in'. All stacked dynamics on a compact plot. In short, a new school prototype. This project shows precisely what the Ghent City Architect means by his urban buildings: fascinating multi-tenant volumes that transcend their programme.

Viewed from the outside, the new Melopee primary school is more structure than building. A demarcation of the maximum building volume marks the corners of the playing field. Once inside (a paradox, because inside is outside and outside is inside), the surprising programmatic interaction is striking. A refreshing alternation of indoor and outdoor spaces that influence, reinforce and confirm each other.

The school is named after a poem by Paul van Ostaijen. The poetry within the industrial structure of the building is surprising. The sensitive stacking and mixing of functions creates an extremely palpable building, one in which it is a pleasure to learn and spend time. The steel structure offers protection and security against the capricious surroundings. This controlled meandering of play areas, which acquire an even more spectacular dimension thanks to their stacking, is actually a direct translation of the need for densification within the city.

A walk through the building tells a story that is both logical and surprising. The accumulation of kindergarten, classrooms, refectory and sports hall, each with its own outside space, is built up from its own logic. It is the mutual interactions and programmatic relations that make the walk so captivating. The outdoor spaces are playful and float within the steel framework. Both child and teacher as well as visitor are offered a wealth of new perspectives on the city. Children are not patronized in this school but are seen as full-fledged city dwellers.

The building does not initially pretend to be architecture. However, the meticulous selection of materials and detailing lend it a great deal of sensitivity and subtlety. A rich and varied material palette not only lends an essential identity to the various functions but is also chosen according to the specific usage needs. For example, the large, wide staircase with a white cast floor serves as a tribune, while the refectory and sports hall each have their own specific colour of perforated glazed bricks, which also provide acoustic insulation. The classrooms have warm, stained interiors in addition to polymer concrete, while the outdoor areas are interspersed with colourful impact-resistant surfaces, concrete and plants.

Everything is enclosed and framed within the galvanized steel framework.

Kiki Verbeeck

MELOPEE MUNICIPAL BUILDING

Office
Xaveer De Geyter Architects
Website
www.xdga.be
Address
Kompasplein 1, Ghent
Client
sogent
Design
May 2015

Delivered
February 2020
Surface areas
4,630 m² (interior) +
3,050 m² (exterior)
Volumes
24,500 m³ (interior) +
28,000 m³ (exterior)
Total building cost
€ 10,000,000 - excl. VAT

Total building cost per m²
€ 1,302 - excl. VAT
(interior + exterior)
Stability studies
Ney & Partners, Watermaal-Bosvoorde
Acoustics studies
Daidalos Peutz, Leuven
Technology studies
Boydens Engineering, Ghent
Photographer
Maxime Delvaux

Situation plan

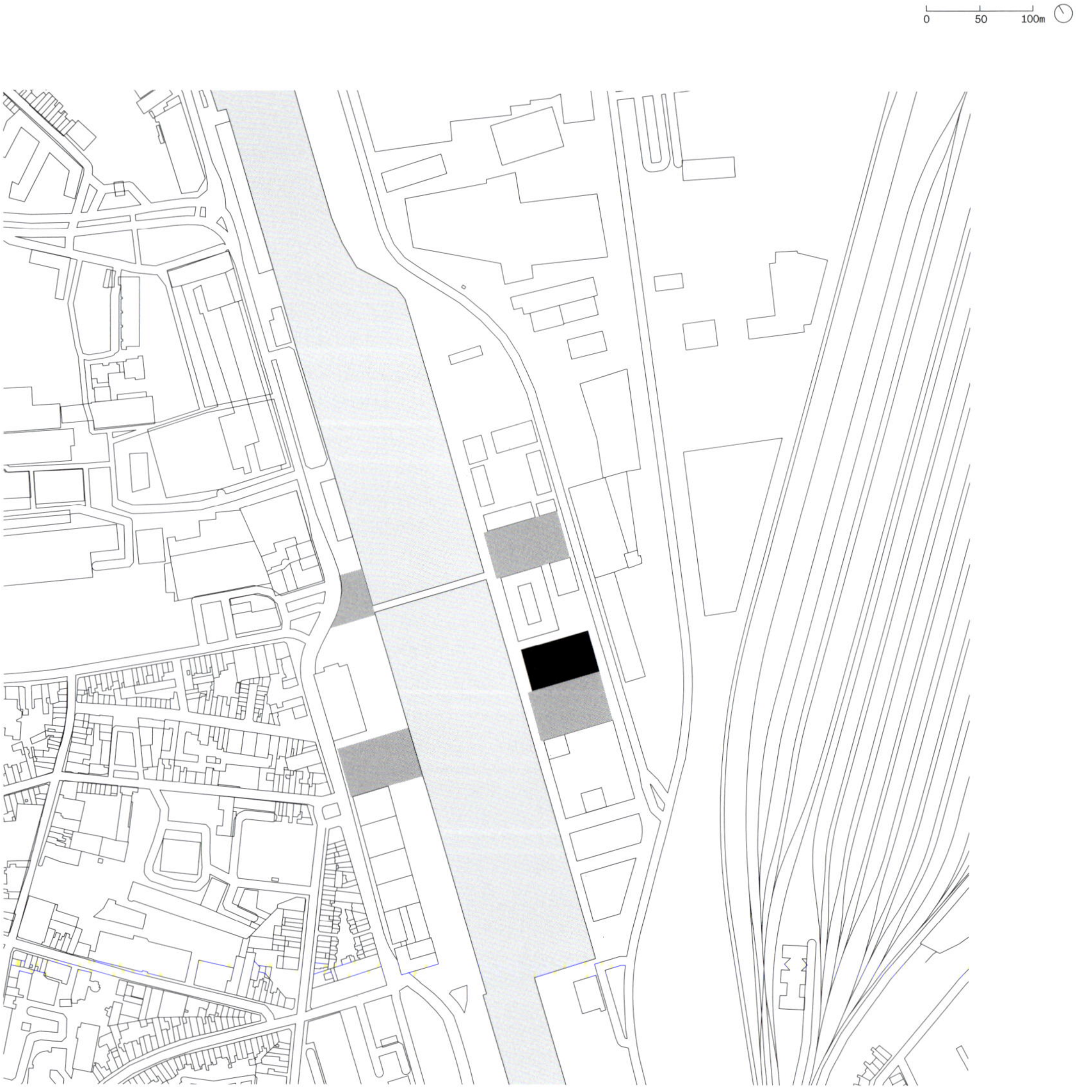

Section Aa

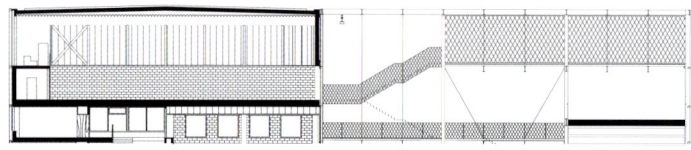

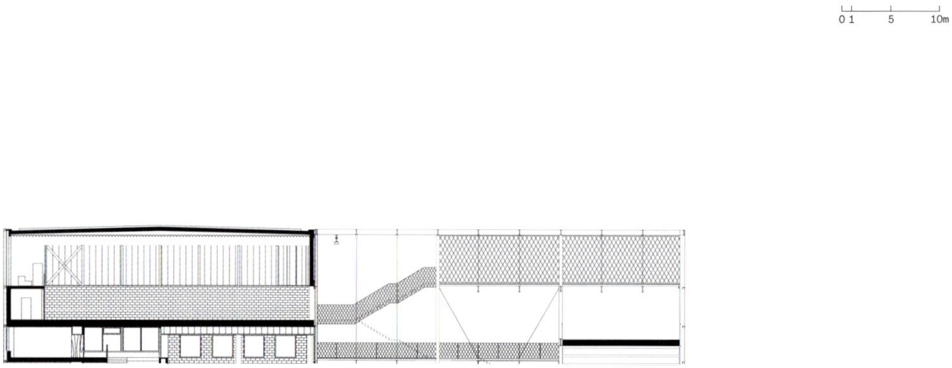

Xaveer De Geyter Architects

Level 3
Level 2
Ground floor

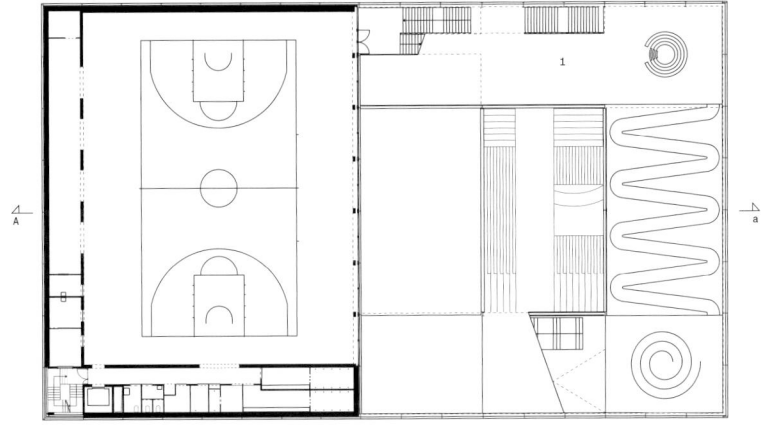

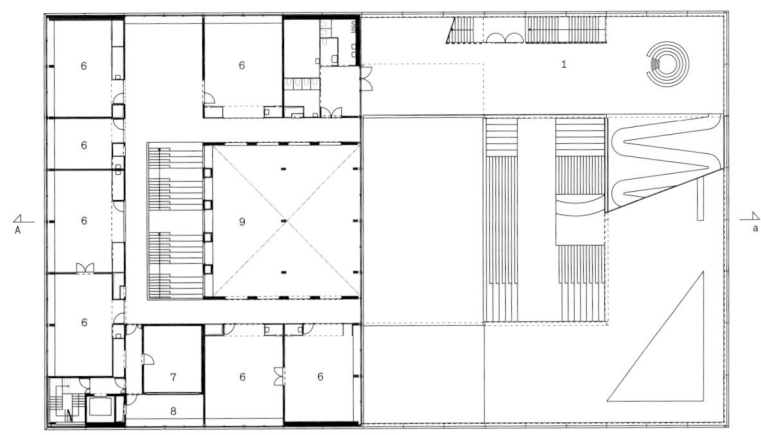

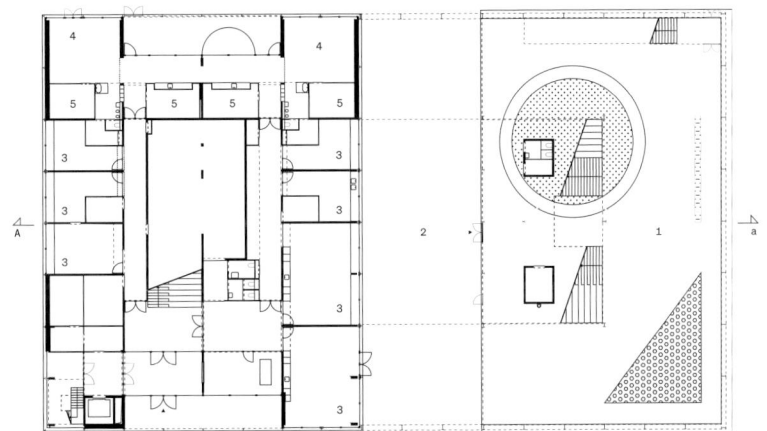

1. Play area
2. Public passage
3. Staff rooms
4. Childcare
5. Relaxation area
6. Primary school classroom
7. Music studio
8. Music theory classroom
9. Cafeteria

Melopee municipal building

Melopee municipal building

Bruges Meeting & Convention Centre, Bruges

Eduardo Souto de Moura and META architectuurbureau

From the Bruges train station, a stroll along the river Reie – the historical centre's natural boundary – leads you towards the Bruges Meeting & Convention Centre (BMCC). Following a series of houses and apartment blocks clad mostly in brick, BMCC appears behind a sequence of trees. With a combination of glazing on the ground level and solid bricks rising towards the square, the façade of the voluminous centre corresponds to the architecture of the trees. The interior of the building on street level can easily be seen through the thin tree trunks while the brick volume above is hidden behind the branches. This helps the building to be accepted more easily into the surrounding neighbourhood by not intruding on the domestic lives of inhabitants. Beech trees were planted on this site after the former convention centre, designed by Group Planning, was built in 1967. The trees were kept during the new construction. To protect their root systems, the size of the underground car park was limited to the footprint of the building and its use to staff and participant companies (the public is directed to the parking lot on the nearby square 't Zand).

The glass façade at street level allows deep perspectives into the volume, stimulating your curiosity and establishing a connection with the other side of the block. As you turn the corner of the building, you reach the new Beursplein. It is on this fairly sized square that the entrance to the building is located, an entrance marked by a sculpture by Philip Aguirre y Otegui. Water trickles slowly down the bronze sculpture leaving wet marks and producing a subtle sound on the square. The rhythmic brick lines that dominate the square and define the building's mass do not reach the street, but stop almost five metres above ground to form a canopy over the entrance. This generates a contrast between the weightiness of the bricks and the floating canopy over the square, emphasizing the presence of the building.

The entrance gives on to the exhibition hall. Besides its function as a trade fair, this space can be shared with the city for the organization of markets or festivals. Its potential to become a public interior is emphasized by its transparency towards the street and its high ceilings. The floor plans are simple and leave no room for confusion among visitors. Taking the stairs on both sides of the main entrance, you reach the auditorium with a background view of Bruges. The second floor is reserved for breakout rooms while the top storey houses a reception space. Here the glazing behind the brick lines defining the main façade is set back to form a terrace overlooking Bruges and its two towers. Behind the circulation on either side of the building lie offices and services such as an industrial kitchen and storage.

'On parle la même langue', Eduardo Souto de Moura told Eric Soors of META architectuurbureau at their first meeting in Porto. The strength of the collaboration is based on this notion of a shared approach to architecture, a balance between monumentality and humble presence, a building that does not promise to be more than a building yet does not compromise rich spatial qualities.

Hülya Ertas

BRUGES MEETING & CONVENTION CENTRE (BMCC)

Offices
Eduardo Souto de Moura and META architectuurbureau
Website
www.meta.be
Address
Beursplein 1, Bruges
Client
City of Bruges
Design
2016
Delivered
December 2021
Surface area
21,035 m²

Volume
121,261 m³
Total building cost
€ 29,399,190 – excl. VAT
Total building cost per m²
€ 1,398 – excl. VAT
Project development
CFE, Oudergem
General construction
MBG, Antwerp
Exterior space design
Landinzicht, Brussels
Art integration design
Philip Aguirre y Otegui
Stability studies
Mouton, Ghent

Technology studies
hp engineers, Ghent
EPB, energy and acoustics studies
Daidaloz Peutz, Leuven
Stability and technology studies
AFA Consult, Vila Nova de Gaia[PT]
Infrastructure studies
Ingenieursbureau France, Lier
Mobility studies
Vectris, Leuven
Fire safety studies
FESG, Ghent
Photographer
Filip Dujardin

Situation plan

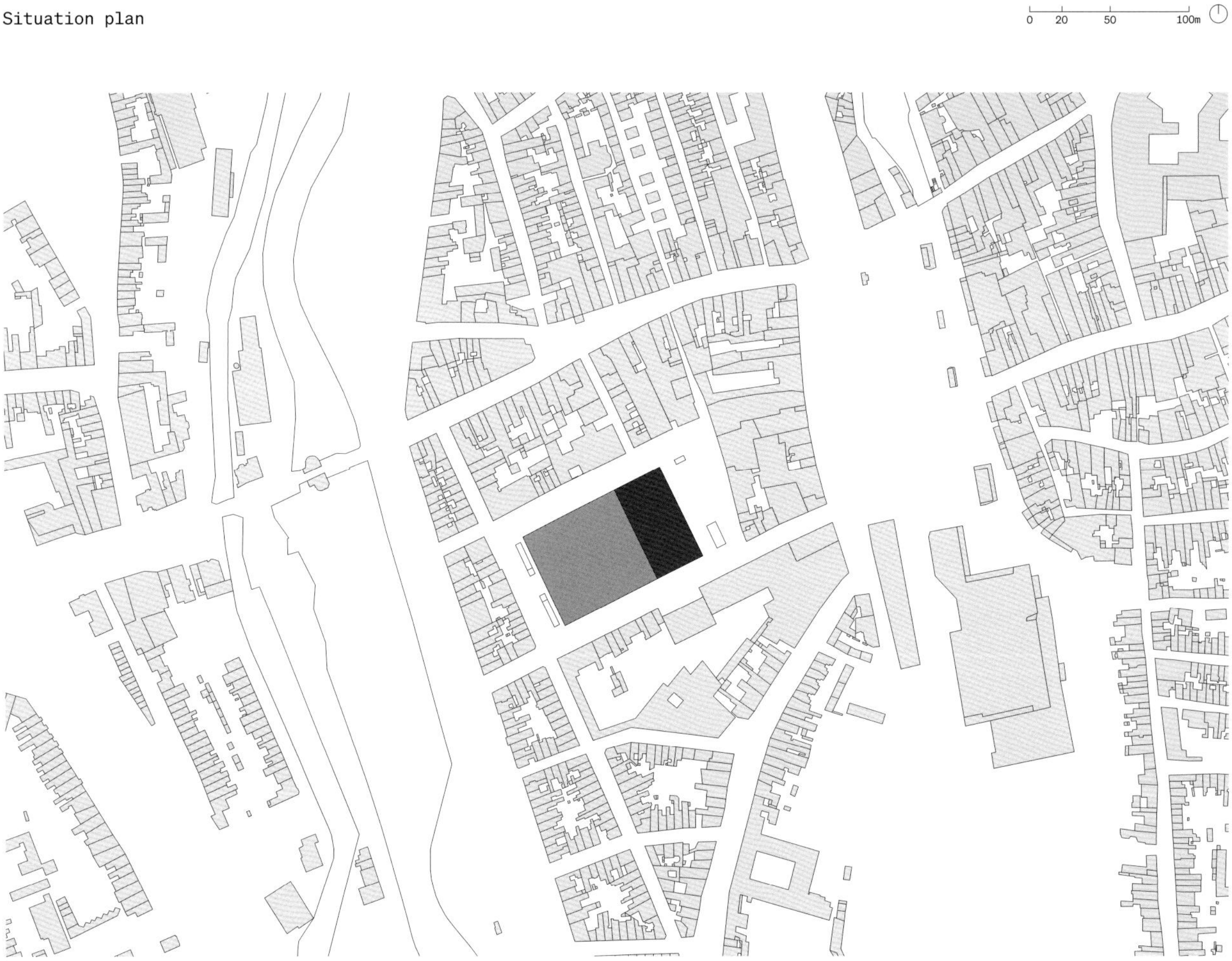

0 20 50 100m

Section Aa

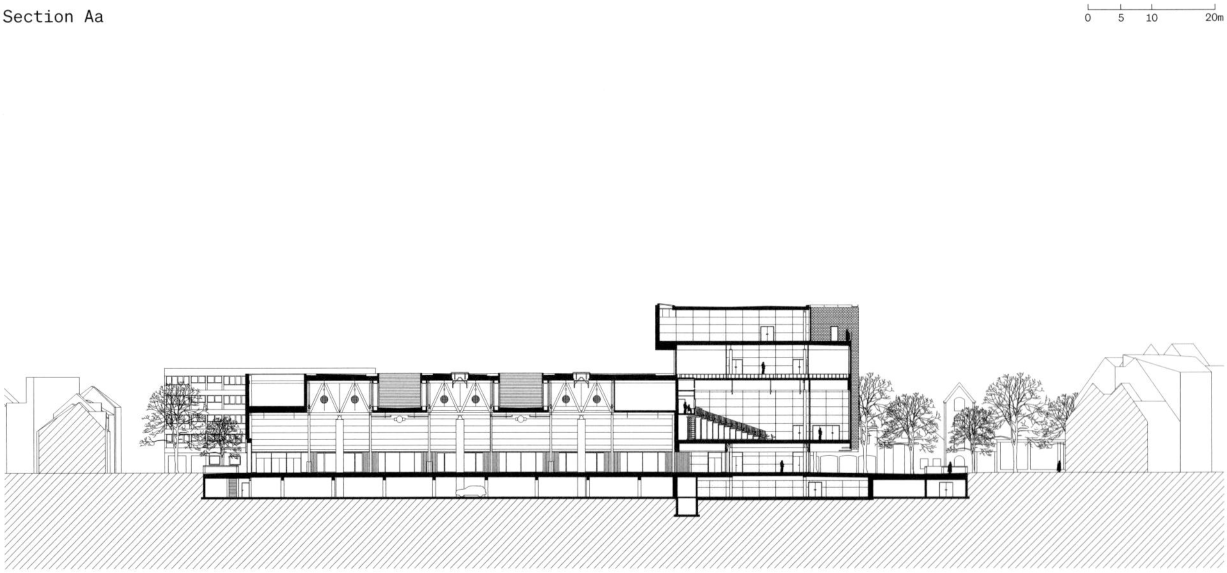

0 5 10 20m

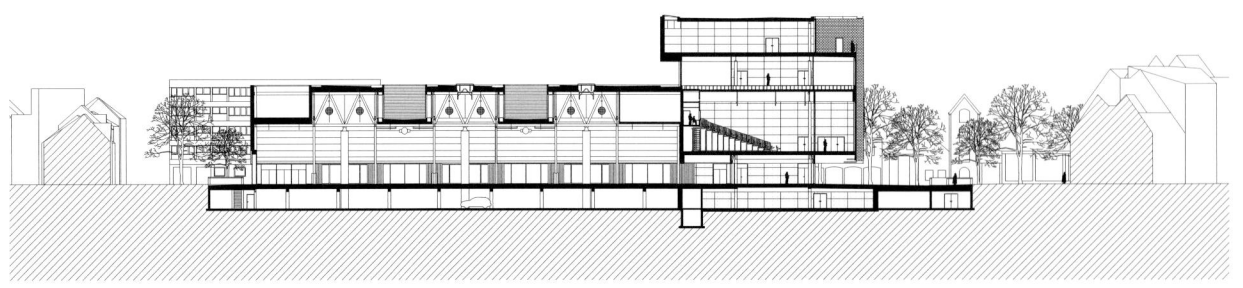

Eduardo Souto de Moura and META architectuurbureau

Level 3
Ground floor

Level 4
Level 2

0 5 10 20m

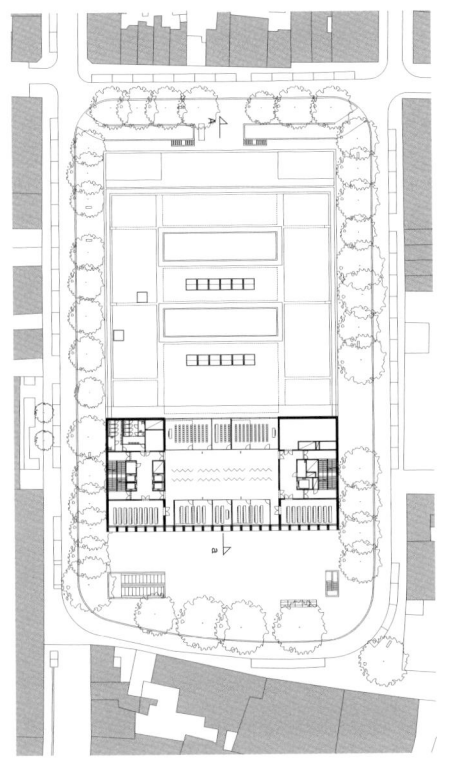
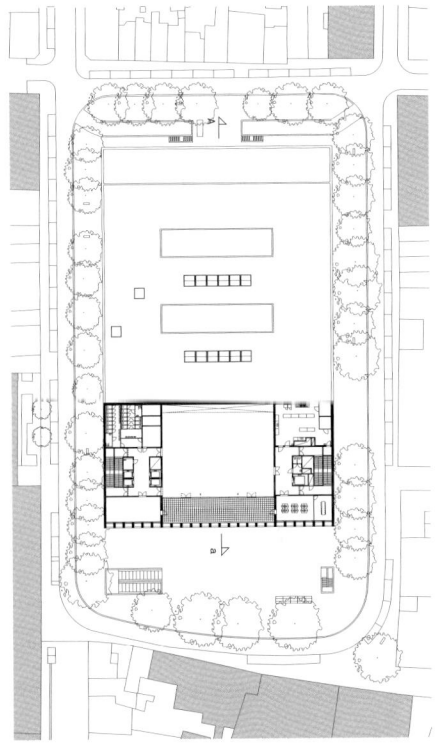
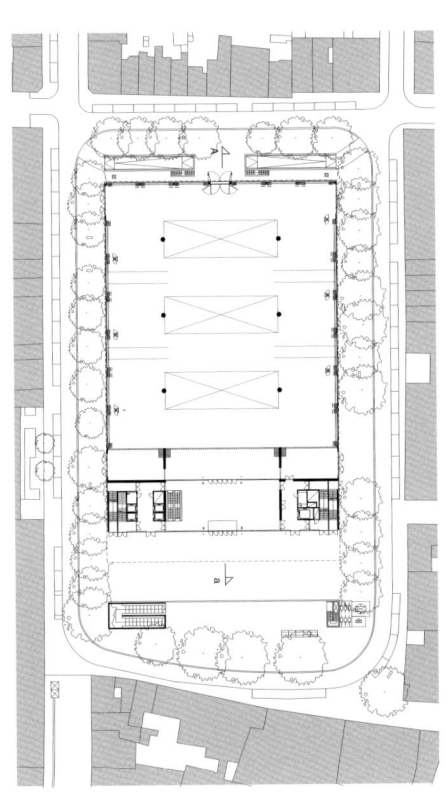
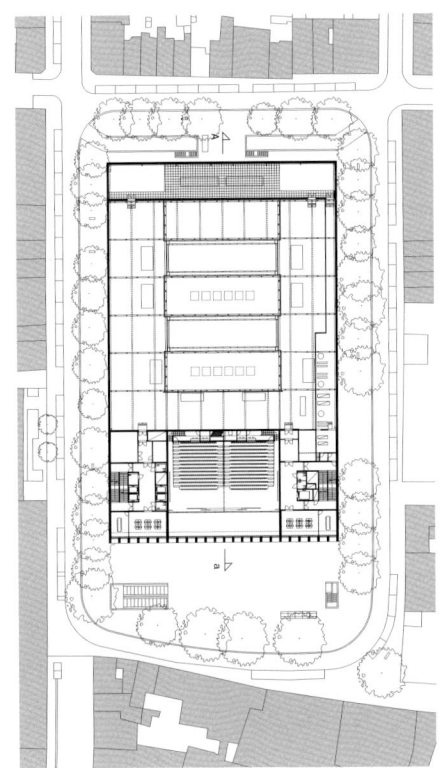

Bruges Meeting & Convention Centre

Eduardo Souto de Moura and META architectuurbureau

Bruges Meeting & Convention Centre

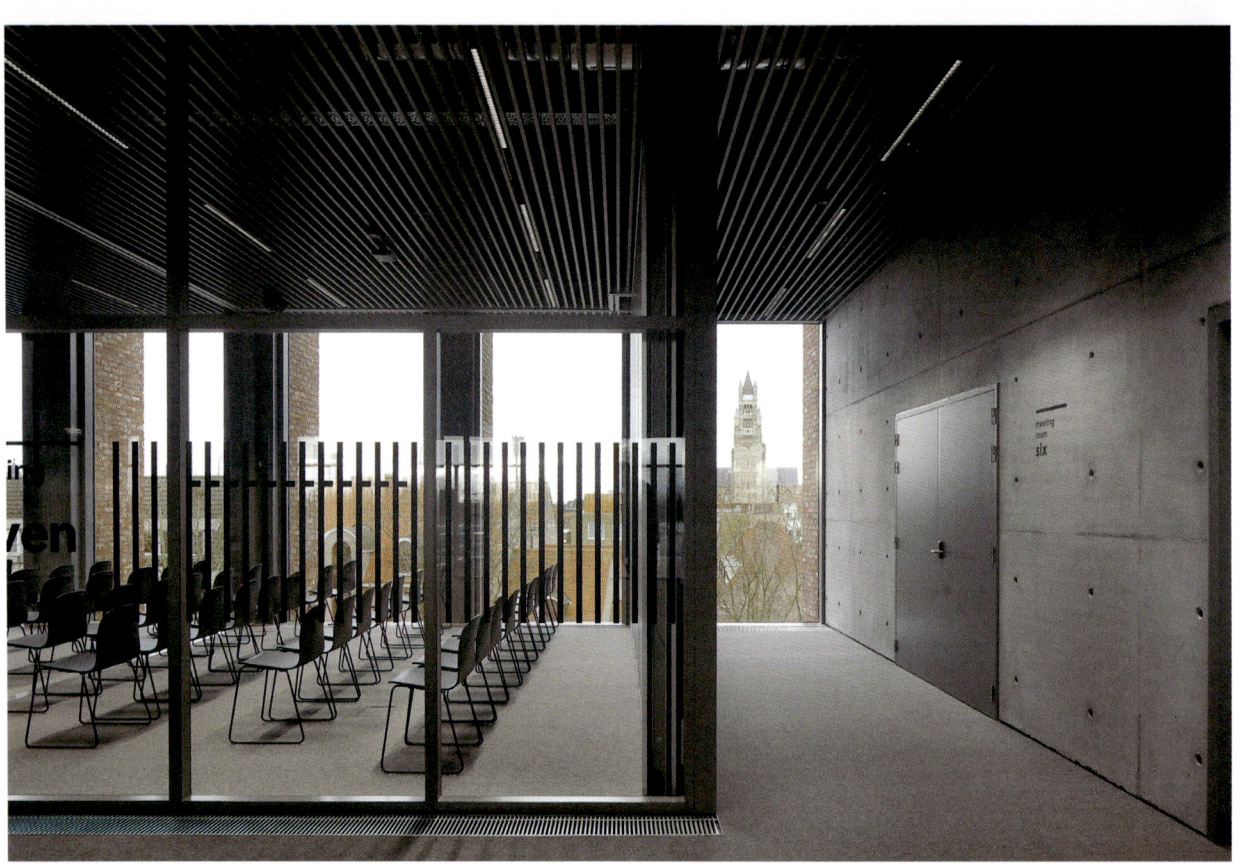

Het Steen, Antwerp

noAarchitecten

Het Steen is a diminutive icon, one that used to be an integral part of the historical centre of Antwerp, adjacent to the Vismarkt. Since around 1890, however, it has cast a lonely figure. The Vismarkt disappeared and Het Steen found itself isolated on the long quay of the straightened river Scheldt. At one point, the quay assumed a public character, with a park and leading to Het Steen's jumble of turrets and houses. Together, these resembled a fortified castle that had been assembled over time, composed of several interdependent structures, both large and small, including a museum and at one time even a prison. Eventually, it became further cut off by roads and rail lines running parallel to the river. In the middle of the twentieth century, another structure was attached, apparently indifferent to the ensemble's almost medieval character, which added to its sense of detachment and waning relevance.

The core elements of Het Steen were restored by noAarchitecten, who cleared away the most recent additions and replaced them with a stack of new spaces and a tower. These included a reception space for disembarking cruise ship passengers at quay level and, above, sets of rooms for the use of an Antwerp visitor centre, which are joined to the original structure's diverse collection of rooms and outlooks. From the outside, the new building elements are added and fused with the existing agglomeration, in sympathy with the ad hoc manner as the original. The renewed rampart is reminiscent of Edwin Lutyens's Castle Drogo, which featured as a point of reference in the architects' entry for the Open Call competition. The architects worked with the artist Pieter Vermeersch on the material of the façades, where bricks of differing tones suggest both natural weathering and the improvised assembly of the existing complex and its additions.

The spatial and material quality of the interiors suggests permanence, that the rooms will remain long after their current uses have been displaced by the demands of succeeding generations. At the ground, these are distinguished by terrazzo floors, concrete columns, brick walls, ventilation shafts as chimneys with large open hearths, and concrete ceilings. Above, the palette lightens: oak floors, plastered walls and ceilings; and on top, oak floors and wood-beamed ceilings. In all rooms, a family of oak furniture – from display and meeting tables to seats for resting and watching the river – assume an almost monumental status. They are designed for use in posterity.

The object of the project is a plausible whole, in which additions share essential characteristics with the main historical fabric, apparently blended with its forms and materials, reflecting the accidental informality of the 'original'; its many articulations echoing those of the various structures clustered within. Even windows contribute to this effort. Either framed in stone or as 'rough' openings in masonry walls, these seem to be placed in relation to imagined outlooks to the river Scheldt rather than any internal function. In their substance, materials and forms, they demonstrate a degree of autonomy from any programme-driven imperative, consistent with the design of the rooms. Indeed, they are placed in relation to the world without and thought of as vehicles for experience. Deep reveals provide places to pause, sit and look at the city and its territories, a gift consistent with the attitude guiding the architects' restoration of existing rooms throughout, as permanent settings for an ever-unfolding sequence of uses, users and interpretations.

Mark Pimlott

HET STEEN

Office
noAarchitecten
Website
www.noaarchitecten.net
Address
Steenplein 1, Antwerp
Client
AG Vespa
Design
April 2017

Delivered
November 2021
Surface area
3,700 m²
Volume
13,229 m³
Total building cost
€ 10,000,000 – excl. VAT
Total building cost per m²
€ 2,400 – excl. VAT
Main contractor
Renotec-Democo

(temporary association), Hasselt
Stability studies
UTIL Struktuurstudies, Schaarbeek
Technology studies
hp engineers, Oudenaarde
EPB and building physics adviser
Daidalos Peutz, Leuven
Art integration
Pieter Vermeersch
Photographer
Kim Zwart
except p. 178 and 179: Michiel De Cleene

Situation plan

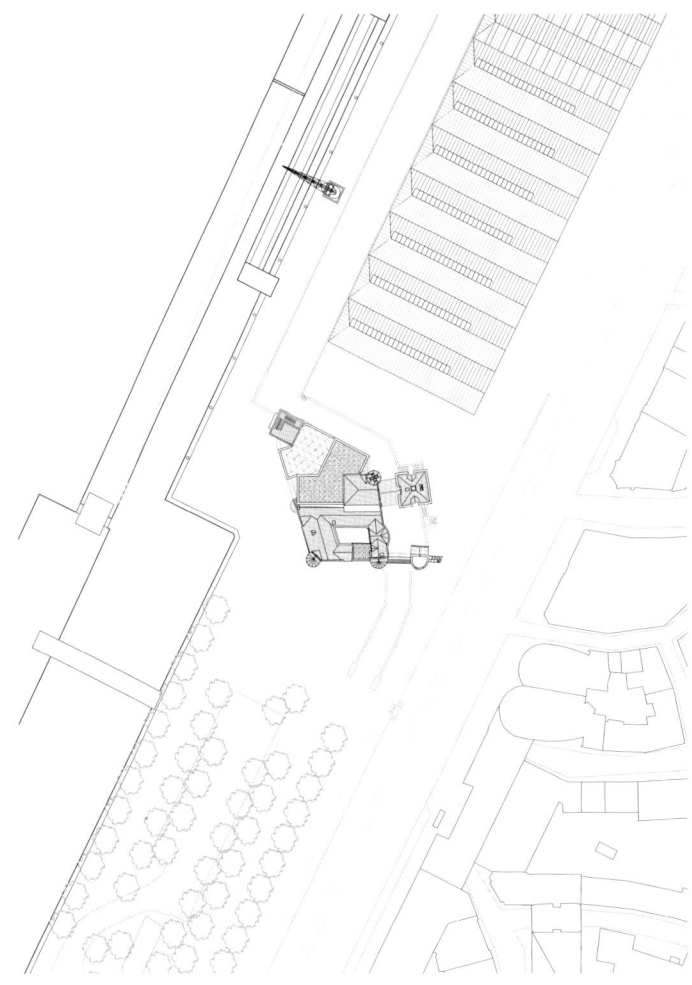

Section Aa

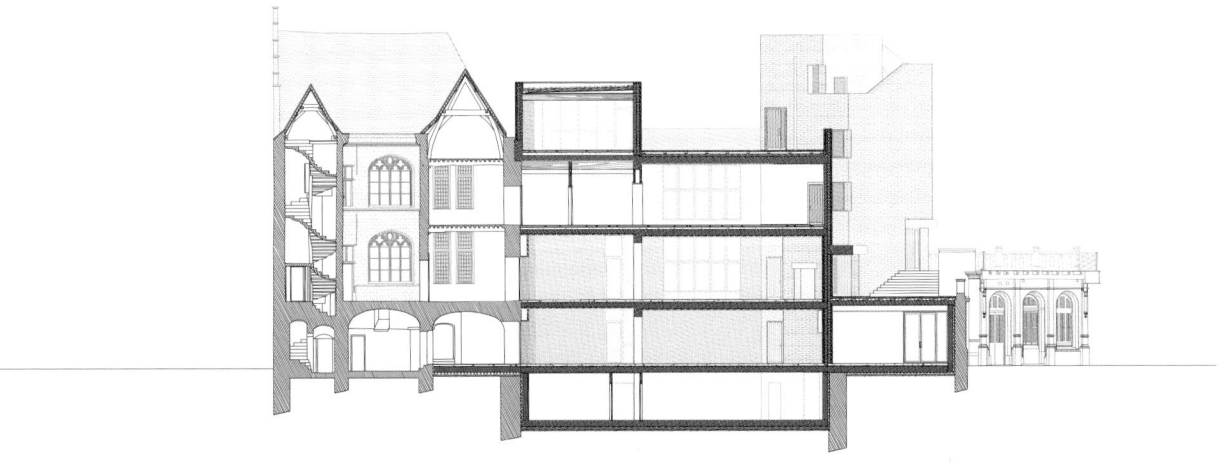

noAarchitecten

Level 1
Level -1

Level 2
Ground floor

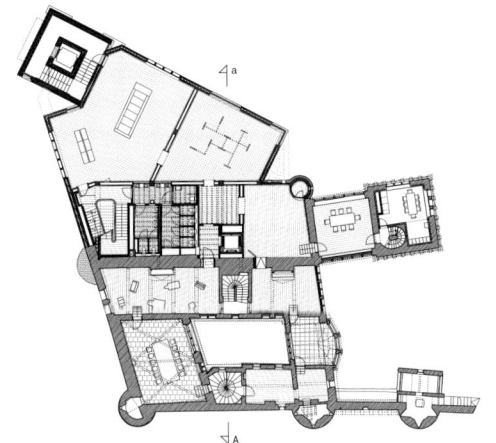
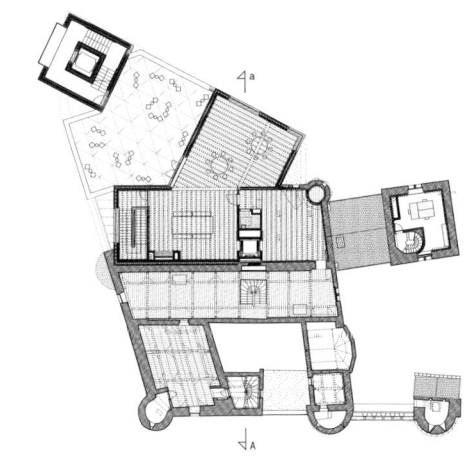
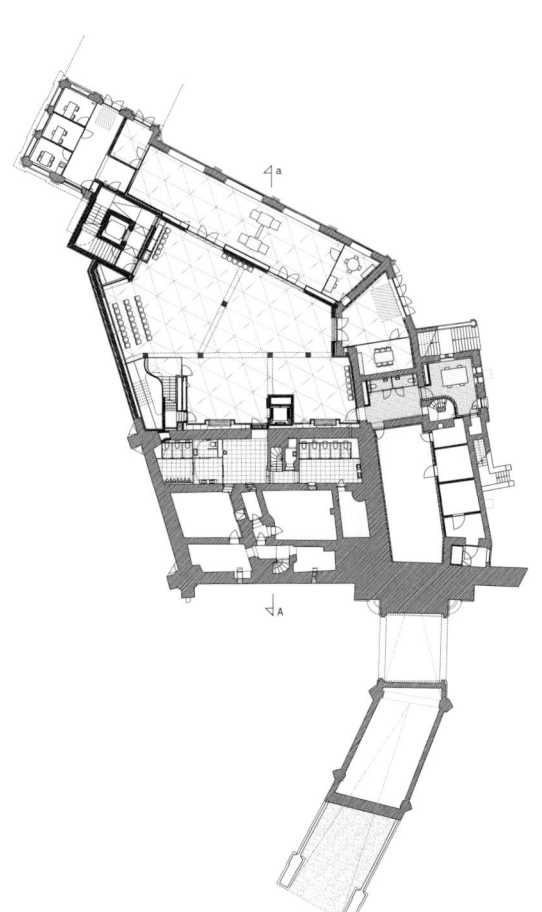
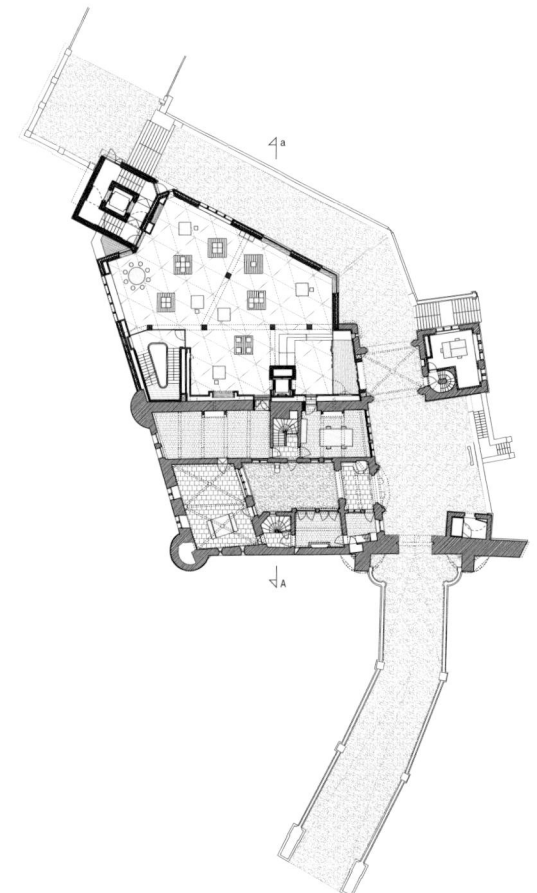

Het Steen

noAarchitecten

Het Steen

Onument #1, Kortrijk

Bureau Bas Smets

Onument is the term coined by psychiatrist Uus Knops to indicate a series of small interventions designed by Brussels-based Bureau Bas Smets to commemorate the victims of the Covid pandemic. Two have already been built: the first in Kortrijk, at the edge of the city's cemetery, the second in the Vinderhoutse Bossen in Ghent. Several others will be built in the coming months around other Flemish cities. While monuments are associated with specific rituals, defined social practices and often formal behaviours, the chosen term, spelt with a capital O, wishes to indicate an alternative approach to the commemoration of victims: Onuments are meant to be inviting, open and freely accessible spaces to be used in a multiplicity of ways, quietly or loudly, day or night, together or alone.

The interventions are inspired by the work of Swiss landscape architect George Descombes, with whom Bas Smets studied in Geneva and whose landscape design is often characterized by a 'humble monumentality'. They reinterpret the memorial for the victims of the Brussels terrorist attacks of 2016 built by Bureau Bas Smets in the Sonian Forest in the south-east of Brussels. Each intervention consists of a low circular wall created by placing side by side thirteen identical curved concrete blocks. Embedded in the ground, these blocks function as a linear bench from where to either observe the surrounding landscape or sit together in a circle for a commemorative moment. Unlike its predecessor in Brussels, each Onument is here an incomplete circle, as if parts of the circumference had been removed. Each consists of thirteen polished concrete blocks measuring 60 centimetres wide and realized with stone aggregates specifically chosen for each location. All the elements are aligned horizontally as a way to reveal, by means of contrast, the topographic condition of the site.

The first Onument stands at the very edge of the Kortrijk cemetery designed by Bernardo Secchi and Paola Viganò in 2000, where the plateaus of the burial fields end in front of the surrounding agricultural fields. Placed sensitively in a hidden corner so as not to interfere with the design of the cemetery, the circle is here broken in two parts, with the thirteen polished dark concrete blocks outlining two semi-circles that integrate the edge of an adjacent field and a small willow grove into the circular space. What is remarkable about this and the other realized Onument in Ghent is, on the one hand, their new approach to mourning, commemoration and grief, and, on the other hand, their 'pedagogical' capacity to make people aware of the beauty and calmness of the surrounding landscape. In a heavily suburbanized region where ribbon developments often make it impossible to perceive and experience the landscape, the Onuments emerge as humble yet powerful devices capable of revealing something that in Flanders is often forgotten, namely the calming and pacifying beauty of the vast natural and agricultural territory.

Martino Tattara

ONUMENT #1

Office
Bureau Bas Smets
Website
www.bassmets.be
Address
Ambassadeur Baertlaan 5, Kortrijk

Client
City of Kortrijk
in collaboration with
Moving Closer and Kunstwerkt
Design
2020-21
Delivered
June 2021

Total building cost
€ 39,615 - excl. VAT
Main contractor
Stadsbader, Harelbeke
Photographer
Michiel De Cleene

Onuments

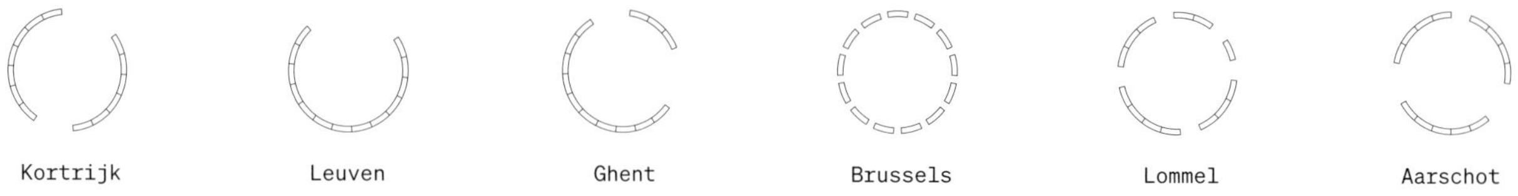

| Kortrijk | Leuven | Ghent | Brussels | Lommel | Aarschot |

Situation plan Kortrijk

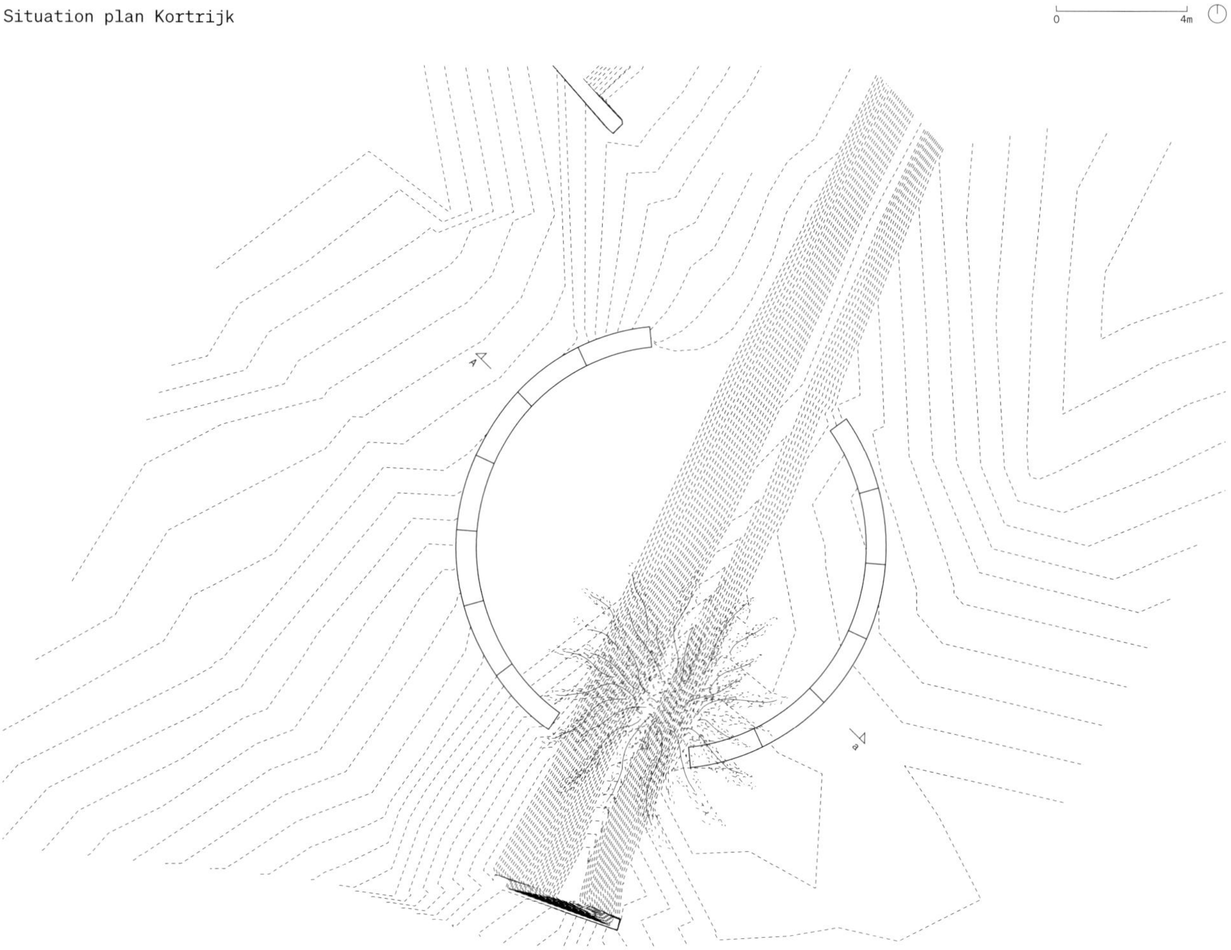

Section Aa

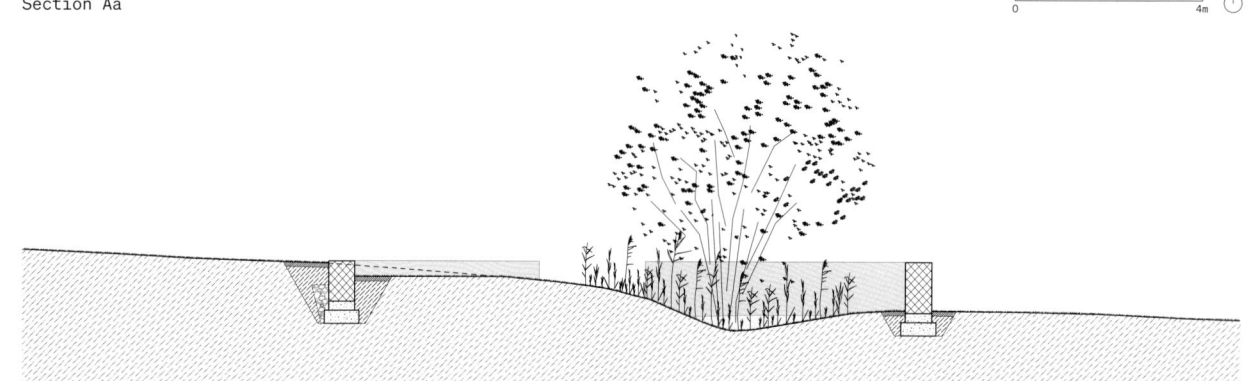

Bureau Bas Smets

Onument #1, Kortrijk

Onument #2, Ghent

Onument #2, Ghent

Miles Fischler

Designing from the Inside

Hülya Ertas

1. Bruno Latour, 'Inside', Zone Critique, 14 February 2018, YouTube video, https://www.youtube.com/watch?v=gzPROcdIMuE.

In his lecture-performance titled 'Inside', Bruno Latour shows the famous *Earthrise* photo of the Earth from outer space and explains *how* such imagery changed our relationship with our planet.[1] Taken on 24 December 1968 from *Apollo 8*, this picture of the Blue Planet became one of the symbols of the environmental movement, leading to the celebration of the first Earth Day on 22 April 1970. However, Latour proposes that this externalized image of the Earth affected our perception and ultimately generated a paradigm that has led us to consider ourselves as separate beings instead of feeling united in one ecosystem.

William Anderson (*Apollo 8*), *Earthrise* (24 December 1968)

Besides this image, a growing awareness of the dangers of pollution and of the threats posed to wildlife also contributed to the environmental movement's increased momentum in the 1960s. In architecture, R. Buckminster Fuller was one of the most public voices. He articulated his ideas in *Operating Manual for Spaceship Earth*.[2] This book offers guidelines for humans to use the planet wisely. In the scope of this work, Fuller developed further the notion of 'ephemeralization', a term he coined in 1938 that refers to the ability to do 'more and more with less and less until eventually you can do everything with nothing'.[3] Fuller advocated technical and technological development to keep progress moving on a planet with limited resources. While he outlined an exemplary approach to technological determinism, Fuller was committed to being careful in the extraction of natural resources. That perspective is still dominant in today's thinking with the introduction of new, greener building technologies.

Timothy W. Luke's rereading of *Operating Manual for Spaceship Earth* and Fuller's life story led him to define Fuller's approach as environmentalism, following Andrew Dobson's classification of environmentalist and ecologist positions.[4] Reminding us of the externalized view of the Earth, 'environmentalism argues for a managerial approach to environmental problems, secure in the belief that they can be solved without fundamental changes in present values or patterns of production and consumption'.[5]

The environmentalist position has become prevalent among architectural practices that have demonstrated an interest in protecting the planet. Following in the wake of Fuller's innovations in the 1960s and 1970s, the approach gained in clarity in the managerial actions of green building certificates such as LEED (Leadership in Energy and Environmental Design) and BREEAM (Building Research Establishment Environmental Assessment Method). Without a holistic understanding of the impact of human actions on the planet, however, these certificates served to maintain the business-as-usual approach in architecture and construction. For example, you could gain points for branding a building green by washing the tyres of trucks leaving the construction site while paying little to no attention to the wider impact of the construction industry. Architecture media was increasingly flooded with 'green' or 'ecological' projects. Branding and greenwashing followed while more and more buildings were being erected worldwide. Few questions were raised regarding the extraction of resources from nature to provide building materials or regarding the expansion of cities towards the outskirts, increasing energy use and pollution. It seemed like architecture was trying to save the planet but in fact it had got it all wrong.

In times of soul-shattering reports by the IPCC (Intergovernmental Panel on Climate Change) and as the devastating effects of climate change become more visible and activists all around the globe are demanding a paradigm shift in climate policies, the environmentalist approach is obsolete. Going back to Dobson's classification, ecologism, as opposed to environmentalism, 'holds that a sustainable and fulfilling existence presupposes radical changes in our relationship with the non-human natural world, and in our mode of social and political life'.[6] In this perspective, a culture change is deemed necessary in our relation with the planet as a whole.

Now, in a world where it is becoming harder to ignore the effects of climate change on our daily lives, the transition from an environmentalist position to an ecologist

2 R. Buckminster Fuller, *Operating Manual for Spaceship Earth* (New York: Simon & Schuster, 1969).

3 Wikipedia, 'Ephemeralization', last modified 20 March 2022, https://en.wikipedia.org/wiki/Ephemeralization.

4 Timothy W. Luke, 'Ephemeralization as Environmentalism: Rereading R. Buckminster Fuller's *Operating Manual for Spaceship Earth*', *Organization & Environment* 23, no. 3 (2010): 354–62.

5 Andrew Dobson, *Green Political Thought* (London: Routledge, 2000), 2.

6 Dobson, *Green Political Thought*, 3.

one seems inevitable. The urgency of this paradigm shift will define how life on Earth needs to be reorganized, especially with regard to human actions before global warming reaches a point of no return. What is the role of architecture in this reorganization? And how can it propose a new kind of living that takes care of the planet and all the species on it? This of course requires a culture change in the practice of architecture and in how we live both in and with architecture.

The following three examples illustrate this paradigm shift from an environmentalist approach to an ecologist one. More than following energy regulations and 'green' building rating systems they provide an insight into how we can rethink the position of architecture in terms of our production and consumption modes, daily habits and our perception of the earth from the inside…

LIVING SEASONALLY

The renovation in Molenbeek of a depot building into an architect's own house had started during the time of impressive climate marches in Brussels. These motivated Harold Fallon of AgwA and Evelia Macal to question the practice of architecture and its effects on the planet. During the transformation, Fallon aimed to demolish as little as possible to prevent new waste. But some volumes of the concrete structure on the ground floor were cleared to make room for a garden. This meant that the soil could reclaim some space in the city, the garden becoming the pathway to the house. The entrance is anything but cosy. It recalls the industrial character of the building. Now reinforced with diagonal wooden columns, the open structure welcomes you. Here you can see the shared atelier through a glass wall and the staircase leading to the living areas. One of the main design principles was 'no more concrete'. The wooden diagonals across the building sit on the foundation and support the existing concrete frame. They also play a role in defining the tone of the circulation spaces, which are non-climatized and rough in their materiality.

The staircase leads to the first floor, from where you can enter the living and sleeping areas. The project almost rests on a 'box in a box' principle. Out of ecological concerns, only specific volumes in the house are heated. Insulated with hemp, these volumes are the living and sleeping areas on the first floor and the sleeping and bathroom areas of the children on the second floor. The rest of the house is not heated, leading the family to live more compactly in winter. This is the most radical design decision, reminding us of premodern times when there was little or no access to artificial energy resources. While the physical efforts necessary to heat a place were higher and resources were limited compared to today, another balance prevailed between comfortable living environment and energy consumption.

Ecologist architecture introduces a new way of living, changing daily habits and questioning conventional comfort standards such as indoor temperature. During the winter you need a warm jumper when moving between the heated spaces, which make up less than half the whole volume. The presence of the atelier on the ground floor also helps to reduce energy consumption and encourages a different life-work balance. The culture change proposed by the project itself challenges the practice of architecture and the daily habits of its architect.

©Séverin Malaud

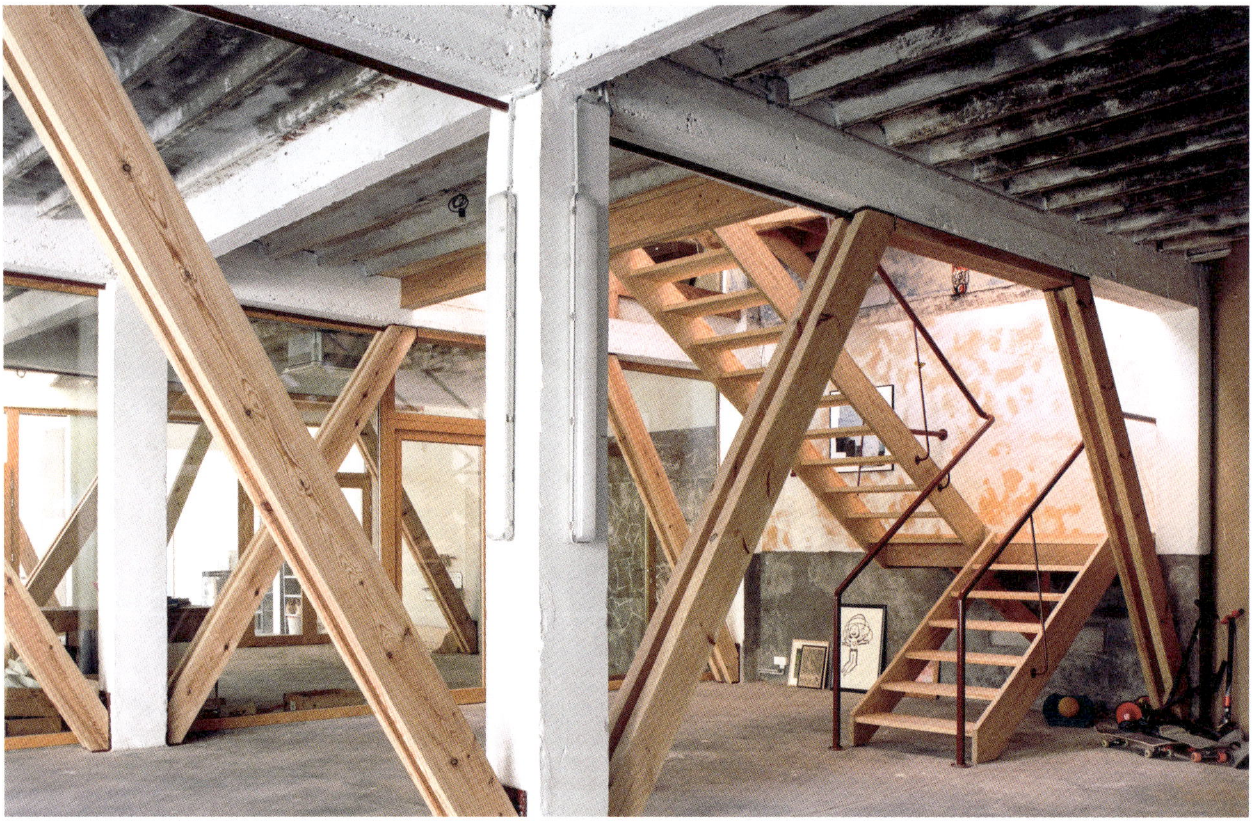

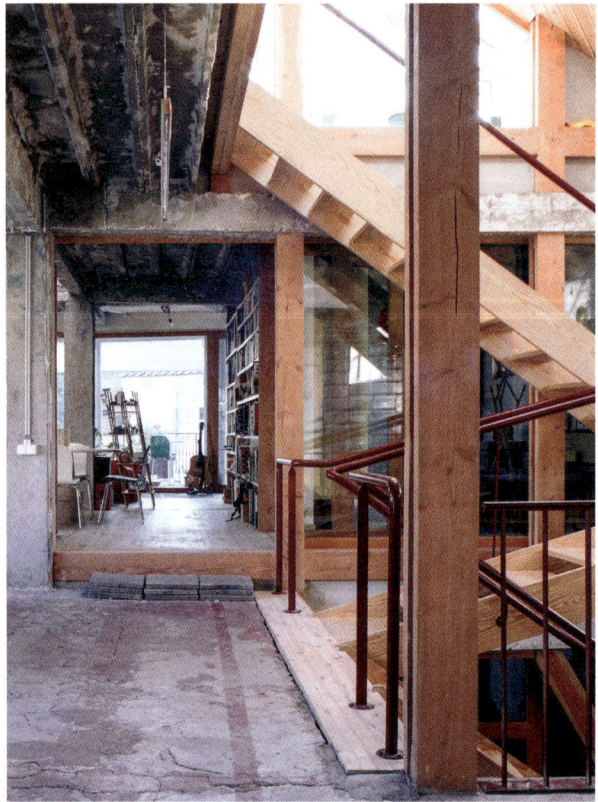

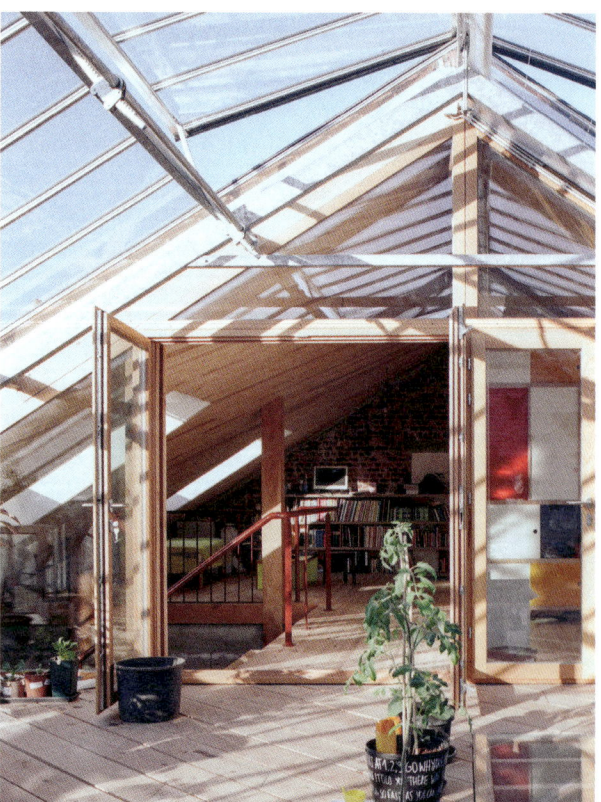

Verbiest house and studio, Sint-Jans-Molenbeek – AgwA and Evelia Macal

CONVERGING APPROACHES

See p. 119

Agrotopia rooftop greenhouse by META architectuurbureau and van Bergen Kolpa Architecten is a research centre for agriculture. In a plot surrounded by a logistics centre, car gallery, hardware shop and wholesale vegetable market, Agrotopia stands out as a monumental structure. That is surprising given the conventional characteristics of the materials used. The greenhouse typology is applied in the building, this time by using the pitched roof modules as façade elements. The repetitive roofs on the entrance façade expand towards the ground floor to welcome visitors to Agrotopia through a staircase. The space accommodates greenhouses, offices and exhibition areas where different organizations such as private companies, NGOs and academies come together to exchange knowledge on food production. In line with the nature of the experiments being carried out in Agrotopia, separate greenhouses cover most of the 9,500 m² area. The offices are designed as volumes that can be climate-controlled, like the living spaces in the house converted by AgwA. In terms of energy use, the architects here took a holistic approach that transcends the singular building of Agrotopia. The building is heated by residual heat from a nearby waste incinerator. Instead of finding a building-specific solution for heating, the design reaches out to the wider context, conceiving the question of energy as an all-encompassing system. The rainwater is collected in the silos below the greenhouse that also support the building structurally. This water is then used to irrigate the plants.

The uncanny semi-industrial, semi-agricultural character of the busy intercity *steenweg* in Roeselare has gained a new hybrid structure on top of an industrial facility on the ground floor. Other than the shared energy with the nearby incinerator, the other important ecologist design decision regards density. By not taking up more space on the ground and by building on top of an existing volume, Agrotopia follows the argument of density as one of the solutions to reduce greenhouse emissions.[7] By demonstrating the potentials of rooftops, the issue of the lack of space in cities for agriculture and that of the nature vs city discourse are approached critically. However, this is made possible by freeing agriculture from its dependence on soil. As the ambition to consume locally produced vegetables becomes more realistic in a soil-independent perspective, the existing culture of growing food remains unquestioned. Researching how to grow tomatoes in winter in Flanders in the highly controlled environment of the greenhouse – detached not only from the soil but also from the social structures of agricultural production – is ultimately questionable. Eating seasonally and locally is not the goal of these innovative experiments. Instead of proposing a paradigm shift in our attitude towards the planet and our relation with its offerings, the building programme aims to improve the already existing practices of soilless agriculture. In this sense, Agrotopia converges the two contrasting positions of ecologism (through its density proposal, rooftop potential and sharing energy) and environmentalism (with the business-as-usual agricultural experiments in its programme).

7   Maanvi Singh and Oliver Milman, 'Denser Cities Could Be a Climate Boon but Nimbyism Stands in the Way', *The Guardian*, 22 August 2021, https://www.theguardian.com/us-news/2021/aug/22/cities-climate-change-dense-sprawl-yimby-nimby.

Agrotopia rooftop greenhouse, Roeselare – META architectuurbureau and van Bergen Kolpa Architecten

Hülya Ertas

HUMBLE EXISTENCE

The unmanned entrance pavilion for the Palingbeek nature reserve by Schenk Hattori Architecture Atelier is a reminder of our interaction with nature. Located at the start of the Palingbeek trail, a twenty-minute bike ride away from Ypres, the information point is part of a wide provincial domain. Entering the first room of the wooden structure, visitors are welcomed by a video about the failed Ypres-Comines canal project. This project was launched in 1864 with the ambition to connect the Ypres-Yser canal with Comines and the river Lys to rekindle economic activity in Ypres after the decline of the cloth industry. However, nature fought back against this engineering logic and, after four failed attempts, the project was terminated in 1913. Even the impressive Sint-Elooi bridge could not tame the Ypres clay, while the remains of the collapsed bridge can still be seen in the terrain close to the information point. It is a memorial to nature's victory. Watching the information video in this small room makes you reflect on your actions in the world and their impact on ecology as a whole once again. As you enter and exit the rooms – which become smaller and smaller as they shrink to the size of a cabinet and ultimately end in a wall – you read 'Adequate environmental management protects and strengthens the rich wildlife at De Palingbeek'. In a world vastly occupied by humans, wildlife can only thrive if it is managed by humans.

Its cabinet-like architecture invites visitors to reconsider the scales on which architecture operates. It is not a building but a sequence of rooms and walls. In this way, the dilemma of protecting the environment while at the same time perpetuating human activity through building more feels lighter, not totally overcome but lighter. The use of wood combined with the simplicity of the structure, its modularity and demountability create an impression of ephemerality on a billion-year-old planet. The modest design tells the story of the landscape while itself not claiming more space than required.

These three projects with different programmes and architectural languages come together in their search for a new position to designing with care for the planet. By going beyond the environmentalist and managerial approach, architecture can play a role in defining a new culture of living. And it is perhaps through this new culture that we can overcome the very pressing reality of climate change. There is, it seems, a greater field of action beyond green building certificates or infrastructural solutions such as insulation and efficient HVAC systems. Illustrated by seasonal living (Verbiest), densification (Agrotopia) and minimized environmental impact (Palingbeek), that paradigm shift requires a new mindset in design. Beyond the palliative solutions of individual choices, the challenge is to find a way to embed planetary thinking in all aspects of our lives, including architectural practices, and to do so from the inside.

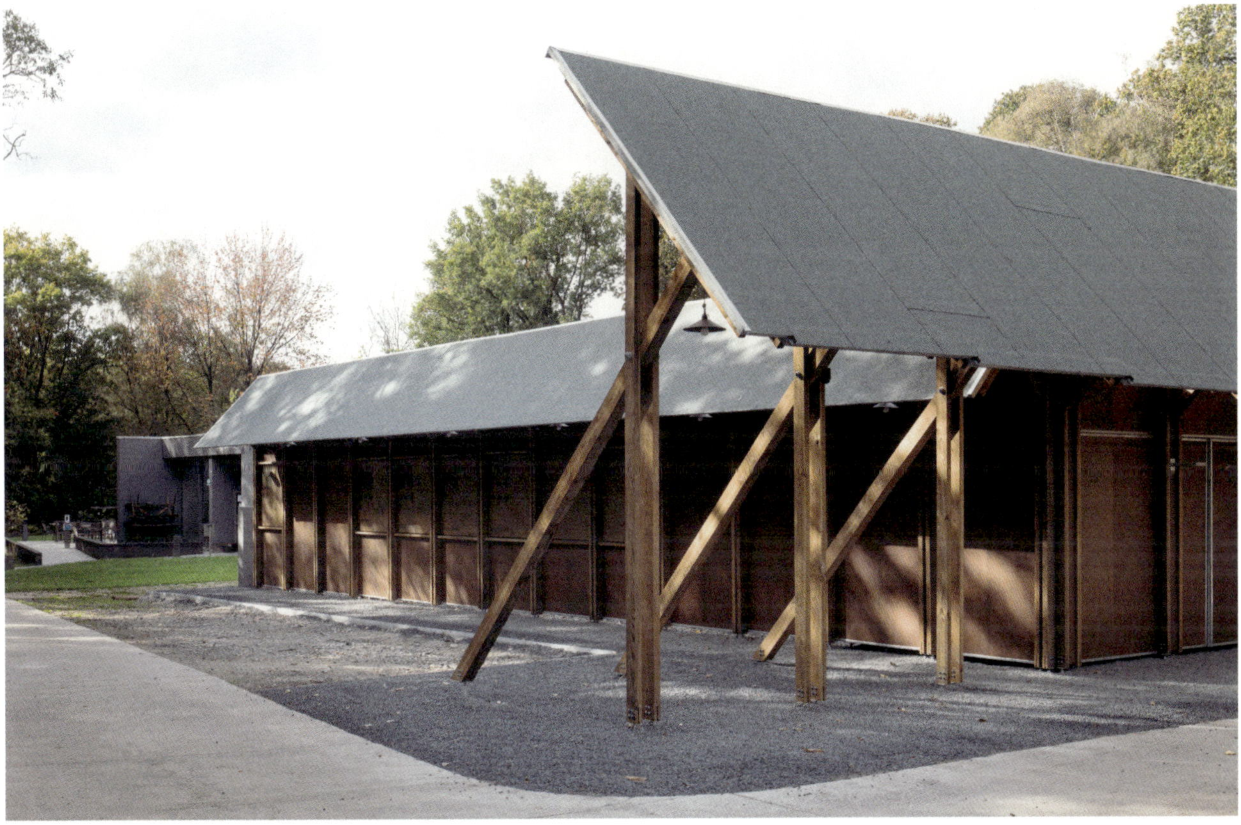

Unmanned entrance pavilion for the Palingbeek nature reserve, Klein-Zillebeke – Schenk Hattori Architecture Atelier

Hülya Ertas

VERBIEST HOUSE AND STUDIO **Office** AgwA and Evelia Macal **Website** www.agwa.be **Address** Jean Verbieststraat 5-7, Sint-Jans-Molenbeek **Clients** Harold Fallon and Evelia Macal **Design** 2018	**Delivered** July 2020 **Surface area** 610 m^2 **Volume** 1,710 m^3 **Total building cost** € 380,000 - excl. VAT **Total building cost per m²** € 623 - excl. VAT **Main contractor** Revgroup, Brussels	**Stability** JZH & Partners, Brussels **Special technologies** AgwA, Brussels **EPB reporting** JZH & Partners, Brussels **Landscape architecture** AgwA and Denis Dujardin
AGROTOPIA ROOFTOP GREENHOUSE	See p. 119	
UNMANNED ENTRANCE PAVILION FOR THE PALINGBEEK NATURE RESERVE **Office** Schenk Hattori Architecture Atelier **Website** www.schenkhattori.com **Address** Palingbeekstraat, Klein-Zillebeke	**Client** Province of West Flanders **Design** September 2016 **Delivered** October 2020 **Surface area** 200 m^2	**Total building cost** € 255,000 - excl. VAT **Total building cost per m²** € 1,275 - excl. VAT **Main contractor** Arthur Vandendorpe, Zedelgem **Stability studies** Tandem Ingenieurs, Leuven

Sofie De Caigny

History and Architecture Entangled

Focus on three Antwerp monuments

Architecture keeps historical values and meanings alive within the urban fabric. While this applies to generic buildings, it is particularly true of monuments. The past is also emphatically present in the social discourse, being used by various political and community groups to inform arguments in support of a contemporary position. This increases the critical, multifocal reading of the past: people no longer accept that only the historical story of the majority is told. This essay examines how contemporary design can meaningfully deal with the topicality of the past, using three recent interventions on Antwerp monuments as examples: the Royal Museum of Fine Arts (KMSKA), Antwerp City Hall, and Het Steen. All three buildings have been extensively renovated. The text focuses on just one aspect of these structural alterations, namely their position in relation to the histories of the said monuments.

The buildings can only be understood through Antwerp's radical transformation in the nineteenth century. This was the period when they acquired their pre-renovation form. As in many Western European cities, it was a time of unprecedented change. The city walls were razed and new districts quickly emerged around the old city. The citadel was transformed into a bourgeois district with a new museum. The port grew exponentially to the north while the quays were straightened to facilitate modern harbour activities. With this last operation, the oldest parts of the city disappeared and the former gateway, Het Steen, was left vacant as a last surviving vestige of a bygone era. Existing monuments, including the city hall, were extensively renovated. The unprecedented urban transformation was the material externalization of various phenomena: increasing mobility; a surge in energy consumption and industrialization; shifting borders and nation-building; colonialism and imperialism; modern news dissemination and bureaucracy; and greater separation between the public and private spheres. The speed of change was accompanied by a sense of loss that acted as a catalyst for unprecedented preoccupation with the past. The rupture had to be mediated. Important public buildings such as Het Steen, the KMSKA and the city hall all bear witness to this nineteenth-century obsession with history. But when it comes to updating them in a meaningful way while respecting their historical integrity, these monuments present twenty-first century architects with challenging design decisions.

RESTRAINT IN THE CITY HALL

Antwerp's imposing city hall has been renovated several times since it was erected in the sixteenth century. Despite this near continuous process of transformation, the original design is still legible. The building acquired its imposing staircase to the *Schoon Verdiep* (*Bel étage*) between 1880 and 1885. As the floor where foreign dignitaries were received, this is the most representative level. It contains, among other things, the mayor's office, the register office, the lecture hall and the council chamber. Dating from the nineteenth century, the vibrant and opulent neo-Renaissance ornamentation deliberately references the city's glorious past, as do the monumental historical tableaux and portraits that adorn the chambers on the Schoon Verdiep. In this way, the tension between past and present was bridged during a period of rapid social change. The nineteenth-century renovation spilled over into a number of smaller twentieth-century adjustments that, nevertheless, were still inscribed within the previous century's vision of the building. The result is a story of almost five centuries of architectural interventions in a building that symbolizes the very heart of local power.

Now, in the early twenty-first century, Antwerp City Hall has submitted to another dramatic transformation. The 450th anniversary of the building and the desire to consolidate all the aldermen's offices under one roof (previously dispersed throughout the city) were the reasons for launching an Open Call via the Flemish Government Architect. In assembling the winning team around the architecture office HUB, the designers expressed their hope that the contemporary transformations would

City Hall, Antwerp – HUB and Origin with Bureau Bouwtechniek

share an affinity with the changes made to the building throughout history. In this, they were referring to Eduardo Souto de Moura's concept of 'domesticating architecture', whereby the building indicates its own needs. This principle can be elaborated in two ways: on the one hand, from the material layers of the building, on the other, from the immaterial meanings of what local power has signified over the centuries. Every renovation in the town hall's long lifespan has embodied the kind of governance desired by the rulers of the day.

The city hall's ground floor and second storey had the greatest potential for transformation. It is here, therefore, that the new programme is accommodated. These levels must also be a consummate expression of the values advanced by the current administration. The ground floor has been made accessible once more. The blue stone around the columns, which has been left visible, and the bare walls and ceilings are sturdy and sober. They mediate between inside and outside and reconnect with the function of storage, which is how the ground floor functioned for centuries. The crux of the design was to create two double-height vestibules on the second floor that link to the offices. The volumes conform to the articulation of the existing city hall and render the threefold division of the underlying floors more legible. On the outside, they remain invisible; inside, they are bathed in zenithal light. Alongside the Schoon Verdiep, the building now also has a *Verlicht Verdiep* (Illuminated floor).

The two vestibules and surrounding offices have the sober materiality, colour scheme and restrained detailing that is HUB's signature. The construction of the flat ceilings

City Hall, Antwerp – HUB and Origin with Bureau Bouwtechniek

on the lower historical floors is given a contemporary translation in steel with oak beams. The same wood is used for the panelling around the doors. The city hall is crafted from ancient oak and the same wood recurs throughout HUB's building interventions, up to and including the new furniture for the council chamber on the Schoon Verdiep and a new staircase leading from the first floor to the new vestibules on the second. The oak floors are identical throughout the building, with only the pattern becoming more subdued the higher you climb. Despite this coherent materialization, it is difficult to make a clear physical connection between what happens on the Schoon Verdiep and first floor, and the new rooms above and below. The sobriety and down-to-earthness are the antithesis of the nineteenth-century opulence. With their uniform language, it is the carpets by Studio Lommer and Jente Hendrickx that weave a coherent thread through the floors.

HUB argues for the pronounced austerity by citing the need for transparency within a twenty-first-century democratic system. This reasoning does not continue in the restoration. A critical restoration or conservation project that leaves the layers of time and deterioration visible in the patina would, in any case, suggest that such a material expression of power is a historical fact. Conversely, for policy to be enacted in the same building after a long succession of administrative changes is nothing short of profound. This field of tension between historical embedding and actualization, and between continuity and change, would probably have been more explicitly expressed in an approach that emphasizes preservation over restoration. It could then connect to the critical social debate that increasingly advocates the contextualization of the historical symbols of power within the public domain. The façade, in which the age-related tonal variation of the different types of stone have been left visible like sticking plasters, nevertheless provides a stimulating impetus for this discussion.

TWO CUT-OFF WORLDS IN THE KMSKA

As with the vestibules in the city hall, KAAN Architecten's starting point for the KMSKA is the articulation of the existing building. The design team responded to the demands for additional space, improved environmental conditions and provided greater opportunities for temporary exhibitions by creating new volumes inside the patios of the existing museum. As a result, this imposing building – which the Flemish Government regards as its most valuable patrimony – does not stray beyond the existing volume in the densely built-up residential neighbourhood of which it is an indelible part, in both architectural and urban terms. Yet the decision not to make any radical changes to the exterior does not imply a genuine commitment to the existing structure. KAAN have explicitly created two worlds: a decorous, seemingly original nineteenth-century museum experience that is complemented by a route through sharply contrasting contemporary exhibition spaces. Apart from a common feature – the existing and the contemporary sections are both 'daylight museums' – the new spaces avoid any dialogue with the nineteenth-century museum interior. At the time of their construction, however, these latter spaces deliberately sought to emulate the international trend in museum architecture while simultaneously allowing Antwerp's artistic Golden Age to resonate throughout the building. While the treatment of history was the leitmotiv in the decorative schemes executed by the original architects (Jean-Jacques Winders and Frans Van Dijk), it remains to be seen which stories will remain in the snow-white rooms of the twenty-first century.

The conceptual and spatial dichotomy between both the nineteenth- and twenty-first-century buildings poses insoluble problems. Two buildings that are so intimately intertwined, with one literally nestling inside the other, will inevitably touch. These contact points, or their deliberate masking, are the pressure points within the design. For example, an eighteen-metre-long staircase takes the visitor up and over the historical rooms in a spectacular but meaningless gesture. The view from the museum shop of the researchers in the reading room might place the researchers in the spotlight, but it also reads like a painful allegory of the relationship between libraries and commercial spaces. In other places, the circulation in the new sections necessitated radical modifications to the existing museum rooms. The latter must conform to the imperative logic of an architectural concept that refuses to seek out an interesting conversation between past and present. The adjustments to the existing spaces are disguised in new ornamental frames with gold decorations, new doorframes and floors that replicate the originals, rendering them as good as invisible within the historic building. They mask the fact that old is also new at crucial moments.

KAAN freezes the existing museum in time, yet the museum sector is never static. Public engagement, education, conservation and such are constantly evolving and have been the cause of justified interventions within the building since its very inception. None of this is addressed in the new public experience of the museum. The result is a timeless and placeless visitor experience. On the one hand, it is devoid of links to the local culture, or to the rich history and scale of the city, which

Royal Museum of Fine Arts, Antwerp – KAAN Architecten

could guide the visitor in the new galleries. Moreover, the high-gloss floors reflect the artworks, which may have a great impact on the visitor's viewing experience. On the other hand, the restoration decisions have locked the building into time as if nothing had occurred between 1890 and today, and as if no new developments could occur. If the past is so removed from the present, what does this say about the future? Any meaningful next steps appear to have already been pre-empted.

TRUTHS AND FICTIONS INTERTWINED IN HET STEEN

Like the city hall and the KMSKA, Het Steen embodies much of Antwerp's history. The city's oldest building was once part of the city wall, later an element within the organic development of the historic city, before finally becoming, in the 1880s, a free-standing volume on a square adjacent to the straightened quays. Het Steen subsequently underwent a thorough restoration that reflected the nineteenth-century vision of the castle. A red brick extension followed in the 1950s, when the building functioned as the city's Maritime Museum. When noAarchitecten responded to the Open Call in 2016, they were particularly fascinated by the nineteenth-century fiction of the castle. The architects appreciated the original remnants of the building and the neo-Gothic architectural approach more than the 1950s extension, which they removed while retaining the footprint.

↪ See p. 173

The question of course is, Can you (re)create a castle that haunts the collective memory and belongs to both the past and present? What remains of the original Het Steen offers a way out: noA has allowed the rooms in the new section to connect with those in the existing one. This unites the old and new Steen into a single, multi-era building. The articulation of the wall thickness, with generous seating areas in the window openings; the chimney breasts; the simple but solid materials; and the wall incisions of medieval inspiration that usher in a sense of plasticity: all of this is inspired by an empathetic reading of the original building. Together with artist Pieter Vermeersch, a gentle gradient of different brick types was designed for the façade, with colour transitions that blend both old and new. Despite this historical inspiration, the extension is unmistakably contemporary. The stainless-steel window profiles, concrete window posts and glass sections make no pretence that the new extension is old. Historical and contemporary elements, facts and fictions: they all receive equal attention and care.

The architects have has turned Het Steen into a robust building, almost an infrastructure, one that is capable of accommodating various functions. As such, a conceptual link is re-established with everything that Het Steen has signified since its inception: a city gate during the Middle Ages and part of the promenade along the Scheldt during the nineteenth, but also a warehouse, prison, sawmill, museum and residential building. The volume is now a visitor centre and cruise terminal, but this programme does not determine its purpose. Het Steen is also part of the Sigmaplan, which is designed to protect the city against flooding from the Scheldt. It is thus resuming its original urban defence function, only this time against the threat of water. From the rooftop of noA's new donjon, one can experience how the building once fitted into the rooftops and turrets of old Antwerp, and from which it is cut-off at ground level by the busy road along the quay. Totally transformed, the building has rediscovered its origins.

CHALLENGING THE PAST FOR THE FUTURE

Het Steen, the KMSKA and the City Hall in Antwerp are all potted versions of local history. The recent building interventions demonstrate that it is precisely the historical stratification that offers both opportunities and pitfalls for designers. Just as in the nineteenth century, the current social transformations are leading to an upending of history that can be felt in every cultural discipline. There is also a debate on how to deal with buildings that bear traces of beliefs about power, one's own past and social differences. The question is, Which architectural positions are still relevant in an age when it is no longer acceptable to ignore the significance of the past or deal with it uncritically? The close reading of the three Antwerp monuments reveals how the monumentality of the nineteenth-century historical gaze brings with it an uneasiness in contemporary design.

The three recent interventions mainly reflect a quest that meanders between the search for the right distance, dominance and an in-depth testing of the historical narrative for its contemporary significance. The articulation of the buildings is appreciated in both the city hall and the KMSKA, yet no explicit statement is made about their nineteenth-century identity. While the path of least resistance might initially seem to lie in avoiding intense engagement with these historical layers, it leaves open the question of how to deal with them. Moreover, the city hall's reticence and the KMSKA's radical dichotomy both create an ambivalence in buildings with highly consistent programming and where, certainly in the case of the museum,

Het Steen, Antwerp – noAarchitecten

Sofie De Caigny

more architectural coherence could have been expected. Conversely, the design for Het Steen's contemporary extension was guided by the building's own history, including the nineteenth-century image of its medieval past. By creating a robust structure that can accommodate changing functions, and in keeping with the historical narrative, history remains unfinished.

LITERATURE

Inge Bertels, Bert De Munck and Herman Van Goethem, eds., *Antwerpen: Biografie van een stad* (Antwerp: Meulenhoff/Manteau, 2010).
Leen De Jong et al., *Het Koninklijk Museum voor Schone Kunsten Antwerpen. Een geschiedenis 1810-2007* (Oostkamp: Stichting Kunstboek, 2008).
Rony De Meyer and Lut Prims, *Het Zuid. Antwerpen, 1875-1890: architectuur en maatschappij* (Schoten: Continental, 1993).
Petra Maclot and Ilse Van Ginneke, 'De bouwbiografie van het Antwerpse stadhuis', in Marnix Beyen, Inge Schoups, Bert Timmermans and Herman Van Goethem, eds., *Het stadhuis van Antwerpen. 450 jaar geschiedenis* (Ghent: Pandora Publishers, 2015), 87–169.
Pieter T'Jonck, 'Form Follows Fiction', *A+ Architecture in Belgium* 294 (2022): 46–52.

CITY HALL

Offices
HUB and Origin with Bureau Bouwtechniek
Websites
www.hub.eu
www.origin.eu
www.b-b.be
Address
Grote Markt 1, Antwerp
Client
City of Antwerp
Design
January 2015
Delivered
March 2022

Surface area
10,300 m²
Volume
46,000 m³
Total building cost
€ 21,835,770 - excl. VAT
Total building cost per m²
€ 2,300 - excl. VAT
Main contractor
Monument Vandekerckhove / Monument Goedleven / Altri Tempi (temporary association)
Electrical subcontractor
Evip, Kontich
HVAC subcontractor
Thermoco, Antwerp

Joinery subcontractor
Potteau, Heule
Structural engineer
BAS, Leuven
Technology engineer
RCR, Herent
Building physics adviser
Daidalos Peutz, Leuven
Fire safety adviser
FPC, Antwerp
Art integration
Germaine Kruip

ROYAL MUSEUM OF FINE ARTS

Office
KAAN Architecten
Website
www.kaanarchitecten.com
Address
Leopold de Waelplaats 2, Antwerp
Client
Flemish Government, Department of Culture, Youth and Media
Design
January 2010

Delivered
December 2020
Surface area
30,000 m²
Volume
170,000 m³
Total building cost
€ 66,000,000 - excl. VAT
Total building cost per m²
€ 2,200 - excl. VAT
Main contractor
Artes Roegiers Artes Woudenberg (temporary association), Kruibeke/Bruges

Stability studies
Royal Haskoning DHV, Rotterdam[NL]
Technology studies
Royal Haskoning DHV, Rotterdam[NL]
Bureau Bouwtechniek, Antwerp
Acoustics studies
Royal Haskoning DHV, Rotterdam[NL]
KAAN Architecten, Rotterdam[NL]
Project support
Bureau Bouwtechniek, Antwerp

HET STEEN | See p. 173 |

Schools, the Gentle Revolution

Kiki Verbeeck

Who can forget the shrill sounds of children's voices ringing in the concrete playground; the smell of pea soup and the clattering of plates in the large, cool, high-ceilinged refectory; the voices of strict headmistresses reverberating through chilly, endless corridors? Flashback to typical school sites, contexts and atmospheres. Where our pristine senses are stimulated for the first time. The smells, sounds and colours of that time are things we never forget. They never leave us, precisely because we were children. Childhood is often the time when we form our first impressions of the power of buildings, of architecture. So let us focus on the beginning: primary school.

SCHOOLS AS A FOUNDATION

Schools mark the start of collective life. They are the place where everyone comes together, where we experience an important part of our youth and develop our vision of the future. The school building has undergone a major evolution. In the past, a school was like a cloister: isolated, walled, separate from the world. A place where a unique set of laws and rules applied. Yesterday's 'seclusion institute' is unthinkable and unworkable in today's diverse society. But the sterile buildings of that era still exist. They remain obstinately erect, standing the test of time again and again in a rapidly evolving world. A lick of paint, a new porch here and there, and *voilà*, the new school is complete.

Interventions of this kind, which barely deserve the title of 'evolution', are inexplicable to our children. Fortunately, in recent decades different insights have emerged which reassess schools as valuable, new, adapted learning and living environments for the youngest members of society. A hopeful, careful renaissance of the school building is under way in Flemish villages and towns.

In the first new school projects in the early 1990s, the spectre of laws and regularity, order and discipline were still tangible. The schools were already opening up more to their surrounding environments but still worked around a classic arrangement of classrooms and corridors. After that, we witness a sea change: there are radical and clear reactions to the school as a machine, a norm-establishing apparatus designed to turn children into decent, neat citizens. From then on, the individual takes precedence over collectivism, rather than the other way round. This development dissociates itself from multiple systems: on the one hand, the typology of the strict school building; on the other, the stringent budgets and strict deadlines within which some schools must be constructed. Take the 'Schools of Tomorrow' campaign, which managed to conjure up 182 schools in a short space of time. Although highly praised at the time, we should question what the innovative pedagogical story was behind a mass movement of this kind.

It is for precisely this reason that we are delighted to embrace the gentle revolution that is paving the way here and there, the child taking the place of the 'apparatus' as the design focus. What follows is a thought process with finger exercises that grow from within: from the perspective of the child in relation to the wider environment. We start with three concrete pavilions.

FINGER EXERCISES: FROM PAVILIONS TO NEW PROTOTYPES

We selected a number of specific projects to put under the microscope: three small-scale schools that began as modest extensions within a larger, 'classic' site. What is immediately striking is the involvement of the clients (the head teachers) and their intensive interaction with the designers. This is only logical: head teachers experience and collide with the reality and limitations of the classic structures on a daily basis. Drawing on their vision, expertise and concern for children's well-being and comfort, they always provided extremely valuable input, which resulted in a daring and comprehensive revolution in terms of approaches and impacts. These three finger exercises have clearly grown out of intensive design research: the typology of the school building has been challenged, taken apart and elaborated right down to the level of the material. These are prototypes, which make a judgement on new typologies.

The great strength of these projects lies in their manifestation of conceptual freedom: the extensive autonomy of the new school set-up vis-à-vis the classic school context. This freedom has distilled and streamlined the combination of classrooms and corridors into the essence of the 'classroom': an open space for learning that is flexible, changeable, light and in close interaction with its environment. This is followed by the interconnectivity of and synergy between the various classrooms. A series of interesting experiments with a range of exciting configurations offering space for new developments within the school context are elucidated below. A new sensory language is created. It is no longer about the smells in the corridor or the sounds in the playground, but about the intense interplay between the child and their direct environment. Continuous consideration is given to the experiential world of the child; the individual amid the environment takes precedence. How does the child look at the world? Their gaze is central and opens up fresh perspectives.

This experimentation reaches its zenith in the extension of the School pavilion in Denderleeuw by ZOOM architecten, in terms of both typology and material use. It comprises a circular pavilion, a quarter of which is opened up as a covered playground. The clever positioning of three door panels in solid wood transforms the pavilion into a single, transparent, covered outdoor space. At a stroke, three classrooms are transformed into a single, large multipurpose space.

Typical of the small pavilions discussed here is the green setting and the short distance to the 'mother ship', which immediately provides the necessary freedom in terms of both usage and materialization. The CLT (cross-laminated timber) walls serve as both structure and finish. A single streamlined design strategy underpins a warm and rich experience for the child. The experiment is in no way abstract or unmanageable but directly tangible and ready to be experienced. Its small scale invites further experimentation at a similar scale.

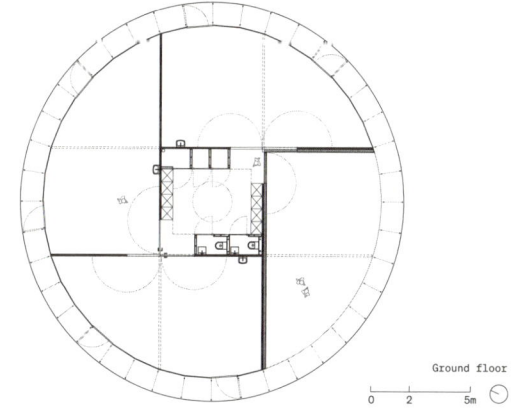

School pavilion, Denderleeuw – ZOOM architecten

These research and execution processes allow for innovation at different levels and layers, the ultimate goal being to arrive at new prototypes and new steps in school architecture. However, school buildings must comply with economic demands. Minimal resources must offer maximal spaciousness and experiences. This project effortlessly succeeds in this: the classroom construction is a decor that opens and closes, adapting to the activity of the day. A light structure defines the transition from in- to outdoors. Standard materials in a fresh composition create a pleasing complement to the sturdier main school. The school as an arbour in the park: what a reversal when compared to the walled institute where, out of sight of the immediate surroundings, order and discipline ruled. Here instead we have a (literally) open building that is inviting and transparent, interacting fully with its (mostly green) surroundings.

The Kosmos primary school by Dierendonckblancke architecten takes this principle the furthest. In the middle of the public Nachtegalenpark in Antwerp, the entire school programme spreads out gently amid the green environment, close to and beyond boundaries. Three stand-alone pavilions face and complement one another while retaining their individual autonomy. And all this takes place in a public park, a huge playground. Who doesn't dream of that? A sustainable approach to available space is self-evident here.

Four volumes – two existing grand buildings and two new additions – enter into a peaceful interrelationship. The programme is always different, yet the buildings are

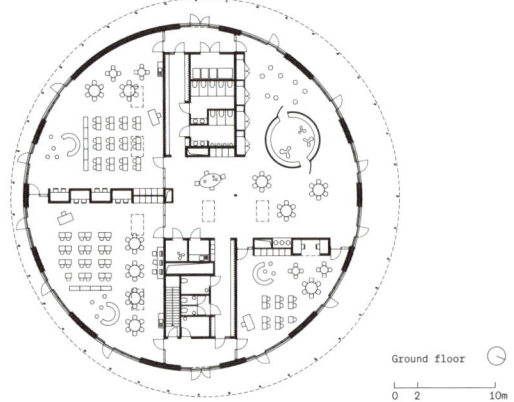

Kosmos primary school, Antwerp – Dierendonckblancke architecten

closely linked. Architectural elements such as porches, windows and doors ensure uniformity and clarity across the site. These are infrastructures that welcome children and immediately offer the warmth of human security. The project as a whole is uncomplicated and invariably focuses on the scale of the child.

The classrooms are located in the circular pavilion. A spacious, covered outdoor passage leads to a play area, changing area and rest space. Entrances to the building have a uniform colour. Entrance grilles point to the proximity of green space. Large windows offer direct views of and access to the classrooms. Infrastructures, materialization and colours are a guiding factor. Minimal circulation leads the children to the building's central point, an open, multipurpose area. Three spacious classrooms with large windows are oriented towards the generous green space. In- and outdoors are just a few steps away. This spaciousness is matched with simple, natural materials. There are no longer separate storage spaces for each classroom, but a single large cupboard in the central space where all the material is stored. At the same time, the prescribed pedagogical choice to work with two classes combined demonstrates the boundaries of the classroom typology. The larger volume of the sports hall also fits seamlessly into this design. The simplicity of the solution is self-evident: a deepened sports hall with high windows offers plenty of space for sports and games, while it is possible to look right through the building from the park. This building also has a similar oversized porch, which is a good place to hang out, both during and outside school hours.

This is the open school! A genuine revolution in the history of the school building that fits smoothly into the existing context. There have been neither barricades nor protests, simply an open vision of the specific needs of the child, constructed and materialized at their scale. The ensemble flows seamlessly into the park. In among large, mature trees, it feels as though this school has always been and will always be there – partly as a school, partly as pavilions in the park.

The same design strategy underpins HUB's Park classrooms in Merksem. Although set within the safely enclosed space of a castle park, a wooden classroom pavilion takes pride of place among the greenery. This is a textbook case of designing from the perspective of and at the scale of the child – in this case, a primary-school first year. We discover a homely tableau of various interlinked living rooms. Large windows with windowsills for working on. Warm colours in the interior, a wooden structure, a living-room ambiance, proximity to nature... Everything is provided to enable the child to grow up in optimal comfort and peace. This marks a permanent shift away from the original approach taken by schools, which saw a school building as no more than an instrument, a functional, practicable object. Such unquantifiable elements as experience, expectation, dreams and memory now come to the fore and are afforded a dominant role in the design. This sea change in the way that we think about schools seems to work perfectly on a small, homely scale. Can this philosophy, at the scale of the child, also be applied to larger interventions? Can we translate this human vision, with the emphasis on the child and their place in the world, into a context in which multiple generations of children come together?

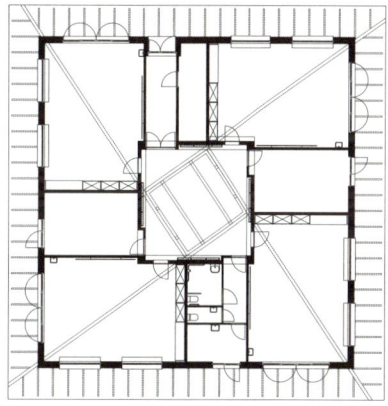

Park classrooms, Merksem – HUB

Kiki Verbeeck

PLAYTIME IS OVER: FROM PAVILION TO BUILDING?

Can small finger exercises also work for bigger challenges? Hofkouter primary school (Geert De Groote Architecten and Isabelle Jacques-Bernard Wittevrongel architecten) in Sint-Lievens-Houtem is the result of an Open Call. This comprises an extension of the existing school estate. On an open and green school site, the new building contributes to the fresh arrangement of the site. The building is fully equipped for changing pedagogical approaches. This flexibility is visible in every part of the building. The contrast between freedom and specifically determined and defined spaces results in an atypical appearance. The structure allows ample opportunity to move classroom walls, while the technical installations have been considered in an equally flexible way by concealing them in a separate 'wooden' cabinet. With the framework created, total freedom reigns within. However, the result is a school building that is anything but neutral. The materiality has been approached with great care, meaning that the children use the building with great respect. The flexible floor plan also makes it possible for the school to be opened up for use by local residents.

Melle is home to the Park School, another winning Open Call project, designed by the double duo Petillon Ceuppens architecten and Schenk Hattori Architecture Atelier. The precise integration of two new volumes hints at an instantly sensitive,

↦ See p. 63

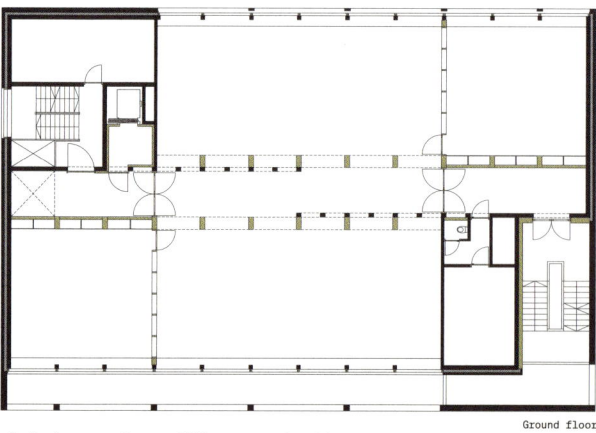

© Corentin Haubruge

Hofkouter primary school, Sint-Lievens-Houtem – Geert De Groote Architecten and Isabelle Jacques-Bernard Wittevrongel architecten

unified approach. The elongated school building meanders carefully through the park. A rhythm of structural lines and windows adds a human touch to the project. The muted but effective materialization is striking, both out- and indoors. The colours and materials are not garish but neutral, acting as a backdrop for the school's everyday activities.

The spatial experience varies from floor to floor. The collective space in the centre is always played off against the linked classrooms. Thanks to an ingenious planting design, the larger scale of the project as a whole is split into two separate entities at ground level. Kindergarten and primary school stand noiselessly back-to-back, offering the children the necessary feeling of safety. If required, the collective space can again be used by the community, simply by opening and closing scissor grilles. On the first floor, a single central space creates multiple spots and corners. The classrooms can be accessed both through this interior and through a gallery that frames the whole and seeks contact with the playground via playfully inserted steps.

The promise of today's school design discourse lies in the fact that it clearly begins with the individual experience of the child. This is the consequence of a force that comes from within. The freedom the designer finds in this provides opportunities for developing pleasant, user-friendly frameworks which mediate between the school and its surroundings.

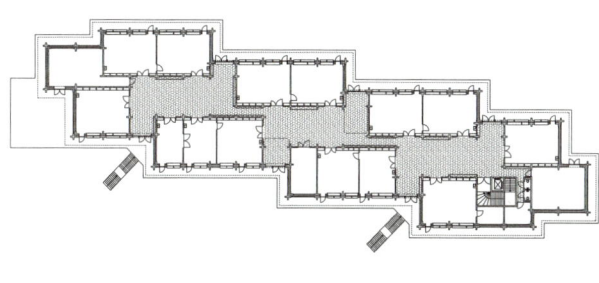

Park School, Melle – Petillon Ceuppens architecten and Schenk Hattori Architecture Atelier

Here we pay tribute to these projects as small, courageous experiments, as silent pioneers. Is the era of chilly, strict, regulated schools as we recall them gone for good? We must dare to dream.

SCHOOL PAVILION

Office
ZOOM architecten
Website
www.zoom-architecten.be
Address
De Nayerstraat 11a, Denderleeuw
Client
GO! Flemish Community Education
Design
2014
Delivered
March 2021
Surface area
244 m²
Volume
786 m³
Total building cost
€ 420,000 - excl. VAT
Total building cost per m²
€ 1,721 - excl. VAT
Main contractor
APK construct, Pelt
Structural engineering and technology
BAST architects and engineers, Ghent

KOSMOS PRIMARY SCHOOL

Office
Dierendonckblancke architecten
Website
www.dierendonckblancke.eu
Address
Gerard Legrellelaan 5-7, Antwerp
Clients
AG Vespa
City Education in Antwerp (AGSO)
Design
November 2016
Delivered
February 2021
Surface area
3,284 m²
Volumes
Classroom building: 3,524 m³
Sports hall: 3,294 m³
Total building cost
€ 5,098,663 - excl. VAT
Total building cost per m²
€ 1,553 - excl. VAT
Main contractor
Brebuild, Antwerp
Sanitation contractor
Aerts EG, Balen
HVAC contractor
Thermoco, Antwerp
Electrical contractor
Kobre, Kalmthout
Landscape design
Fris in het landschap, Ghent
Acoustics studies
De Fonseca, Meise
Stability studies
Mouton, Ghent
Technology studies
Tech3, Ghent
EPB studies
EA+, Ghent
Safety coordination
Macabo, Tessenderlo

PARK CLASSROOMS

Office
HUB
Website
www.hub.eu
Address
Gagelveldenstraat 71, Merksem
Client
KOBA
Design
July 2016
Delivered
June 2019
Surface area
445 m²
Volume
169,226 m³
Total building cost
€ 685,000 - excl. VAT
Total building cost per m²
€ 1,539 - excl. VAT
Contractor
Thys BP, Westerlo
CLT contractor
CLT-s, Westerlo
HVAC contractor
Sig-air, Aartselaar
Structural engineer
UTIL Struktuurstudies, Schaarbeek
Engineering technologies
ESTA Advies, Ravels
Interior
Vanhout.pro, Turnhout

HOFKOUTER PRIMARY SCHOOL

Offices
Geert De Groote Architecten and Isabelle Jacques-Bernard Wittevrongel architecten
Website
www.gdga.be
Address
Schoolstraat 4, Sint-Lievens-Houtem
Client
GO! Flemish Community Education
Design
December 2009
Delivered
January 2020
Surface area
1,570 m²
Volume
7,100 m³
Total building cost
€ 2,470,923 - excl. VAT
Total building cost per m²
€ 1,574 - excl. VAT
Building contractor, exterior joinery and flooring
Detrac, Vichte
Special technology contractor
Matthijs, Lochristi
Interior joinery contractor
Van Den Rijse, Erpe Mere
Stability studies
Studieburo Mouton, Ghent
Technology studies
Boydens Engineering, Ghent

PARKSCHOOL

See p. 63

Care and Homes

Petrus Kemme

Exercises in scale and silent hearts

In 2012 the then Flemish Government Architect Peter Swinnen and Flemish Minister for Welfare, Public Health and Family Jo Vandeurzen launched five Pilot Projects for innovative care architecture.[1] Design teams explored new spatial models for the care sector, elderly care in particular. Existing care institutions put forward specific questions for the selected designers who would go on to develop and execute the institutions' projects. The Government Architect aimed to harness specific projects to react to structural and urgent challenges for the elderly care sector, specifically the increased demand due to population ageing, the over-representation of large-scale and often remote care centres, and the shifting socio-economic and political view of elderly care, with core words such as 'client', 'self-reliance' and 'informal care'.[2]

Against this backdrop, the Pilot Projects advocated the Invisible Care initiative, 'care that is no longer isolated but integrated into social and urban life'. The motto was fleshed out in seven key strands or 'invisibility factors', all of which approached care architecture as 'embedded' on the basis of broad social lenses such as the market, urban life and regulation.[3] Collective living was thus given a preferential position: as a fundamental social ambition in itself, but also as a primary 'invisibility factor' and a common thread throughout the rest of the argument. In its most condensed form, therefore, Invisible Care advocated approaching care architecture initially as a collective living specification.

This essay will not attempt a comprehensive discussion of the Flemish Government Architect's Pilot Projects. Instead, it will start with recent realizations in order to review a wide range of newly executed projects against the backdrop of the Invisible Care initiative. The integration of care and living thus serves as the common thread for a tour of residential and/or care projects in Flanders that will underpin a broader interpretation of the 'invisible care' concept.

INVISIBLE CARE

On the edge of Gooreind, a village in the Campines municipality of Wuustwezel, noAarchitecten has constructed a new home for the Coda palliative care centre. The mission of the contracting non-profit organization – to take people in the final phase of life out of their isolation – ties in seamlessly with the ambition of Invisible Care. This translated into the versatile programme of an open house with hospice, a day centre, and an operational base for palliative care, grief counselling and home care.

---

1 Joeri De Bruyn, Stijn De Vleeschouwer and Peter Swinnen, eds., *Pilootprojecten Onzichtbare Zorg: Innoverende Zorgarchitectuur* (Brussels: Flemish Government Architect, 2014).

2 Peter Swinnen, 'Onzichtbare Zorg', in De Bruyn, De Vleeschouwer and Swinnen, *Pilootprojecten Onzichtbare Zorg*, 6.

3 Swinnen, 'Onzichtbare Zorg', 6.

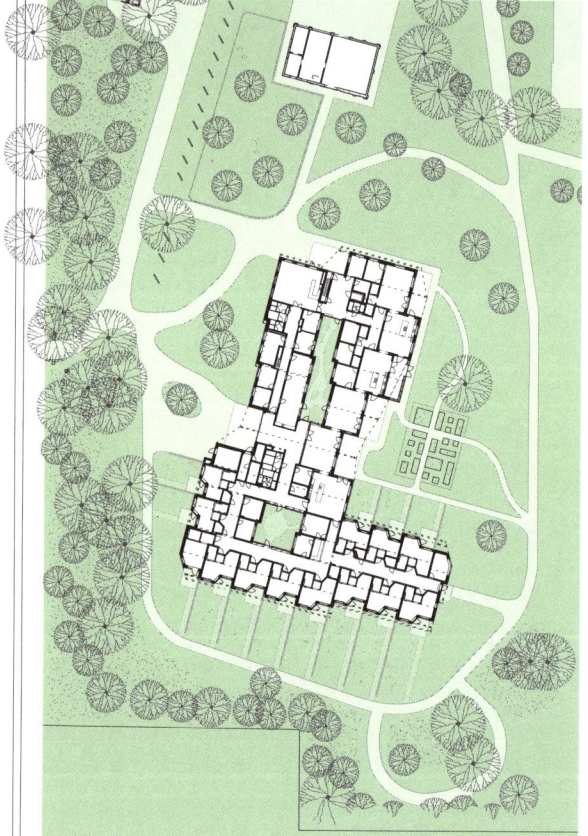

Coda palliative care centre, Wuustwezel – noAarchitecten

Situation plan

Although the programme does not really centre on residential provision, homeliness is a starting point for the architectural ambition.

To achieve this homeliness, noA refers in the first instance to the pastoral backdrop of the marshy Campines landscape and the partially preserved abbey farm on the same site where the client is based. Emphasized by the parallel saddle roofs, the new sequence of volumes echoes the familiar sight of farm architecture in the landscape with piecemeal extensions while camouflaging the true scale of the care centre. Inside, two patios make up the silent heart of the building: they provide the surrounding rooms with daylight and ensure that they all retain a relatively homely scale despite the building's large footprint. Around the patios, the corridors informally link all the offices, meeting spaces and individual rooms. The physical and visual accessibility of the landscape is central to every room, with wide doors that afford level access to the outdoors, under the protection of the overhanging roof. One significant detail is the recurring theme of a window seat, a place that allows you to be alone, talk to someone, look outside, focus your gaze inwards. In terms of colour usage and materials, noA also embraced the idea of the farm as a visibly inhabited yet large-scale structure embodying homeliness for care.

A literal example of elderly care as a collective living concept is De Korenbloem residential care home in Kortrijk. A pair of historic villas on either side of an inner courtyard serve as the starting point for two complementary sub-projects by Studio

Jan Vermeulen and Tom Thys Architecten (north side) and Sergison Bates architects (south side). The respective new-build blocks containing various types of residential care units were designed independently of one another but always in connection to their respective villas. The two old buildings themselves were renovated and equipped for the shared functions. In so doing, the architects not only preserved as many of the former houses' authentic elements as possible, but also focused on the site's core asset: the inner courtyard. With entrances on both sides of the block, the former villa garden is a potential green oasis in the city, and in theory the ideal place for the social integration of care home residents with people living nearby.

However, the radical splitting of the project into north and south results in a fragile constellation. The old wing of the care home borders almost the entire west side of the block, while greenery and fences screen the street on the east side. Therefore, the entrances to the courtyard are only visible from the sub-projects, and the architecture of the historic villas is not conducive to signposting a place with a potential public function. Despite their intrinsic qualities, the new wings look like mid-sized apartment blocks, each of which further knits into the eclectic architectural fabric of the mid-sized city. The intended integration therefore stands or falls with the policy adopted for the inner courtyard, which is controlled by the care centre, even if only in a spatial sense. Add a gate or two and the ambition to frame elderly care as collective living soon threatens to be downgraded to the considerably less socially integrated phenomenon of the gated community. Here too, care as collective living appears to be colliding with resistance to this type of dwelling in privatized Belgium.

De Korenbloem residential care home, Kortrijk – Sergison Bates architects (south) and Studio Jan Vermeulen and Tom Thys Architecten (north)

A comparable order of magnitude as regards construction programme and budget is visible in the Pilot Projects that have already been completed.[4] In each case the clients have a certain institutional weight. Understood as collective forms of housing, these projects always express themselves on the scale of a large-scale housing construction project, albeit in very different contexts and forms. Not only are these Pilot Projects chiefly focused on answering a single care need (namely that of the elderly), but they are therefore limited to a relatively specific scale level within the prescribed social integration of care. Collective living can take on a range of scale levels, however. This observation begs the question of how 'invisible care' might look at a different scale and with other care needs.

MORE INVISIBLE CARE

In recent times, small care projects clearly have increasingly taken the form of a very large house.[5] They thus come one step closer to the disputable but still dominant housing model of the nuclear family. It is for precisely this reason that, both architecturally and irrespective of their care programme, they can be regarded as projects that collectivize living rather than domesticate care. Could collective living as a care model on precisely this scale not form a link in the 'cultural shift' towards collective living advocated by Invisible Care? And could small-scale collective living as a model for care architecture not lead to *more invisible* care?

The Monnikenheide care campus in Zoersel has a rich tradition of interaction between care and contemporary architecture.[6] In a parcelled-out section of the former castle estate that also houses the care campus, FELT architecture & design constructed Villa Kameleon residential care home, a house for nine people with an intellectual disability. The project is conceived as co-housing where the residents largely live together independently, supported by carers during the day. In terms of both its operations (which include remote overnight security) and its intention, the house draws on the expertise and infrastructure of Monnikenheide. Nevertheless, the striking thing about this project is that it is underpinned by a private initiative (from the family of one of the residents). From this perspective and also as regards its location, it is in the first instance a house like many others in a residential area. With its green checked tiles and plasterwork, this somewhat large and hexagonal property merges into the wooded environment of the former castle estate.

In the interior, the floor plan is laid out in such a way as to ensure that each studio looks out onto the green surroundings from two corners and that each of the compact individual bathrooms also has a window. The ground-floor living space and the entrance hall accord with the dimensions of the studios above, while also being fully oriented towards the garden. A striking spiral staircase in the centre of the building connects the two building layers – perhaps more as a sculpture or a medium for light and sound in the shared core of the building than in the functional sense. Somewhat hidden between the central stairwell and the living spaces are also a spacious shared bathroom, a laundry room and storeroom, a lift and a less ceremonial staircase to the basement. With its large surface area and robust materialization, the latter begs to be used to house a secret party, a riotous table tennis tournament or a comfortable sofa on which to hang out – an informal counterpart to the living space.

---

4   One of the three completed care Pilot Projects – Klein Veldekens assisted living (Aster) in Geel by osar – is not discussed in this article. However, Gideon Boie's critical analysis of the project is worth noting. See: Gideon Boie, 'Intrede van de architect-ondernemer', *Apache*, 25 January 2021, https://www.apache.be/gastbijdragen/2021/01/25/149164.

5   For example, the latest edition of the *Flanders Architectural Review* featured Huis Perrekes in Oosterlo by NU architectuuratelier. See: Sofie De Caigny et al., *Flanders Architectural Review N°14. When Attitudes Take Form* (Antwerp: Flanders Architecture Institute, 2020).

6   Monnikenheide, a care campus for people with an intellectual disability, includes projects by firms such as 51N4E, Dirk Somers and UR architects. The campus has a direct connection with the development of the architectural field: as Flemish Minister for Finance and Budget, Health Institutions, Welfare and Family, Wivina Demeester, one of the driving forces behind Monnikenheide, was involved in the foundation of both the Flemish Government Architect role and the Flanders Architecture Institute.

©Stijn Bollaert

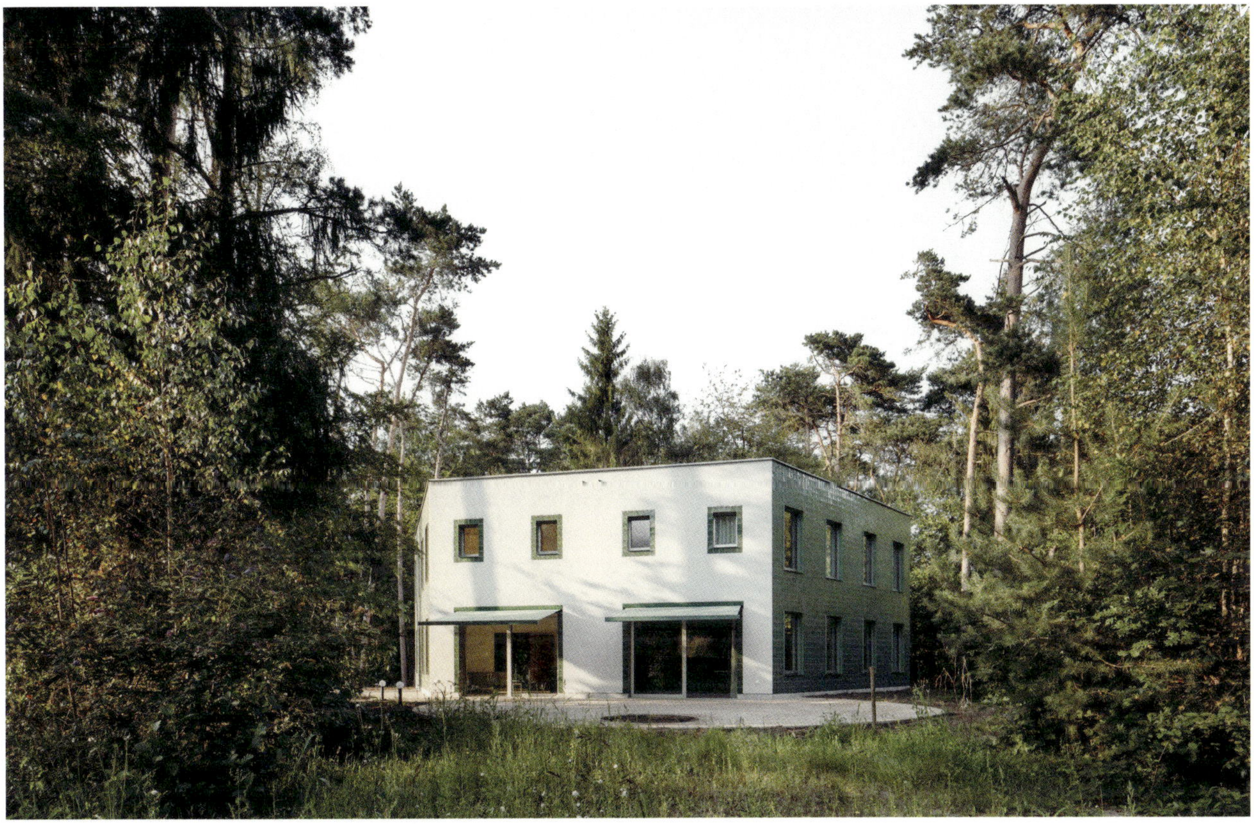

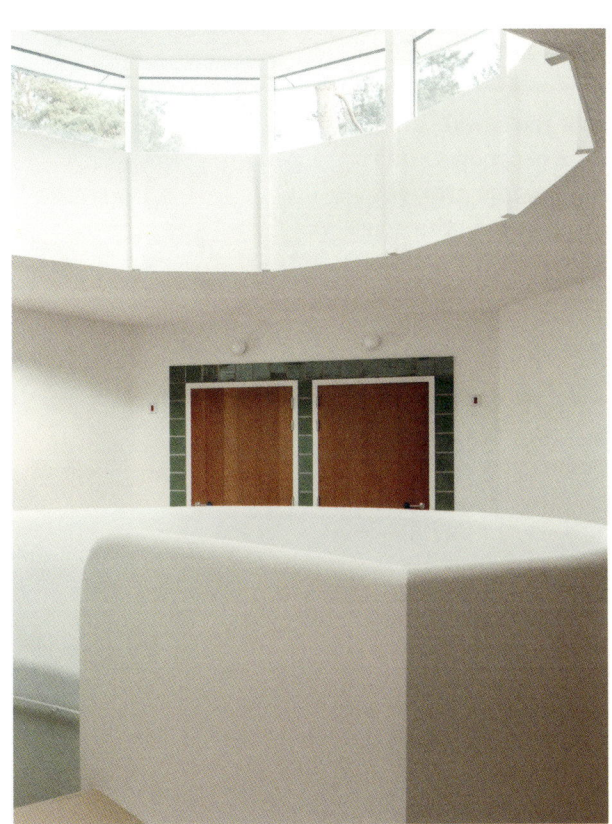

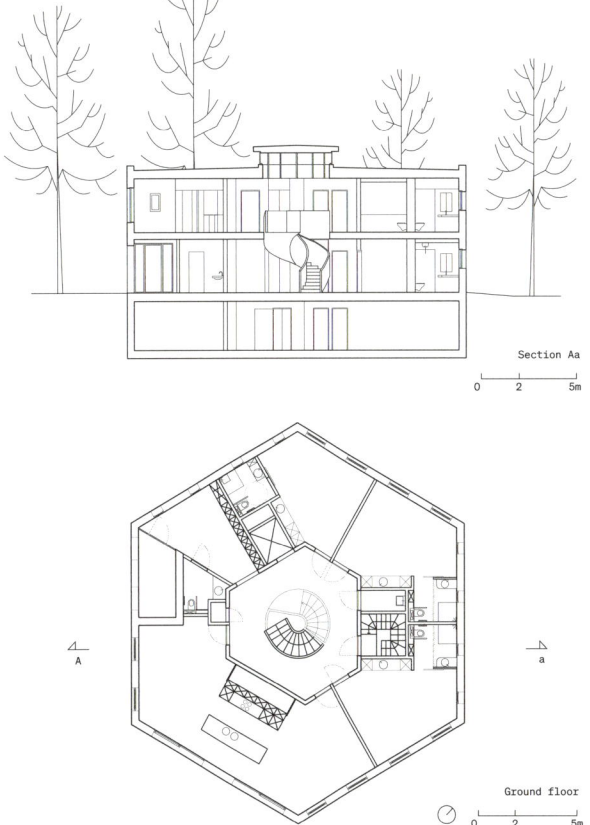

Villa Kameleon residential care home, Zoersel – FELT architecture & design

The stairwell assumes a central position within the Kameleon residential care model, both literally and figuratively. The shared spaces and individual rooms are never directly linked, but always require a journey through the stairwell. This also encourages informal encounters and tempers the spatial dominance of the night-time over the daytime parts. Although a spacious stairwell is certainly not an exotic phenomenon in a villa quarter, here one can even read into it a typological relation to care infrastructure (the same hall could also have connected six residential groups, in a star-shaped floor plan with three wings). Thus, by analogy with the outdoor spaces in both Pilot Projects under discussion, the stairwell serves as the 'silent heart' of the residential care model.

In Levenslust shelter by B-ILD in Gussenhoven (Linter), a typical roadside village near Tienen, the circulation space plays a central role in the extension of a home for care purposes. The house provides a collective home environment for twelve children who, for various reasons, cannot live with their families, whether temporarily or in the long term. The starting point was a generic pair of houses beside the road: to the left a grand, hundred-year-old head teacher's house with a symmetrical stone façade, to the right an unremarkable terraced house, around half its age. To the rear of the head teacher's house, B-ILD extended the ensemble with two sequential volumes. The largest is a square block that turns away from the existing volumes at an angle of around thirty degrees. A small, circular volume connects old and new and serves as the informal entrance to the home, in the centre of the composite whole.

In the square new-build section, a half-disguised spiral staircase divides up the floor plan into a primary living space that gives onto the garden, a more intimate living space at the back, and the strategically located kitchen. In-between the latter two, the sanitary fittings and the storeroom narrow down the remaining space into a space for homework. The plan thus combines a variety of opportunities to be together and alone with the necessary oversight. Upstairs, the spiral staircase occupies a central position in a spacious landing leading to six bedrooms and two bathrooms. On both levels, a hall in the circular in-between volume provides an angled link to the central stairwell of the former head teacher's house. In this sense, the connection between the stairwells is at the heart of the collective living, and this again mediates between the institutional scale of the whole and the more intimate scale of the connected houses and individual rooms.

In both Linter and Zoersel, the client's specific request was to first design a home, and only then a care institution. The villa quarter and the small roadside village stand in stark contrast to the typical environment for a collective living project – indeed, there the term 'density' is never far away. Although neither of the two projects is a textbook example in that sense, care programmes in the heart of low-density Flanders can perhaps accustom us to the idea of collective living.

VISIBLE LIVING

On the other hand, collective living can also accustom us to the idea of integrated care. On the outskirts of Leuven, Carton123 architecten constructed Korbeek Winners collective housing. The ensemble was designed for four connected families with diverse compositions, including a couple who are grandparents. The patio home on the ground floor was therefore designed to be wheelchair-accessible – with a

© Jeroen Verrecht

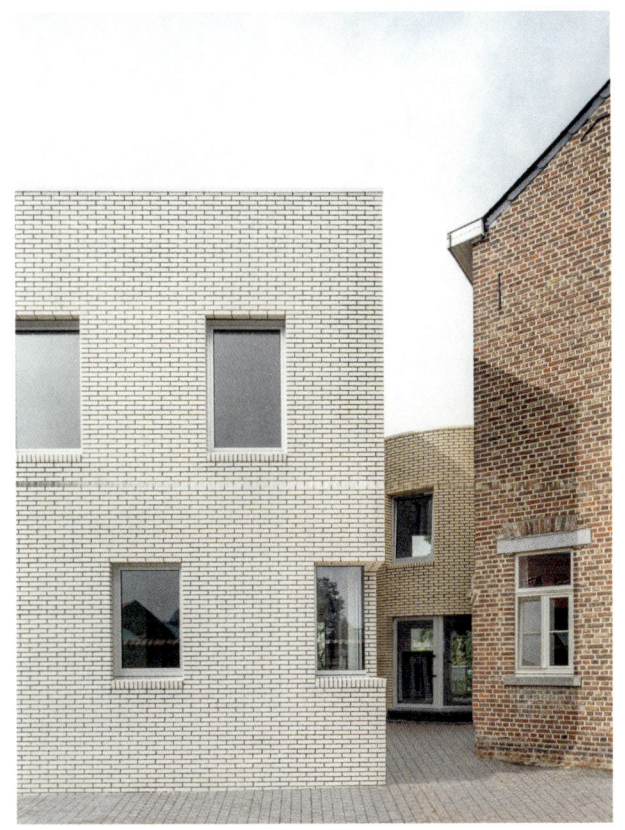

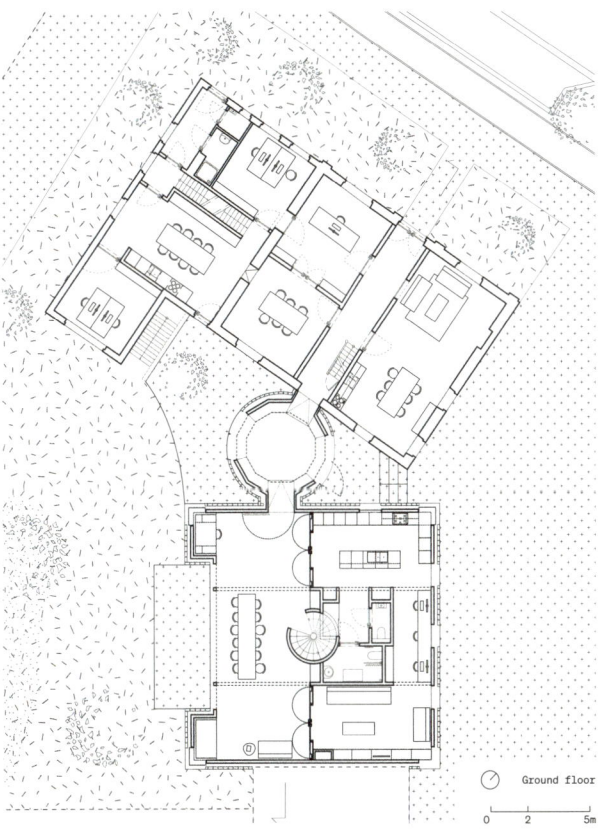

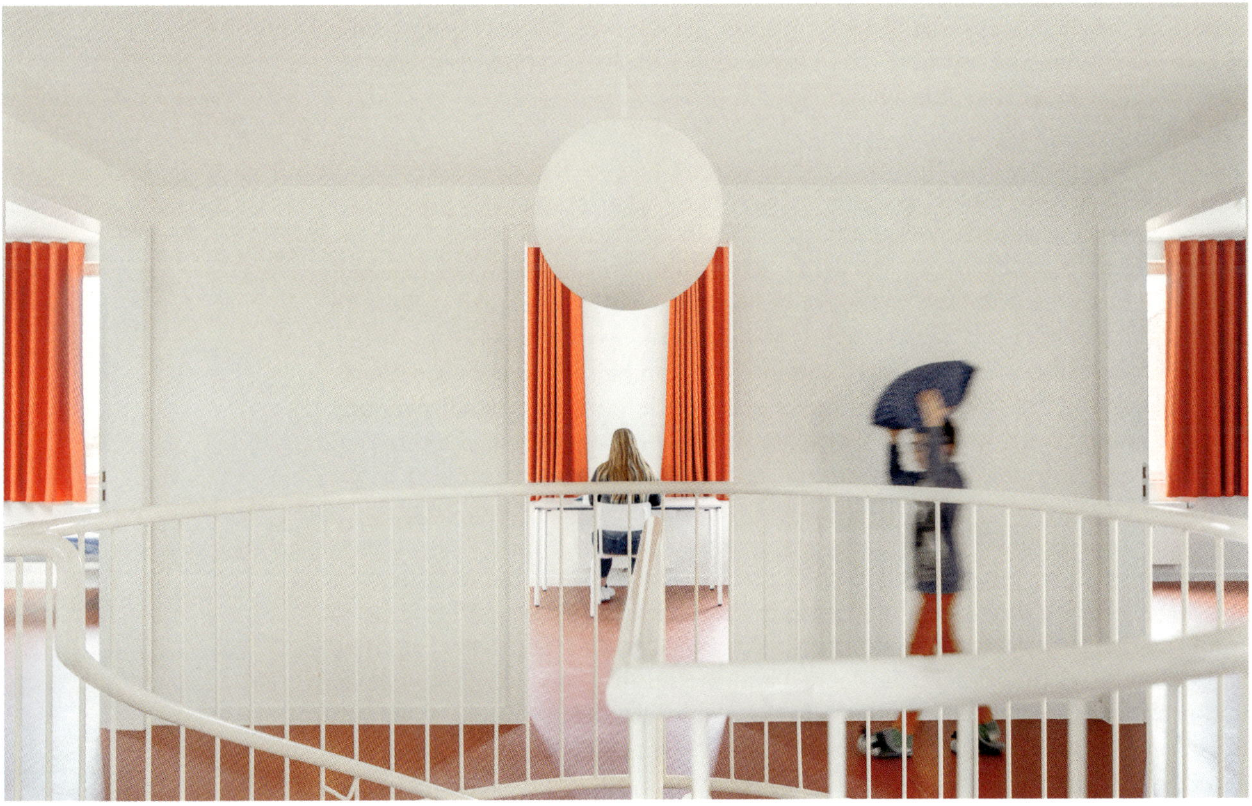

Levenslust shelter, Linter – B-ILD

view to the future, but also to be able to welcome wheelchair-bound friends. On the other side of the site, the five bedrooms of a larger unit are located in the basement, which, thanks to a double-height patio at the back and high ceilings at the front, enjoys a modest amount of daylight. The high ceilings flow into the double-height living room of the home above, where a mezzanine rests on a separate studio for two older teenagers. A simple duplex with two bedrooms above the grandparents' home completes the picture. The project as a whole offers an impressive variation on small-scale forms of housing.

At the heart of the project, a covered walkway runs from the street side to the spacious back garden via a shared terrace between the living units on the ground floor that extend out to the rear. The walkway leads to the front doors in two opposite façades that run perpendicular to the street and are linked by an outdoor staircase and a spacious outdoor landing that can serve as an additional outdoor space when needed. Windows and balconies are carefully balanced to ensure privacy while providing oversight of the shared outdoor space (and the connection with it). Thus, a mutual understanding is created in the oversized circulation space between the inhabitants, an understanding that contravenes the norms of traditional terraced living.

A coincidental combination of household compositions and a need for secondary care have here given rise to a modest form of collective living which, aside from the clients' specific situation, invites caring and visible living. The highly distinct units within the project – superficially the wheelchair-accessible apartment and the studio – enable the integration of care, among other things, and probably encourage this more effectively than a stacking of almost identical units modelled on the 'average' family. Moreover, it is possible to propose the integration of a variety of care needs, of short or long duration. This approach thus injects a kind of collective living and Invisible Care into probably the least self-evident context for it: small-scale, private housebuilding.

PILOTS AND STEWARDS

In the aftermath of a pandemic and with a new refugee crisis fresh in our minds, it seems useful to recall the key strands of Invisible Care, also on a small scale, with a broad understanding of care and with a forward-thinking view of collective living. In this sense, the smaller residential care projects can be seen as complementary to the Pilot Projects. The cultural shift towards which these are partially working is such a fundamental revolution that it seems unthinkable without projects that lead the way in the still-dominant mass of small-scale construction projects in the dispersed city.[7]

In that respect, we focus attention on the fact that the clients and architects of the projects being discussed found one another in a more or less informal way: from the institutional framework of the Pilot Projects, via the private initiative supported by Monnikenheide in Zoersel and the self-initiated call from a local non-profit care organization in Linter, to the almost classical private commission in Leuven. Moreover, the practices behind the three smaller projects (FELT, B-ILD and Carton123) are in a similar phase: all are relatively young, but experienced and recognized in the field. Projects of this kind also seem to contain an opportunity for

7 See also the collective living Pilot Projects in: Joeri De Bruyn, Anne Malliet and Peter Swinnen, *Pilootprojecten Collectief Wonen: Vijf Masterplannen Uit Startblokken – Fase 2* (Brussels: Flemish Government Architect, 2014).

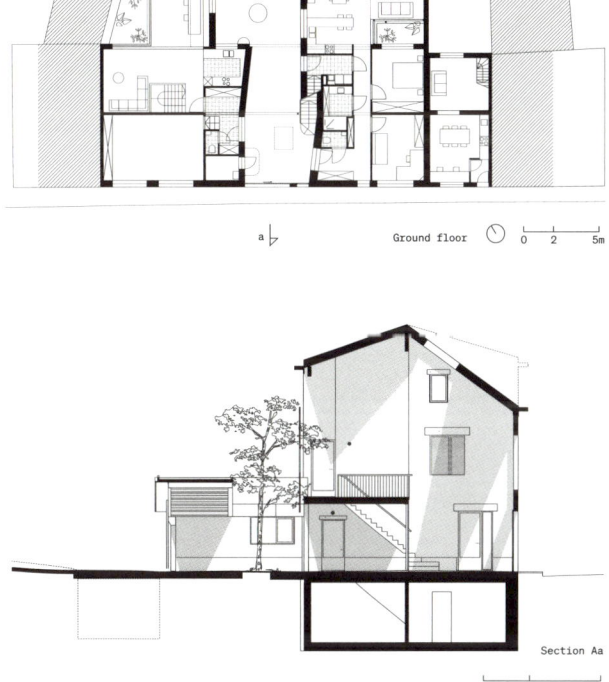

Korbeek Winners collective housing, Leuven – Carton123 architecten

the architectural field: the small residential care projects are located on the interface between the individual commission (still paramount for most young practices) and the institutional environment of public commissions (meanwhile with several generations of established architects as competition).

Commissions of this kind therefore occupy the space between living and care, between young and established practices, between institutional and informal commissioning, between inherited individualism and a collective future, and between inspiration and realism. Perhaps, within the framework of a cultural shift towards collective living and *Invisible Care*, in a strongly developed field full of relatively young practices and alongside the institutional weight and exemplary ambition of the Pilot Projects, it will also be possible to focus on supporting small-scale and informal care and/or residential projects, step-by-step interventions that give a nudge in the right direction, in the midst of the fragmented, individual and decentralized construction culture that we are still far from having escaped. In the cabin behind the Pilot Projects, in among the passengers, lies a *Stewardship of Invisible Care*.

CODA PALLIATIVE CARE CENTRE

Office
noAarchitecten
Website
www.noaarchitecten.net
Address
Bredabaan 743, Wuustwezel
Client
Coda
Design
2013
Delivered
June 2020
Surface area
2,577 m²
Volume
8,899 m³
Total building cost
€ 5,052,292 - excl. VAT
Total building cost per m²
€ 1,960 - excl. VAT
Main contractor
Vanhout.pro, Turnhout
Art integration and garden
Jan Minne, Brussels
Acoustics
Kahle Acoustics, Brussels
EPB and safety coordination
Danafix-EVC, Brasschaat

DE KORENBLOEM RESIDENTIAL CARE HOME

Offices
Sergison Bates architects (south)
Studio Jan Vermeulen and Tom Thys Architecten (north)
Websites
www.sergisonbates.com
www.studiojanvermeulen.eu
www.tomthysarchitecten.be
Addresses
Sint Jansplein 13A, Kortrijk (south)
Pieter de Conincklaan 12, Kortrijk (north)
Client
De Korenbloem
Design
2013
Delivered
October 2021
Surface area
4,250 m² (south)
5,307 m² (north)
Total building costs
€ 6,900,000 - excl. VAT (south)
€ 7,600,000 - excl. VAT (north)
Total building costs per m²
€ 1,623 - excl. VAT (south)
€ 1,488 - excl. VAT (north)
Main contractor
Strabag, Ghent
Site supervision
Katrol Architecten, Antwerp
Surroundings
BuroGroen, Roeselare
Stability, technology and EPB studies
VK architects + engineers, Merelbeke
Safety coordinator
DCC, Roeselare

LEVENSLUST SHELTER

Office
B-ILD
Website
www.b-ild.com
Address
Sint-Truidensesteenweg 190, Linter
Client
Huize Levenslust
Design
2018
Delivered
June 2021
Surface area
765 m²
Volume
3,148 m³
Total building cost
€ 1,137,016 - excl. VAT
Total building cost per m²
€ 1,486 - excl. VAT
Main contractor
Postelmans-Frederix, Beringen
Stability engineer, technology, EPB
STir, Dilbeek
Art integration
Something Els (Els Vandekerckhove)
Grau (Anthony Jammes)

VILLA KAMELEON RESIDENTIAL CARE HOME

Office
FELT architecture & design
Website
www.felt.works
Address
Langebaan 91, Zoersel
Clients
Chris De Roo and Emmaüs
Design
October 2017
Delivered
September 2021
Surface area
843 m²
Volume
2,768 m³
Total building cost
€ 1,357,000 - excl. VAT
Total building cost per m²
€ 1,610 - excl. VAT
Main contractor
vanhout.pro, Turnhout
Stability studies
Robuust architectuur & onderzoek, Ghent

KORBEEK WINNERS COLLECTIVE HOUSING

Office
Carton123 architecten
Website
www.carton123.be
Address
Oudebaan 456, Leuven
Clients
Martens and Verheyden families
Design
September 2017
Delivered
November 2020
Surface area
735 m²
Volume
2,418 m³
Total building cost
€ 1,160,000 - excl. VAT
Total building cost per m²
€ 1,578 - excl. VAT
Main contractor
Easy Bouw, Linter
Stability studies
Lambda-max, Aalst
Technology studies
David Martens, Leuven
EPB
EMS, Deinze
Safety coordination
VK Robyn, Drongen
Roofing contractor
Roothans, Lint

A Critical Appraisal of New Domestic Architecture in Flanders

Martino Tattara

It has repeatedly been stated that Flanders is facing a housing shortage and that there is a high need for new housing units in the region. A few years ago, for example, the Flemish Government Architect announced that Flanders would need to build 300,000 new units by 2030 to face the region's rising housing demand, a call that was wholeheartedly embraced by architects. While the population is certainly on the rise (mainly due to internal and international migration), to explain such numbers and the ensuant alarming tones, one needs to consider other relevant factors beyond pure demographic variations. Among such factors we find the growing number of singles, couples and very large families compared with the traditional four- or five-member family (which has mostly been at the centre of local housing production); the inadequate conditions of parts of the existing housing stock; the mounting attractiveness of cities over suburbs; and, ultimately, the ways in which existing housing is capable of accommodating new forms of living and working. The growing housing need also seems to be confirmed if we look at public-sector rented housing, which, in contrast to neighbouring countries, occupies a relatively marginal role within the overall housing provision.[1] In 2018 the demand for social housing units reached 150,000 units, with a third of this concentrated in the province of Antwerp. While all this would suggest that we need more, and more affordable, homes, residential real-estate prices have, alarmingly, been rising for quite a while, with yearly increases of about 9 per cent in the last few years. This confirms that real estate remains one of the most profitable forms of investment in Flanders. Since the number of newly built homes has continued to grow, the fundamental question that needs to be answered is whether the new domestic landscape of Flanders can accommodate current societal needs.

To answer this question, one should look into multiple fields, including policymaking, urban planning, economics and of course architecture. While I will not be able to explore all these dimensions in a systematic manner, I would like to highlight the active role of architecture in responding to these and similar societal strains. Many examples can be illustrative in this regard. Think of the ways in which architects were able to innovate typologically the residential market in American cities in the late nineteenth and early twentieth century. They did so, for instance, through the invention of such types as the residential hotel for middle-class families that moved to the city to work as well as through the rise of SRO units (single room occupancy) for singles and Home Clubs for middle-class families. Despite being in most cases commercially driven developments, these initiatives were able to promote technological innovation but also social emancipation by supporting a lifestyle based on

1 Only around 6 per cent of the housing stock in Flanders ranks as a dwelling owned by a social housing corporation or sublet by a social rental agency. See Kristof Heylen, *Grote Woononderzoek 2013. Deel 2. Deelmarkten, Woonkosten en Betaalbaarheid* (Leuven: Steunpunt Wonen, 2015). See also Hilde Heynen, 'Belgium and the Netherlands: Two Different Ways of Coping with the Housing Crisis, 1945-70', *Home Cultures* 7, no. 2 (2010): 159–77.

professionalized domestic labour. Or consider architectural experiments that, inspired by Charles Fourier's idea of the *phalanstères* (developed in the early nineteenth century), emerged across Europe[2]: in London, 'service apartments', a mix of elegant flats with hotel-level services; in Denmark, the *kollektivhus*, which offered living spaces supported by services such as housekeeping and catering carried out by service staff[3]; or, in Germany, the ideas of Lily Braun, who proposed to develop apartment buildings with centralized food preparation, housekeeping, childcare, an in-house kindergarten and recreational facilities. While we tend to see these as exceptional and experimental projects, they represented a diffuse and accepted alternative way of living to the traditional family house, at the time preferred by many as these types were identified as more capable of responding to the labour conditions of the time and the needs of a transient society.

While these examples might seem to be 'historically' distant from the present condition, in recent years too, alternative housing projects, often initiated by architects themselves, have supported typologically innovative domestic schemes for both middle-class and less privileged households. Take, for example, the recently completed San Riemo block in Munich (Germany), resulting from the collaboration between the offices of Summacumfemmer and the German (now Ghent-based) architect Juliane Greb. After winning an international competition launched by the local Grossstadt cooperative, the architects developed a collective housing scheme offering a range of housing possibilities, from small studio to large, shared apartments. But the scheme's clear differentiation between primary structure and partitions, together with the position of the kitchen at the centre of the living unit, made it possible to renegotiate the unit's size and the number of rooms according to the changing needs of inhabitants. Alternatively, think of Lacol's La Borda housing project in Barcelona, winner of the 2022 EU Mies Award for Emerging Architecture. In this case, the design is based on the reduction of the private space and the maximization of communal areas that can be freely used by inhabitants for leisure, domestic work, care and distribution. Organized around a central covered courtyard, the design subverts many of the dominant logics of contemporary housing production, where circulation, for example, is generally seen as a mere technical space with the goal of steering inhabitants as quickly as possible into their apartments.

2   Norbert Schoenauer, 'Early European Collective Habitation: From Utopian Ideal to Reality', in *New Households, New Housing*, eds. Karen A. Franck and Sherry Ahrentzen (New York: Van Nostrand Reinhold, 1989), 47–70; Dick Urban Vestbro, 'History of Cohousing – Internationally and in Sweden', in Dick Urban Vestbro, ed., *Living Together: Cohousing Ideas and Realities around the World. Proceedings from the International Collaborative Housing Conference 1st Stockholm May 2010* (Stockholm: Royal Institute of Technology. Division of Urban and Regional Studies, 2010), 42–55; Dick Urban Vestbro and Liisa Horelli, 'Design for Gender Equality: The History of Co-Housing Ideas and Realities', *Built Environment* 38, no. 3 (2012): 315–35.

3   Vestbro, 'History of Cohousing', 45.

San Riemo cooperative housing project, Munich[DE] – Summacumfemmer and Büro Juliane Greb

Cadix group housing, Antwerp – Bovenbouw Architectuur – BULK architecten – Sergison Bates architects

Cadix group housing, Antwerp – Bovenbouw Architectuur – BULK architecten – Sergison Bates architects

When looking at contemporary housing production in Flanders, it becomes crucial therefore to ask whether it is capable of meeting contemporary social, economic and environmental demands. These include socio-demographic transformations (the shift from a society made of medium-sized families to one based on either small or very large family households as well as the emergence of new subjects beyond the traditional nuclear family); the recent call towards new forms of 'ageing in place'; the wish for new forms of collectivity, especially for those who could enjoy this, such as migrant families or the young and elderly; the idea of the house as a place where the relation between reproductive and productive activities could be rethought and redistributed; the rising housing prices and maintenance costs; and ultimately the need to upgrade and transform a rapidly ageing housing stock.

The Cadix group housing in Antwerp's Het Eilandje is a new urban block resulting from the collaboration between BULK architecten, Bovenbouw Architectuur and Sergison Bates architects. The project is part of a series of recent residential interventions in the city's old port area. In this case, the architects proposed a rectangular building block on what was an empty site used for a long time as a parking facility. The block itself consists of seven different buildings, all sharing the same façade materials (brick) and a central courtyard. With one exception, typologically speaking, they are all apartment buildings. While the architecture – through its forms, materials, decorations and urban typology – seems eager to establish a relationship with history, it remains unclear whose history this is. The architects paid close attention to the detail of their buildings' elevations rather than to the units' plans, with the risk of translating this effort into a new façadism. Entrances at ground level are conceived as large, elegant and somewhat monumental spaces and yet, with the exception of the graceful staircases of Bovenbouw's palazzo, as soon as you go through this intermediate space, you are immediately brought back from the monumental scale of the lobbies of New York apartment blocks into the awkward conditions typical of internal circulation spaces of average apartment buildings in Flemish cities. Instead of celebrating a collective dimension, the careful design of the lobbies and their rich materials seem to be there to primarily glorify the social status of the inhabitants.

In terms of units and types, apartment plans clearly prioritize living rooms and large kitchens, often accessible through dark circulation spaces whose dimensions are remarkably large when compared to the number and size of bedrooms. One immediately feels compelled to ask for whom these apartments have been designed. You would certainly expect that, in such a part of the city, especially considering that this block is built on what previously was public land, priority would be given to young families with children offering living spaces in which to accommodate the complexities and struggles of domestic life, or what Lewis Munford described as the 'intimate union of domesticity and labor'.[4] Instead, apartment plans reinforce the sharp division between work and home – a distinction traditionally used as a sign of class privilege – and therefore seem a better fit for wealthy ageing people or perhaps transient Airbnb users.[5] The architecture of the Cadix block seems to be the architectural embodiment of what Madden and Marcuse have defined as the hyper-commodification of housing, where, in other words, 'real estate speculation becomes the principal source for the formation of capital'.[6] Although Flanders has long been characterized by relatively low real-estate value and affordable prices, especially when compared to other Western cities, commodification processes of housing have found in the region's asset-based welfare system a fertile ground for its reproduction.[7]

Probably it would have not been possible to expect something different from a project initiated by a private developer, yet the role of the city and its policies in relation to the privatization of public land remain questionable. In Ghent's De Nieuwe Dokken, a similar former harbour area undergoing transformation, the city, through its urban development company, forced

4   Lewis Mumford, *The City in History* (New York: Harcourt, 1989), 281.

5   Such a distinction was nevertheless challenged by the recent pandemic, when white-collar workers were able to work from home while blue-collar, care and distribution workers had to continue going to their traditional workplace.

6   Henri Lefebvre, *The Urban Revolution* (Minneapolis: University of Minnesota Press, 2003), 160.

7   See Pascal De Decker and Caroline Dewilde, 'Home-ownership and Asset-based Welfare: The Case of Belgium', *Journal of Housing and the Built Environment* 25 (2010): 243–62.

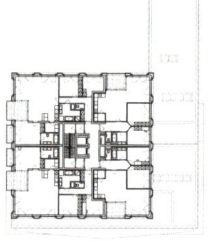
Tower level 6

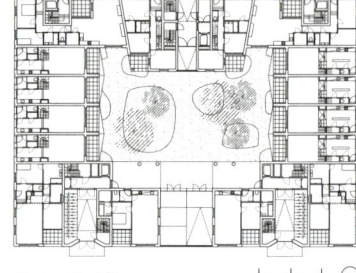
Palazzo ground floor   0 5 10m

© Stijn Bollaert

Stapelplein group housing, Ghent – 360 architecten (Tower) – BULK architecten (Palazzo)

private developers to incorporate a percentage of affordable units. Building on the general master plan drawn up by OMA in 2004, BULK architecten and 360 architecten proposed a series of buildings on the south-west side of the dock, including two palazzos and one tower. While the architecture of the tower contains many of the tropes already described for the urban block in Antwerp, in BULK's adjacent palazzo, of which only the first has so far been built, the architects have attempted to develop a compact open block as a conglomerate of different types, with apartments and terraced houses gathered around a collective central courtyard. The opening of this central space towards the canal and the future public space along the docks have the potential to literally connect the water with the very collective core of the block and become a significant space in the life of residents.

See p. 135 ↵

Another example of the fruitful relationship between architects and municipal urban-development companies is represented by the recently completed housing project by Architecten Broekx-Schiepers in the Borgerhout district of Antwerp. In the context of AG Vespa's somewhat debatable strategy to develop housing for sale at controlled prices in deprived neighbourhoods (often resulting in the displacement of the local population), the architects have been able to challenge many of the traditional tenets typical of Flemish domestic architecture. In a larger plot spanning two streets, the architects placed, on one side, a series of four terraced houses and, on the other, an apartment block, with a collective garden in-between. Especially the apartment building, of which one unit was furnished according to the architects' ideas, reveals a plan configuration that differs radically from the contemporary Flemish domestic landscape. By concentrating the kitchen and bathroom in the central part of the unit, by using large doors that either slide or disappear into the thickness of the wall, by highlighting structure and partitions through different materials, the result is a domestic space that can constantly be reinvented and that allows multiple ways to inhabit the space. Rather than define a rigid choreography of daily life (as most apartment plans do), the Broekx-Schiepers project suggests how charged with possibilities the role of the architect is when given the opportunity to go beyond the façade and the development of standard plan units, and instead to engage with typology, interior design and furniture. And yet, perhaps because of the central shared garden or the uncertainties regarding the future of an adjoining plot, this project has not been commercially successful so far.

While all the above projects concern either private or public-private developments, it remains to be checked whether the situation is different in the sphere of public housing interventions, where one would expect architecture to play an even more fundamental role in accommodating pressing societal questions. In this respect, it is important to recall that the future for social housing agencies in Flanders is full of challenges. These include the need for internal reorganization following the recent reform that supports the merging of local social-housing agencies, the need to increase their housing offer and ultimately upgrade their rapidly ageing housing stock, especially housing built in the second half of the twentieth century. [8,9] For social housing agencies operating in the main Flemish cities, this last issue mostly concerns large-scale apartment blocks, slabs or towers waiting to be either demolished or reconstructed. In case of demolition, besides environmental concerns, the risk is often the impossibility of being able to rebuild the same volume and the ensuing reduction in units. The alternative – namely, launching into a radical project of retrofitting – presents its challenges and limitations, as architects in this case

8   Thomas Detombe, 'Hervorming sociale huur duwt mensen in handen van huisjesmelkers', 18 May 2021, https://sociaal.net/achtergrond/hervorming-sociale-huur-duwt-mensen-in-handen-van-huisjesmelkers/.

9   Isabelle Blancke and Jürgen Vandewalle, 'Beneath the Wheel', *Flanders Architectural Review N°14. When Attitudes Take Form* (Antwerp: Flanders Architecture Institute, 2020), 137–44.

Collective housing, Borgerhout – Architecten Broekx-Schiepers

need to work within the limitations given by the existing structure. Social housing agencies such as De Gentse Haard in Ghent and Woonhaven in Antwerp have courageously chosen this option and engaged with architects on projects that propose the complete retrofit of existing blocks. The recently completed project by DBLV architecten (Dierendonck-Blancke-Lust-Van De Ginste) in Ghent belongs to this category of interventions. It follows the project by Atelier Kempe Thill and RE-ST for the retrofitting of two blocks in Antwerp's Rozemaai social housing complex (discussed in the previous edition of this book).[10]

10   Blancke and Vandewalle, 'Beneath the Wheel', 137–38.

↦ See p. 49

In this case, an existing social housing slab, built in 1971 and characterized by apartments facing either east or west, has been radically transformed by removing all secondary partitions and reinventing the typological organization of the block. Instead of dwellings with single orientation and accessible through a corridor running longitudinally to the slab on every floor, the architects designed larger transverse dwellings organized over two levels, with windows on both sides and with a small private balcony. The reduced number of units has been compensated by two new volumes, each located on either side of the existing slab and that together are capable of better integrating the volume in its urban context. The proposal seems to answer many challenges: the retrofitting of existing social housing blocks built in the second half of the past century, the need to transform the offer of units from medium-size to either very large or very small flats, and the capacity of dwellings to better respond to the lifestyle of large families in particular.

In terms of typological transformation, duplex apartments have the capacity to offer a higher level of privacy to inhabitants of the same unit compared to single-storey flats, while the living room stretching between the two sides of each unit with the kitchen positioned in the middle supports simultaneous uses among different residents of the same household. Positioning the kitchen at the centre of the flat rather than in a 'hidden' corner (as often happens in traditional domestic space) reinforces the idea that the house is a place of productive and reproductive labour and that the recognition of this constitutional condition is the prerequisite for social transformation. The addition of an extra volume on the outside next to the existing slab seems to be a replicable strategy that could be reproduced in other situations as in many cases post-war housing blocks were placed in the middle of large areas that represent an often-unexplored potential.

Reforming the domestic landscape in Flanders remains a difficult undertaking, especially in a region where 70 per cent of households own their home and almost 80 per cent of the housing stock is made up of single-family houses. In the region, the legacy of the twentieth-century housing policies that favoured family houses and rooted out any possible diversification in the housing offer seems very strong still. The dominant idea of home is yet that of a private place, where our sense of intimacy is cultivated, naturalizing domestic labour and rendering it an intimate activity done only for the sake of the family and not for society at large. The recent emphasis on urban living, density and the city as ideal living space has not diverged from these ideas. When housing is produced by private developers with little control by public authorities, architecture has proved to be unable to challenge the traditional shortcomings of domestic space and produce new emancipatory domestic forms. The situation seems different in the few other instances when housing projects are the result of direct public interventions or when city authorities are able to retain a certain level of control on housing development. In such cases, architects are able to experiment and their work often seems not only capable of upgrading living standards but also of meeting some of the demands of inhabitants and society at large.

Nekkersput social housing, Ghent – DBLV architecten (Dierendonck-Blancke-Lust-Van De Ginste)

SAN RIEMO COOPERATIVE HOUSING PROJECT

Offices
Summacumfemmer and Büro Juliane Greb
Websites
www.summacumfemmer.com
www.julianegreb.com
Address
Elisabeth-Mann-Borgese Strasse 24, Munich[DE]
Client
Kooperative Grossstadt eG

Design
December 2019
Delivered
December 2020
Surface area
5,257 m²
Volume
17,082 m³
Stability studies
Lieb Obermüller + Partner Beratende Ingenieure mbb, Munich[DE]

Technology studies
Energieagentur Berghamer and Penzkofer GmbH & Co. KG, Moosburg a. d. Isar[DE]
Building physics studies
Müller-BBM GmbH, Munich[DE]
Landscape design
BL9 Landschaftsarchitekten PartG mbB, Munich[DE]
Site supervision
SRW Plan. Architekten GmbH, Munich[DE]

CADIX GROUP HOUSING

Offices
Bovenbouw Architectuur (London residence)
BULK architecten
(Venice/Stockholm/Quebec residences)
Sergison Bates architects
(New York residence)
Websites
www.bovenbouw.be
www.bulkarchitecten.be
www.sergisonbates.com
Addresses
Londenstraat (London residence),
Kattendijkdok - Oostkaai
(Venice/Stockholm/Quebec residences),
New Yorkkaai (New York residence), Antwerp
Client
CIP Construction & Investment Partners
Design
2015-16

Delivered
March 2021 (London/New York residences)
July 2021 (Venice/Stockholm/Quebec residences)
Surface areas
6,197 m² (London residence)
8,000 m² (Venice/Stockholm/Quebec residences)
8,800 m² (New York residence)
Total building costs
€ 8,348,000 - excl. VAT (London residence)
€ 10,110,000 - excl. VAT (Venice/Stockholm/Quebec residences)
€ 13,100,000 - excl. VAT (New York residence)
Main contractor
STRABAG Belgium, Antwerp
Stability studies
ABT, Antwerp
Technology studies
Stabo - Macobo, Leuven

Landscape design
Landinzicht, Brussels
Acoustics studies
VENAC, Anderlecht
Safety coordination
2B-safe, Glabbeek
Control agency
Seco CVBA, Brussels
Sustainability engineer
(London/New York residences)
DGMR, Arnhem[NL]
BREEAM reporting
(London/New York residences)
Bopro NV, Ghent
Executive architect
(New York residence)
eld architecten, Antwerp

STAPELPLEIN GROUP HOUSING

Offices
360 architecten (Tower)
BULK architecten (Palazzo)
Websites
www.office360.be
www.bulkarchitecten.be
Addresses
Handelsdokkaai 1,
Klipperstraat 2, 4, 6, Ghent (Tower)
Stapelplein, Ghent (Palazzo)
Client
Adelaar projects (Acasa-Urban Link)

Designs
November 2014 (Tower)
June 2015 (Palazzo)
Delivered
April 2021 (Tower)
May 2021 (Palazzo)
Surface areas
8,500 m² (Tower)
5,300 m² (Palazzo)
Volumes
26,500 m³ (Tower)
16,500 m³ (Palazzo)

Total building costs
€ 12,000,000 - excl. VAT (Tower)
€ 7,000,000 - excl. VAT (Palazzo)
Total building costs per m²
€ 1,400 - excl. VAT (Tower)
€ 1,300 - excl. VAT (Palazzo)
Technology studies
EDV, Ghent
Stability engineer
Nico Terryn, Ghent
Landscape design
LAND, Antwerp

COLLECTIVE HOUSING BORGERHOUT | See p. 135 |

NEKKERSPUT SOCIAL HOUSING | See p. 49 |

Life As It Is

Marleen Goethals

Urban development of Ghent's Oude Dokken in the interim period

---

URBAN DEVELOPMENT IN THE INTERIM PERIOD

Over the past few years in Flanders, the results of large-scale urban development in obsolete industrial or infrastructure zones and along waterfronts have started to become visible. Antwerp was a pioneer in this respect. Ghent took its time over the redevelopment of its Oude Dokken (Old Docks). The first four residential projects have only been in use for a year now. The new quarter is far from finished, but in this interim period we can already discern a combination of urban design qualities.

The plan by the architectural firm OMA, winner of the 2004 design competition, was not to every Ghent resident's taste, however. The municipal development agency sogent, which was assigned the lion's share of the land holdings and has been directing the project ever since, retained the goal laid out in OMA's plan (to afford as many dwellings as possible a view of water and vegetation), but gave progressive insight a chance. The narrow strips in OMA's plan became construction zones interspersed with parks both large and small. A broad pedestrian and cycling boulevard was added along the quays. Several construction zones at the Houtdok were scrapped, while the broad slipway at its head became a beach, since the interim usage had shown the importance of water-based recreation and open space. During the long lead time, popular and experimental activities such as DOK vzw, the gravel bins, and Smoke & Dust (019) sharpened the expectations of Ghent residents.[1]

Diversity and inclusion were among these expectations. To mitigate the growing social and spatial segregation caused by urban development and to address the urgent shortage of affordable homes for low-income groups, sogent's project management aimed for construction zones with a broad mix of housing typologies, target groups and facilities. On sites owned by the city and sogent, there is therefore a rule that, spread across the various residential blocks, 20 per cent social housing and 20 per cent budget homes will be constructed.[2] If sogent has a limited land holding, it is also permitted to deviate from this division: for example, the Stapelplein on Handelsdokkaai (Palazzo and Tower) includes 40 per cent budget homes for sale.[3] Alongside classic apartments, there are ground-level homes, cohousing options and a forthcoming project with a Community Land Trust development model. However, a glance at the selling prices for the residential offering teaches us that developers are using the sale of luxury dwellings (which enjoy the best views) to compensate for the profits they forego on the budget homes.

---

1   For DOK vzw, the gravel bins and 019, see Els Vervloesem, 'Architecture for Use and Appropriation: From Ephemeral to Permanent Practices', *Flanders Architectural Review N°12. Tailored Architecture* (Antwerp: Flanders Architecture Institute, 2016), 27–32; see also Christoph Grafe, 'Multilingualism: Design Methods and Aesthetics in a North Western European Architecture', *Flanders Architectural Review N°11. Embedded Architectures* (Antwerp: Flanders Architecture Institute, 2014), 280. No one wanted to take on the imposing concrete plant and this industrial relic has now been demolished.

2   Whether or not these budget homes end up permanently in the hands of the target group is another story; this is still being investigated. In the meantime, on its land sogent has switched from budget homes for sale to budget homes for rent. This is the case on the construction areas on Schipperskaai. Here sogent's direction led to pioneering applications of circular concepts. The sustainability cooperative DuCoop – of which all residents or business owners are shareholders – collects waste water for purification and supplies heat with biogas from sanitary waste water (vacuum toilets), heat from waste water from showers, and residual heat from the Christeyns soap factory. The deployment of locally produced renewable energy for local heat and energy usage will make this area a smart energy quarter.

3   These buildings are connected to the city heating network.

De Nieuwe Dokken and the Melopee municipal building (left), Ghent – Xaveer De Geyter Architects

The quarter is not just residential. Offices can be found around the Dampoort railway station. And with the centrally located Melopee municipal building, the neighbourhood also has a broad-based school that includes a crèche and sports hall, attracting children, young people and adults from both the local area and the wider city. In the bases of the housing, cafés, small shops and practice spaces for healthcare providers are encouraged; the first construction area on Schipperskaai has a few of these.

↦ See p. 157

Although still under development, a Ruimtelijk Uitvoeringsplan (RUP) is intended to organize the transition from the declining industrial area to the east of the Oude Dokken (between Koopvaardijlaan and the train tracks) to a mixed residential and commercial area.[4] This site borders the construction zones on the Schipperskaai and has a view of the docks through the strips of parkland. Manufacturing companies, offices and hybrids will be stacked in multi-storey buildings and combined with ground-level homes. At the same time, the level of public amenities will also be increased with outdoor sport facilities, a youth centre, a district library, childcare and healthcare facilities, and a social restaurant doubling as a company canteen: the combination of living and working seems to be taken seriously here.

4   RUP 175 Afrikalaan.

But we have not yet reached this point. What we can learn from this interim period is that the success of an urban development project depends not only on the diversity of the programme and on the design of the buildings, but also on the formatting of its public space.

DOCKSIDE ENCOUNTERS

Wednesday 27 April 2022, between 6 p.m. and 7.30 p.m., twelve encounters

A young woman from Waregem is enjoying the sun on a bench at the Kleindokkaai. She works in an office building at the end of the quay beside the turning basin. During her lunch break she often walks to the Kapitein Zeppospark on Houtdok to look out over the water and watch the passers-by.

Two Afghan men are sunbathing on the lowered wooden quay at the start of Schipperskaai. Both have lived in Belgium for six years and they got to know one another at the dock. The older man has a car wash on Koopvaardijlaan with a view of the quay. When business is quiet, he comes here to enjoy the water and sun. His friend lives in Mariakerke. He takes the number three bus and alights at Dampoort.

A man and a woman with Eastern European accents make a complete tour of the docks on an almost daily basis, setting off from Muide. The open water, the light, the construction sites and the people on the quay give them a sense of calm. In fine weather they sometimes swim in the Houtdok.[5]

A young lawyer's firm relocated from Brussels to the Entrepot building at the Handelsdokkaai, where they rent office space. He lives in Brussels and is about to catch his train home at the Dampoort Station. He crosses the Handelsdok via the Bataviabrug: 'It's nicer walking here in the sun.' He is surprised about the Melopee. 'Is that a school? Wow, it's beautiful!'

A young woman with a headscarf crosses the Bataviabrug with her two daughters and a baby in a pushchair. They were shopping at Action in Dok Noord and are now walking back to Sint-Amandsberg. She always comes on foot and thoroughly enjoys ambling along Schipperskaai.

A man waves at me from a balcony in the Dek building on Schipperskaai. Keen to chat about the quarter he comes down. Sitting on the retaining wall between the promenade and the raised pedestrian zone before the building, he describes the home he lives in with his wife and two teenage children. He is happy with it, even though noise from the city ring road and the floating bars on the opposite bank reverberates off the water. Not all of the homes have direct access to the inner courtyard, meaning that the people living around it don't consider it a place to meet. Nevertheless, residents are in close contact. 'Simply because we can look into each other's homes, but also because we all came to live here at the same time and are like-minded.' They used to live in a large town house on the busy Voskenslaan. The bike route before their door encourages them to cycle more and to car-share.

A young couple walks along Schipperskaai. They live in a ground-floor apartment in the Palazzo building across the dock. This walk to the Schipperskaai, which is bathed in sunlight in the evenings, is one they do almost every day. They like living here and are happy with their home, but their inner courtyard is also underused and is not the place for social contact. 'Our neighbours mainly

[5] Swimming is forbidden, however, and is strongly advised against due to the poor water quality.

Kapitein Zeppospark, Ghent – City of Ghent

stay on their terrace. We often go and sit in the inner courtyard because we don't get much sun on ours.'

A young woman jogs along Schipperskaai. 'My boyfriend has digs in Sint-Amandsberg. I come here to run when I'm staying with him. It's flat and there's plenty of air.'

A group of young women clad in cycling gear stand before the terrace of the CUP café. It's the starting point for their twice-weekly bike rides. The rides normally end with a drink in the café. 'Give us some free advertising!'

A woman from Tolhuislaan enjoys the evening sun on Schipperskaai and the warmth in the air on fine days. She discovered the walk during the Covid lockdown. She usually heads straight to the Bataviabrug via Doornzelestraat. For a longer stroll, she takes the Gardeniersbrug to the Wondelgemse Meersen business zone and then via the railway bridge to Muide and Houtdoklaan. She likes the unfinished nature of her surroundings and the raw, surprising mix of expensive homes and old, less majestic apartments (Scandinaviëblokken), historic industries, such as the renowned glass firm Meyvaert, and small businesses run by newcomers in the vacated industrial buildings. She believes that the quayside promenade links different socio-economic groups together. 'Everyone comes here, even though the expensive buildings on the other side [she points to the former ACEC building] create a frontage towards the water that blocks access for those who live behind it and generally don't have a garden. You must first cross a car park.' She disapproves of the plans for a marina in the Houtdok. 'The big differences between the visitors might give rise to tensions.'

Two young Ukrainian mothers push babies in buggies across the Koopvaardijlaan in the direction of the Kapitein Zeppospark. They do not understand me. Below the seats, the buggies are loaded with shopping.

'One thing I love about this place is being able to walk at the same level as the water.' The young woman from Muide does this circular stroll around the Houtdok almost every evening. 'The birds are so funny when they rush to dive into the water or clamber out again once I've gone past.'

Thursday 28 April 2022, between 6 p.m. and 7.30 p.m., four encounters

A young woman parks her bicycle on Handelsdokkaai. She has come from her work in the city centre. Together with her boyfriend, she purchased an apartment on the fourth floor of the tower. They chose this spot because it gives them air and openness, a pleasant counterweight to the narrow, enclosed streets in the city centre. Their living room, kitchen and terrace have a lovely view of the water and the opposite side. She walks or jogs around the docks every day, sometimes a short tour via the Bataviabrug, sometimes a longer route. 'It's good that the cranes, the rawness and the spontaneous nature still evoke the port atmosphere.' There is more cycling and walking now that there is a better crossing point over the city ring road and the quayside promenade was finished with a broad, smooth strip of concrete.

An older man of Turkish heritage has been living in the Muide for forty years, on Meulestedesteenweg on the other side of the railway. He comes to the park daily, with his granddaughter who wants to visit the playground, or in the evening with friends. 'It's really nice now. The park is important for Muide residents. The dock was here before too, but you couldn't walk around it, everything was broken and dangerous.' The park has caused the price of homes in Muide to double. But he loves the new young white people in the quarter. They are not racists like their predecessors, he asserts. He enjoys talking to them and sharing in activities. The atmosphere has really improved as a result! However, he is worried about the drug dealing and drug use that he has observed in the park in recent weeks, mostly at night but also during the day. Residents are also concerned. There are often arguments and shouting. 'It's not a good idea to come and walk here alone in the evening', he tells me.

Five young men are playing spikeball on the beach of the Kapitein Zeppospark. Some live and work on the Muide and in the Wondelgemse Meersen. This is their first visit. It was a choice between this or the Blaarmeersen. They like it here. The small dog with them is also enjoying itself on the beach.

Kapitein Zeppospark, Ghent – City of Ghent

> Three young men drink a beer on a bench between the beach and water. They discovered this place during the Covid lockdown and have been meeting here regularly ever since. They come from Ledeberg or the Rabot – 'so, from the local area', as they perceive it – and travel by bike. Their bicycles are parked on the beach. The openness of the water and the far-reaching views bring them peace.

GHENT DISCOVERS ITS NEW QUAYSIDE PROMENADE

While construction is still under way on the city development project, Ghent residents have discovered and come to appreciate the Oude Dokken quarter, with its 4 km pedestrian and cycle promenade around the quays. It was a conscious choice indeed by sogent and the city of Ghent to start the project, in 2016, by creating the public space, i.e. before work commenced on the first building site of the new residential area. They began with the Schipperskaai and Bataviabrug (2012), which made the activities of DOK vzw more accessible from the city centre for walkers and cyclists. Today, the promenade is largely finished. It is only in zones where construction sites are yet to commence that there are still earth paths or old road infrastructure. The noisy ring road, which creates a barrier between the Oude Dokken and city centre, still needs to be relocated to Afrikalaan, to the east of the project area. The construction of the Verapazbrug (to the north) and the reorganization of the Dampoort crossroads (to the south of the new quarter) have begun. They will connect the existing and the relocated city ring road. Of the planned park zones, the largest, the Kapitein Zeppospark at Houtdok, has already been in use since 2020. The spontaneous green shrubbery that has sprung up in the remaining planned park zones helps to set the tone. These are occasionally used by urban farmers, or for a game of Kubb.

Oude Dokken as a link between previously separated quarters

The geographical location of Ghent's Oude Dokken makes it clear why it was useful to prioritize the implementation of the public space. While Antwerp's Het Eilandje marks the end of the city before the active port begins, the Oude Dokken are surrounded by residential areas: Muide, Sint-Amandsberg, Ham, Heilig Kerst, Dok Noord, the business zone on Afrikalaan and, here too, the port. The quayside promenade transforms an obstacle into a link: the Oude Dokken quarter lies within easy reach of diverse socio-demographic communities. Attractions along the route such as the Gent-Dampoort train and bus station, the retail warehouses along Vliegtuiglaan, the Dok Noord shopping centre, the Wondelgemse Meersen business park and several other business locations both old and new ensure that the quayside promenade is well used. As a result, this urban development feels truly public even while under construction. People are on their way to work, to the station, to the shops or to school. The early construction of the broad-based Melopee school proved to be a smart move.

The connective power of the Dokken also has a flip side, literally. This becomes visible in the completed construction area on the Schipperskaai, where the square that lies behind it, in among the residential tower blocks and Melopee, temporarily looks out onto the blind warehouses in the neighbouring industrial zone. The new build on Handelsdokkaai is also obliged to embrace the city ring road at its rear. In both cases, a renewal of the threshold to the adjacent quarters is urgently needed.

A leisure destination

The Oude Dokken are also a leisure destination in themselves. The docks and quays offer Ghent residents an extensive open space in which to get a breath of fresh air and enjoy vistas over the water. The fact that the rawness of the port is still so tangible, combined with the minimal and unpretentious reconstruction of the public space, is what makes this location so attractive.[6] The old quay walls were renovated and relics such as tracks, cable ducts, mooring posts, pieces of old cobbles and concrete surfacing, as well as zones with spontaneously sprouting pioneer vegetation, were all integrated into the city floor. Along the way, the quayside promenade has become an open-air museum of historical port cranes. Straddling the promenade, they mark the parking zones.

The promenade invites you not only to move, but also to stay. The lowered wooden quays by the houseboats, the benches and walls you can sit on, all encourage one to linger at the Schipperskaai. In the future, a further two neighbourhood parks will be added, as will the public green living space between the construction areas.

6 The municipal services were themselves responsible for the design and coordination of the public space, which they based on a handbook published by the design agency Stramien. Public official Marc Pinte, co-designer of the Kapitein Zeppospark, stood firm on the retention of port relics and became the point of contact for anyone looking to get rid of a port crane, both in Belgium and abroad. As project leader at sogent, Agnieszka Zajac has been directing the Oude Dokken urban development project since the start of the process.

De Nieuwe Dokken and Oude Dokken collective housing, Ghent – BLAF Architecten

De Nieuwe Dokken and the Melopee municipal building, Ghent – Xaveer De Geyter Architects

At the imposing Houtdok, the promenade widens out into a more layered landscape. Steps that follow the incline of the old natural stone quay wall give access to a concrete path just above the water level. Between the path and the sloping quay wall are two additional walls with arch-shaped excisions. Once floating deliveries of wood had ceased, an extension of the quay floor was laid on these to connect the quay more effectively to the mooring boats. This floor has been removed and the red walls with their leached grouting have been left exposed. Some curves have been reinforced with iron supports. Bluestone caps or clicker-brick planting beds protect against water infiltration. Biologically valuable climbing plants are given free rein. Between the two walls, water seepage causes a swamp-like landscape to form. The experience of this ribbon-shaped biotope varies dramatically from a silent place for birdwatchers to colourful, noisy 'sunbathing areas' (including a beach and boat ramp) around the popular but forbidden (due to pollution) swimming spot for Ghent's young people. Above the quay wall, the scrapped construction zones, in-between spontaneously sprouting vegetation and freshly planted trees, allow space for grassy fields for sports and recreation.

Super-diversity in the public space

For urban anthropologist Lyn Lofland, the public space facilitates fleeting encounters between strangers.[7] These meetings are essential building blocks for intercultural tolerance. In the public space, all the minorities in our super-diverse society should

7 Lyn Lofland, *The Public Realm: Exploring the City's Quintessential Social Territory* (New Brunswick: Aldine Transaction, 1998).

be able to find their place. In serving as an interface between the different quarters of Ghent with their varied communities, and in exerting a recreational pull on the whole city, the Oude Dokken supports this mood of public mingling. This is apparent in the colourful passers-by and those lingering on the promenade.

On the Schipperskaai, a slightly raised and broad threshold zone separates the construction areas (and the disturbance they cause) from the quay. The low wall marks the boundary of the construction site for the early execution of the promenade; the higher section was only implemented once the buildings had been completed. On this higher section, the CUP café sets out its terrace and parents wait for their school-age children without blocking the way of passers-by. The quayside promenade is thus separated from life in and around the buildings, which prevents passers-by from feeling unwelcome. At the same time, it makes room for a quieter, more local and, in Lofland's words, 'parochial' atmosphere, one that can be instrumental in stimulating relations between neighbours and acquaintances. The boundary between both spheres acts as a magnet for couples and friends, who use the retaining wall as a bench.

On Houtdoklaan, the homes of the Muide look out over the Kapitein Zeppospark. The side streets of the Muidepoort, the quarter's main artery, connect to paths that divide up the park. Diverse groups from the Muide and other quarters make themselves at home here. A diverse mix of families are tangled around a playground beneath a gigantic port crane upon which climbing is also possible. The football and basketball cage is teeming with young people. Concrete seating blocks draw the port ambiance into the park. The lower-lying beach, the water path and the plateau of the former ship winch are more adventurous meeting places for young people from different backgrounds. Spots much loved by all groups are the classic benches with views of the dock and of the passers-by.

And what about the art? This is in line with the rebellious, officially condoned atmosphere of the early days. The graffiti panoramas in the gravel bins are popular on social media. The changing flags on Schipperskaai and the unrestrained artist posters on 019's headquarters compete with the inevitable advertisements. This fierce group of artists is proud to display its subversive and frequently funny codes in the public space, thus arousing the curiosity of a different, wider audience.

During the interim period

The Oude Dokken and the business zone between Koopvaardijlaan and Afrikalaan are undergoing a total transformation. Housing projects are gradually being completed and scaffolding is going up on new projects. Many entrepreneurs have already left their business premises, which are now in the hands of developers. In the expectation that the new urban development will expand across their land, they are renting out their buildings to non-profit associations that organize temporary summer bars, concerts and open-air film screenings there. On weekend evenings, these breathe life into the public space. But the industrial buildings that have been freed up are also highly valued business locations for new, capital-poor and low-threshold enterprises. On Koopvaardijlaan behind the Melopee, for example, there is a business that trades and stores second-hand cars. What is desirable and what is troublesome, and which inclusive entrepreneurship has a future, is a necessary but far from simple challenge for urban policymaking.

What does the future hold?

The interim period in the Oude Dokken project is inspiring. The city and its urban development enterprise have used their strong land-holding position to set the tone, in terms of both the programme and quality of the buildings, and of the atmosphere in the public space. But a part of this promise is still to be realized. Today the new residents do not yet reflect the diversity that is already visible in the public space. Most social homes and the alternative forms of living or management are still to be implemented, although they have already been guaranteed in signed agreements.

Nevertheless, the early characteristics that have proved so popular with Ghent residents in the interim period have not yet been permanently secured. Of crucial importance will be the developments in the remaining zones, which the city does not own and in which its negotiating hand is weaker. In these areas, much will depend on whether strong architecture continues to be the hallmark of the Oude Dokken and whether the combination of local amenities, residential units and manufacturing businesses retains the upper hand. The RUP for Afrikalaan mandates strong objectives. The list of permitted manufacturing businesses creates hope that low-skilled work will also be part of the offering. But whether the required facilities will be afforded attractive positions on the quayside promenade – as they have been in the Melopee – remains to be seen. Will the unruly charm remain if new builds dominate? Will the future marina users and exclusive homeowners be as tolerant as the current residents? Another concern is the city ring road. Its relocation will remove a barrier from Dok Noord but will only increase the barrier on Afrikalaan. Would it not have been better to leave the city ring road where it is and further downgrade it? And is a marina really necessary in a place where visitors to the beach are eager to swim? Inspired project management and the enthusiastic reception by Ghent's diverse population made the Oude Dokken a success in the interim period. It is to be hoped that in the next phase, the city authorities will continue to prove themselves worthy of that support.

MELOPEE MUNICIPAL BUILDING | See p. 157 |

KAPITEIN ZEPPOSPARK

Design
City of Ghent
Website
www.stad.gent/en
Quay renovation
Flemish Waterways – sogent
Address
Houtdoklaan 36, Ghent

Client
City of Ghent
Design
July 2016
Delivered
June 2020
Surface area
31,500 m²
Total building cost
€ 5,500,000 – excl. VAT

Total building cost per m²
€ 175 – excl. VAT
Main contractor
Ghent Dredging, Eke (park)
Hye, Kruibeeksesteenweg, Zwijndrecht (quay renovation)
Studies
Studiebureau Lobelle, Jabbeke (park)
SBE, Sint-Niklaas (quay renovation)

In Pursuit of Imagery

Mark Pimlott

1   Sofie De Caigny, Dirk Somers and Maarten Van Den Driessche, eds., *Composite Presence* (Antwerp: Flanders Architecture Institute, 2021).

The exhibition *Composite Presence*, curated by Dirk Somers for the Belgian Pavilion at the Venice Biennale in 2021, brought a collection of painted timber models of buildings together in a quasi-urban yet highly heterogeneous ensemble, in a manner that could be ascribed to Flanders.[1] This could be sensed through the eclectic and individualized nature of buildings' appearances and forms that reflected not only their diverse purposes in reality but also the idiosyncratic nature of recent architectural production in the region, where the invocation of historical prototypes, and appearances suggesting the knowing 'distance' of representation, can be understood as a kind of trademark, signs of the specific condition of 'urbanity' across much of Flanders. The installation drew representative figures of recent architectural practice together. One could not help noting that the appearances of the work, perhaps exaggerated by the character of the models themselves, tended towards a certain pictorial quality that was not limited to the models but, on reflection, was embodied by the originals from which they were derived. The picture-like character of those originals, and the diverse modes of appearance that inform,

Bovenbouw Architectuur, *Composite Presence*, Belgian Pavilion, Architecture Biennale 2021, Venice

surround and announce them, is the subject of this essay. Buildings that 'look like' architecture from Flanders are both intriguing as a historical phenomenon, associated with the production of a native style and yet, in their mimetic proliferation, problematic, suggesting either contentment with repetition or, perhaps, an aversion to reality. The 'problem' echoes a criticism levelled at postmodern architecture of the 1980s. Conversely, this use of the pictorial may indicate a desire to invoke deeper aspects of the Real through an understanding of Representation, which, in our current climate of minimal investment for maximum return, may be a consummation devoutly to be wished, yet impossible to fulfil.

Composite Presence established the feeling that one was looking at a representation of a hypothetical urban settling even more plausible than one might expect to find in a typical excursion to Flanders, one that shared qualities with the previous Flemish representation at the Biennale, *Bravoure Scarcity Beauty*, curated by architecten de vylder vinck taillieu (advvt).[2] In that installation, one was asked to consider a series of scenes that were at once acts, re-enactments and representations. The re-enactments were constructed fragments, both fully present and dislocated representations of the original acts from which they derived. They produced an uncanny effect. Large photographs of these *elsewheres* attested to the gap, or lack, between the 'original' and its re-staged 'double'. Furthermore, there were other large-scale photographs, purporting to be evidence of profoundly re-configured realities, realistic representations of impossible or implausible conditions. The exhibition deployed a strategy of making representation present, inviting viewers to occupy its fictions, as a means towards seeing and experiencing architecture,

2   Christoph Grafe and Jan De Vylder, eds., *Bravoure Scarcity Beauty* (Antwerp: Flanders Architecture Institute, 2016).

architecten de vylder vinck taillieu, doorzon interieurarchitecten and Filip Dujardin, *Bravoure Scarcity Beauty*, Belgian Pavilion, Architecture Biennale 2016, Venice

3   'Architecture and Representation', a discussion with Filip Dujardin, Bas Princen, Jan Kempenaers and Mark Pimlott, Belgian Pavilion, Giardini, Venice, 26 August 2016.

4   Mark Pimlott, 'Ornament and Picture-making', *OASE* 65 (2004): 6–25.

5   Irina Davidovici, 'Communities of Practice: Reflections on a Latter-day *Tendens* in Flemish Architecture', in De Caigny, Somers and Van Den Driessche, *Composite Presence*, 26–39.

its ideas and tangible realities: an architecture, in this case, that was made of modest materials in inventive and unconventional configurations. In a parallel discussion concerning photography and the representation of architecture[3], the problem of representations of architecture was raised as an issue, and (by this author) architecture that, correspondingly, appeared in the world as a representation or a picture of itself, thereby becoming strange. It is important to note that the representational lens used by both advvt and Bovenbouw Architectuur formed a context to all architectural practices in these exhibitions, situating those practices that did not subscribe to it, as well as those that did, within its 'atmosphere'.

In present conditions, one continues to think about the presentation of architecture, the simulations of architecture and its mediated appearances, and whether picture-making affects architectural production itself, not only in terms of what it looks like, but in terms of what it is and how it is encountered.[4] Furthermore, given the prevalence of what seems to be a shared language of representation of architecture in the practice of architecture in Flanders beyond the confines of this exhibition – from drawings, models, renders and various hybrid forms of illustration, and finally, photographs of completed buildings – one might ask whether these representations create a culture of their own, one that can be recognized, in this case, as specifically 'of Flanders': a consistent trope within what might be described as a local *avant-garde*, emulated or imitated by those riding in its slipstream. For the former group, it would seem to be, as so carefully described by Irina Davidovici, a *tendens*, through which an architectural culture expresses and extends itself, consciously and unconsciously[5]; for the latter group, less a *tendenza* and more a *maniera*.

The distinctiveness of this *tendens* requires some examination, beyond its shared ideas concerning the difficult urban form of Flanders, its extreme heterogeneity, the complexities of its governance, and the necessity of strategies of autonomy in response to these conditions. The *tendens* is recognizable through its various forms of appearance, which, as one consequence of their significance, find themselves repeated within architectural culture. Its effect can be seen in those representations described above, in its ways of communicating its ideas to itself within its working processes, in presentations, in communications to its clients, and then, through the outlets of publicity, outward: to students of architecture, to other architects and to consumers of architecture (of which visitors to the Biennale or the Flanders Architecture Institute are representative). What, finally, might be called 'Belgian architecture' is recognizable through its actual appearances in the world, as architecture that is experienced, seen, read and interpreted as, and that resembles –and this is a central concern – its own mediated representations. It is not always possible to say that this is good.

One can remark on a high degree of similarity to the representations that are produced by architectural practices within this culture. These are models, drawings, montages, renderings and renders that take the form of *pictures* that display a degree of spatial and tonal flatness; that convey the atmosphere of the almost-photographic, the hand-made or the cartoon; that favour illustration over rendering (perhaps a consequence of the difficulties and expense of computer-generated imagery); 'naive' line drawing and the almost archaic oblique or cavalier projection, worm's-eye axonometric and one-point perspective; constructed, 'deep' drawings; and the prevalence of *décor*, of garden and household plants, utilitarian furniture and kitchen utensils, bunting; and people either borrowed from paintings or dressed in clothes from COS or TOAST. Such pictures are used to develop, share or promote the architectural project, and even to reflect on it upon completion.[6] This characteristic is even to be found in agency-produced renders, which offer 'soft' quasi-photographic rather than hyper-realistic imagery, as though a fog has settled on its subject on a grey, early spring day. These last types of pictures constitute a *lingua franca* for an international community of architects, to be found emulated in Switzerland, Scandinavia, Britain, Ireland and even Portugal (all of them prone to drab, wet weather).

Then, there is the photography of realized buildings, which, given the sumptuously chaotic contexts of Belgian cities and their territories, assumes the tropes of topographic photography, influenced by Bernd and Hilla Becher and the Düsseldorf School that resonates through fashion and design media. This 'style', which signifies its precursors in topographic and art photography, lends another order of legitimacy to that specific quality of contemporary Belgian architecture, its necessary yet modest autonomy in the midst of heterogeneous circumstance. Finally, there is that photography that is edited (all photography is) in order to achieve *the condition of a picture*, frequently exuding an aura of artifice, strangeness or icy distance, in which its representational character is enhanced and its features adjusted to approach, what would seem to be a tautology: a picture, or, perhaps more precisely, a Double of a photographic image.[7]

One's concern is not with these stylized conventions of representations of projects or the uncanny 'views' exchanged within this community of architects, but with their effect on the experience and presence of architecture made in Flanders, upon which *picture-making*, as a convention, threatens to impose an orthodoxy, or more problematically, an uncanny 'reality'. The picture-making within Belgian architectural culture that has emerged from the *tendens* has become a currency that *simulates* both real life and the Real. The constructions that arise in emulation of the *tendens* suggest an awareness of substituting the Real for a pictorialized version of the Real. What follows is a knowing kind of picture-world, aware of its artifice and its privileged position (say, in the depiction of a plywood panel, brick wall or household plant). The pictures made are fresh, beguiling, benign. They suggest, through a limited array of signifiers, a Real that the viewer believes they know, in the same way wood-grained Formica laminate surfaces did (or still do) suggest real wood through its 'photographic' representation.

Throughout his career, the artist Richard Artschwager made such sculptures as *Description of Table* (1964) that worked with Formica to both allude to the Real and stand at a distance from it.[8] The viewer of the object was left with an encounter with a surrogate, a substitute for the Real, a representation made present. This was not an experience of quite the same order as Yakov Petrovich Golyadkin encountering his *doppelgänger*[9]; it was not quite uncanny, but there was something missing – a *lack* – in the way it presented itself. The work demonstrated a strategy that one must confess an attraction to: in making my own sculpture in the 1990s, I tried to bring objects forth that were 'pictures of themselves', bearing affinities and incomplete resemblances to other objects that were commonly known. Their artifice dragged the 'originals' from which they derived – ordinary and real – into the mind of the viewer, despite their absence. The unease was integral to their presence with

6 Dirk Somers, in Bovenbouw Architectuur, eds., *Living the Exotic Everyday* (Antwerp: Flanders Architecture Institute, 2019), 163.

7 The work of Filip Dujardin and Bas Princen is representative of this edited picture-making's 'altered reality'. For further discussion, see: Jesús Vassalo, *Seamless: Digital Collage and Dirty Realism in Contemporary Architecture* (Zurich: Park Books, 2016); see also: Mark Pimlott and Bas Princen, 'Utopian Debris: A Conversation between Bas Princen and Mark Pimlott', *OASE* 76 (2008): 3–18.

8 Richard Armstrong, 'Art without Boundaries', in Richard Armstrong, *Artschwager, Richard* (New York: Whitney Museum of American Art, 1988), 12–46; see also Mark Pimlott, 'Richard Artschwager', *Frieze* 14 (15 January 1994): 51–52.

9 Fyodor Dostoyevsky, *The Double* (1846).

Artschwager, Richard (1923–2013): *Description of Table*. 1964. Melamine laminate on plywood. Overall: 66.4 × 81 × 81 cm. Gift of the Howard and Jean Lipman Foundation, Inc.. Inv. N.: 66.48. New York, Whitney Museum of American Art.

the viewer. But it was art, not architecture. The centrality of artifice seems to be ingrained in high-minded architecture being made in Flanders now and in that which would like to be considered in its company.

As the 'picture of itself' increasingly comes to characterize the mediated appearances through which one increasingly recognizes Belgian architecture, particularly from Flanders, one is tempted to bring corresponding expectations to that architecture's realized forms. One might seek a continuity between those appearances made in anticipation of its realization, and their fulfilment in building: something tantalizingly artificial or pictorial or even picturesque. Or one might seek something more solid, specific to the demands of presence and the Real. A few instances of current architecture produced in the region indicate that some effort has been made to achieve a condition in which a close resemblance to its representations has been sought. That architecture either tends to disappoint or to create a sense of unease, as the gap between the representation and presence, or the absence of substance is too great: it is too much like the picture of itself and so it creates unease. The architecture within the *tendens* that transcends the representations that preceded it and addresses the specificity of realization, materiality, spatiality, movement and relations does *more*; yet it, too, tends to create something close to strangeness. In the former case, one confronts the *lack*, an absence of qualities, or a withdrawal from qualities that are to be found in the Real, leaving one in the presence of something artificial. In the latter instance, the very resolution of the project brings one in confrontation with something beyond or within the artificial. One is not in the presence of a stage prop, but another proposition entirely: an ideation made Real.

One can appreciate the fruitlessness of the first path. The props of the stage set are charming yet ephemeral. If the artefact is very good, it may endure – and carry its artifice through the ages – as an ornamental carapace. The problem with the first is that – given the widespread reiterations of certain representational tropes, whether in modelling, drawing, montage, illustration or 'soft' quasi-photographic renders – an orthodoxy may be reinforced and instituted among both students and practitioners that *signifies* architecture (it *looks* like architecture) but fails to transcend a pictorial programme, forever binding it to the image, and deferring the possibility of architecture engaged with the Real and with real life. The latter path – which seeks a kind of tension between Representation and the Real and so uses Representation to bring the Real forth – is more intriguing and more promising. However, it raises once more those questions struggled with in the late 1970s and early 1980s, when the problems of Postmodernism haunted architects and students. Then, the attraction to the effects of pre- or not- or off-Modern architecture seemed vital, yet no amount of semiotic play could bring its charms back to life. Postmodern architecture tended to avoid the issue of presence, and the realities of the pasts it purportedly honoured.

Now, in architecture that derives from the pictorial (not to discount an engagement with the typological), a similar unease arises about its capacities to provide *real* experience through its artifice, by which it might genuinely consolidate the quality of everyday life.[10] Its depictions can be merely artificial, superficially engaging, clever, flat or disappointing, amusements or disillusionments. Conversely, it can bring forth the Real, through something akin to those direct encounters with Representation, wherein one almost touches the Real through a materialized 'image' that, intensely animate, seems to contain the Real within it. Yet within such encounters, there are still two possible outcomes: in one, as with the meeting between Leontes and the statue of Hermione in Shakespeare's *The Winter's Tale* (the statue moves and comes alive, 'restoring' the presumed dead Hermione – it *is* Hermione): a redemption is realized, and Life becomes doubly vital. In the other, as with Golyadkin in Dostoyevsky's *The Double*, the uncanny persists: the Real is vanquished, dissolved in the face of his own Representation (his identical other); all meaning is lost.

Beyond the achievement of innovations and revived forms of picturing in architecture from Flanders that has created an internationally recognized language of representation, it is important to hold on to the purpose of its picture-making as a means, its aim and its precise obligation to the experience of the Real, so that it might endure and so be meaningful.

LITERATURE

Richard Armstrong, *Artschwager, Richard* (New York: Whitney Museum of American Art, 1988).

Roland Barthes, 'Rhetoric of the Image' (1964), trans. Stephen Heath, in *Image-Music-Text* (London: Fontana Press, 1977), 32–51.

Bovenbouw Architectuur, eds., *Living the Exotic Everyday* (Antwerp: Flanders Architecture Institute, 2019).

Sofie De Caigny, Dirk Somers and Maarten Van Den Driessche, eds., *Composite Presence* (Antwerp: Flanders Architecture Institute, 2021).

Fyodor Dostoyevsky, *The Double* (1846).

Jantje Engels and Marius Grootveld, eds., *Building Upon Building* (Rotterdam: NAi Publishers, 2016).

Christoph Grafe and Jan De Vylder, eds., *Bravoure Scarcity Beauty* (Antwerp: Flanders Architecture Institute, 2016).

Mark Pimlott and Bas Princen, 'Utopian Debris: A Conversation between Bas Princen and Mark Pimlott', *OASE* 76 (2008): 3–18.

Michael Podro, *Depiction* (New Haven: Yale University Press, 1998).

William Shakespeare, 'The Winter's Tale' (1623), in Stephen Greenblatt et al., eds. *The Norton Shakespeare* (New York: Norton, 1997): 2873–954.

Jesús Vassalo, *Seamless: Digital Collage and Dirty Realism in Contemporary Architecture* (Zurich: Park Books, 2016).

Robert Venturi, *Complexity and Contradiction in Architecture* (New York: Museum of Modern Art, 1966).

Caroline Voet, Katrien Vandermarliere, Sofie De Caigny and Lara Schrijver, eds., *Autonomous Architecture in Flanders* (Leuven: Leuven University Press, 2016).

10 Michael Podro, *Depiction* (New Haven: Yale University Press, 1998).

It's the Way That You Do It

The sustainability of engagement

Maarten Desmet

If we look at the latest architectural developments in Flanders and Brussels, we will see several experiments that flirt with the boundaries of the profession while also aiming to make a positive contribution to society. This is nothing new, of course. In 2015 the Canadian Centre for Architecture published *The Other Architect*, a collection of analyses and portraits of architects who, in their capacity as designers, had adopted socially engaged roles.[1] Peter Eisenman has also examined these 'other roles'. He distinguishes between architectural *project* (in which the architect determines the appearance of the world) and *practice* (in which the world determines the architect's work).[2] In his view, the distinction between project and practice is influenced by how the architect views their relation to the world and the 'why?' that drives them. For Eisenman, every project is a critique of the status quo of the architectural discipline, but merely wanting to 'save the world' does not actually count as a project. To him, a project always includes the discipline of architecture, which both defines and resonates with, in a critical way, the world as we know it.

Today, a growing group of designers in Flanders and Brussels are working on *projects*, often driven by increasing social inequality or the inescapable ecological transitions we face. These designers are probing the boundaries of the discipline or using its synthetic and visionary capacity to actively engage with contemporary social and ecological challenges. This development undeniably challenges the definition and legal meaning of 'architect' as a profession. Equally, it raises questions about the sustainability of the actual engagement. This essay examines how that engagement is organized so that it can also be sustainable.

I talked to architects committed to what could be called 'projects'. More specifically, I questioned eleven practitioners about their recent socially innovative ventures and the organizational structures that have helped them to fulfil their mission. In other words, I sought to discover whether or not their engagement is sustainable.[3] These firms were selected on the basis of submissions to the *Flanders Architectural Review* and a quick scan of recent projects. It is not an exhaustive list. The root questions were: To what extent are these socially innovative projects also community or impact-driven enterprises? And can any specific models be identified?

---

1 Giovanna Borasi, ed., *The Other Architect: Another Way of Building Architecture* (Montreal: Canadian Centre for Architecture, 2015).

2 Peter Eisenman, 'Peter Eisenman: Project or Practice?' (2011), *School of Architecture Lectures Series* 5, https://surface.syr.edu/architecture_lectures/5.

3 Paul Steinbrück (Pool Is Cool), Marie Vanderghote (Broei), Lucas Devolder (ConstructLab), Annekatrien Verdickt (Filter Café Filtré Atelier), Michiel Van Balen (Miss Miyagi), Dieter Leyssen (51N4E), Florence Meessen (RotorDC), Laurens Bekemans (BC Architects and Studies), Eva De Clerck (Buurman Antwerp), Hanne Mangelschots (Architecture Workroom Brussels) and Mattias Staelens (Onkruid).

FROM SOCIAL INNOVATION TO SOCIAL ENTREPRENEURSHIP

Social or impact-driven entrepreneurship has many definitions. Central to them all, however, is a reference to businesses that develop commercial activities with the aim of tackling a social issue. In other words, they pursue a social or ecological mission.[4] If we use this prism to scrutinize an architectural practice that aims to have a certain (social) impact, then it stands to reason that we must also examine the sustainability of the enterprise itself.

Various organizational and revenue-generating models come to the fore, ranging from a non-profit association that relies on external funding or grants to a cooperative that breaks even or actually makes a profit. In essence, a mission-driven social enterprise measures its success by the social benefit it seeks to deliver. Within a social enterprise, community and financial returns will ideally reinforce each other – this is called the 'hybrid' model.[5] The critical question is how architects can combine these social and financial returns and, in so doing, be good hybrid entrepreneurs.

4   Filipe Santos et al., 'Making Hybrids Work: Aligning Business Models and Organizational Design for Social Enterprises', *California Management Review* 57, no. 3 (2015): 36–58.

5   Santos et al., 'Making Hybrids Work'.

ELEVEN PROJECTS, THREE MODELS

Model 1 – Support
Largely dependent on external support

The external financing model is one of the first we identified among the selected case studies. This category includes various types of external funding and several kinds of organizational model.

StamEuropa is essentially a project rather than a company or organization. It is a temporary public programme in the European Quarter that was developed in partnership with the European Quarter Fund (which also provided the funding under the umbrella of the King Baudouin Foundation) and was designed by the architecture firm 51N4E. The building is owned by the Federal Government. Part of it is open to free, temporary use by the European Quarter Fund. As a result, no vacancy tax is due. The money saved can then be invested in the design of the new infill, among other things. Might this be a model worth scaling up and applying to the many unoccupied office buildings in the capital? If we look at 51N4E as a company, it is a committed architectural firm that integrates social innovation into its operations. Thanks to a balance between the social and commercial profits it generates, the firm can conduct pilot projects such as StamEuropa at a reduced rate.

Filter Café Filtré Atelier (FCFA) was launched in Brussels four years ago as a movement for improving liveability and air quality. It is now structured as a non-profit run by architect Annekatrien Verdickt. Those involved are all committed citizens, including many architects who, like Verdickt, volunteer time in the association alongside their professional practice. FCFA does not want to become a large structure. As soon as its mission is accomplished, the organization loses its *raison d'être*. In the literature on social entrepreneurship, this endgame is called 'mission achievement': you cease to exist when your objectives are fulfilled.[6] The architects who initiated and who steer the FCFA appear to have chosen a model that combines classic architectural practice with social commitment and a non-profit structure.

6   Alice Gugelev and Andrew Stern, 'What's Your Endgame?', *Stanford Social Innovation Review* 13, no. 1 (2015): 40–47.

Pool Is Cool is a non-profit that seeks to reintroduce open-air swimming to Brussels through campaigns, actions and interventions (like the temporary open-air swimming pool, Flow). While the association typically relies on grants for its survival, it also generates income, for instance through the sale of drinks at Flow. From a business perspective, it is interesting to note that Pool Is Cool recently spawned a spin-off operation called POP vzw (Project Operation Partner). POP uses the knowledge gained from Pool Is Cool's activism (like managing open-air pools) to provide a consultancy service to other cities and municipalities. Architect Paul Steinbrück is particularly active on this front. The business model can be described as a hybrid enterprise with its own revenue model – especially if you consider Pool Is Cool and POP as one and the same initiative. In terms of the endgame, Pool Is Cool dreams of government adoption, a scenario in which the authorities scale up the enterprise's impact, its activities and methodologies thus becoming institutionalized. In the case of Pool Is Cool, this would mean that cities – Brussels, in particular – would organize outdoor swimming on a structural basis following the Pool Is Cool model.

Model 2 – Mix
Mix of external support and self-generated income

In this model, external support (in the form of grants, sponsorship, etc.) goes hand in hand with income-generating experiments, although the organization has yet to break even.

Broei is a non-profit that helps young people to both discover and develop their talents. Operating from the Duivelsteen Castle in Ghent, its *raison d'être* is derived from the added social value of its activities. Although currently reliant on project grants, Broei also generates income from bars, rentals and collaborations. Falling somewhere between models 1 and 2, it aims to evolve into a hybrid self-funding social enterprise. Broei would ideally like to arrive at a consistent revenue model that can be supplemented with project grants, the latter of which would further enhance its ability to deliver its mission. The non-profit is thus weighing up different kinds of corporate structure, including a cooperative. As with every hybrid enterprise, the

Filter Café Filtré Atelier

StamEuropa, Brussels – 51N4E Acte with Chevalier Masson, Mathilde Pecqueur and Salomé Corvalan

challenge lies in translating the mission into the business model. Broei's purpose is location-specific (creating a safe place in Ghent where underprivileged young people can develop their skills). As regards the endgame, the model could also be scaled up or down via replication, either in the form of a franchise or by making it open-source. Government adoption could also be considered as this kind of service provision often falls within the structural remit of (local) authorities.

ConstructLab is a European network of architects, builders, designers, chefs, artists and sociologists who build according to identical values and principles. They pool their knowledge and communicate to the outside world as a collective. ConstructLab staff have a loose relationship with the network and organize themselves as they see fit in their respective countries. In Belgium, ConstructLab is a non-profit that accepts paid commissions but only charges for the materials and the project team. It relies on volunteers for its day-to-day operations. ConstructLab staff mainly earn their living via second jobs. This is a model that we also encounter elsewhere in networks of engaged architects, like New Generations.[7]

[7] Gianpiero Venturini, *Atlas of Emerging Practices: Being an Architect in the 21st Century* (Rezzato: New Generations Cultural Association, 2019).

Architecture Workroom Brussels (AWB) encourages citizens, authorities and companies to transform their living environment in function of social transitions via design and culture. It generates income through tenders and also receives operating subsidies (through the Flanders Arts Decree) and project grants. This enables it to accomplish its mission with a relatively large team comprised mainly of architects. AWB positions itself as a platform for innovation that complements the existing market and helps to broaden the field by creating opportunities for new types of projects. In terms of business model, AWB is a non-profit similar to Broei, as it combines grants with self-generated income.

Onkruid began life as a service provider that gradually chose to concentrate on its main project, the Horst Arts & Music Festival. The spatial and commercial side of the event is managed by Onkruid (a limited liability cooperative) while the artistic elements, such as a lab, exhibition and workshop, are handled by Onderstroom (a non-profit). The latter receives the all-essential grants while the cooperative generates income through ticket sales, drink consumption and sponsorship, thereby ensuring a break-even festival. For the grant providers, it is interesting that the applicants also

Broei Duivelsteen, Ghent – ConstructLab

HORST Arts & Music, Holsbeek – Onkruid

make a financial contribution to the project. The two aspects of the organization were initially linked closely in terms of management and operational structure. Nowadays, however, the two divisions are much more distinct and each structure has developed its own operating logic and business model. The partners considered scaling up the festival – by offering it to foreign countries, for example – but having identified that interaction with the location is the essential ingredient within the model, they opted for deep scaling instead. This will increase the impact on the Asiat site by transforming it into a stimulating public place based on a sustainable business model.

Model 3 – Hybrid
Hybrid social enterprise

An impact-driven model and a revenue-generating one are mutually reinforcing in the hybrid model. Because the enterprise is less dependent on external funding, this is considered a sustainable business model for social enterprises. According to Santos, a hybrid social enterprise is as promising as it is vulnerable because it treads a thin line between achieving its social mission and meeting market expectations.[8] There is a danger of mission drift, whereby financial goals take precedence over the company's purpose. The case studies below are all experiments in this type of hybrid model.

8   Santos et al., 'Making Hybrids Work', 36-58.

One way of keeping the mission in sharp focus is to choose a cooperative structure.[9] Social enterprises have historically tended to organize themselves into this type of framework. Firstly, because staff can become co-owners (the workers own the company), but also to facilitate capital investments (and the attendant impact). Thus, through crowdfunding, crowdlending and other forms of investment, money can be raised to finance growth.

9   For more information on cooperatives, see: Cera, 'Coöperaties', https://www.cera.coop/nl/cooperaties.

Miss Miyagi is a private limited company that accepts commissions from public and private clients. It has also recently generated two spin-offs or new structures. Te Herbestemmen (To be repurposed) is a private limited company that acts as a broker and matchmaker, with the aim of connecting people seeking a location with

Hal 5, Leuven – Miss Miyagi

Demolition at Brussels North station – Rotor DC

immovable heritage sites. The Stadsmakersfonds (City Makers Fund) is structured as a limited company that invests in socially responsible real estate. Miss Miyagi's three companies all share the same mission but accomplish it via three different routes and business models. They are hybrid enterprises with a direct relation between social impact and financial profits.

Established in Brussels in 2005, the non-profit Rotor is one of the oldest architect-entrepreneurs on the list. In addition, the limited liability company Rotor DC, launched in 2016, operates as a broker for recovered building materials. Furthermore, Rotor set up the Opalis platform to publicize other like-minded initiatives. In so doing, the non-profit remains the thought leader on this particular issue. Rotor, Rotor DC and Opalis are three different models with an identical mission. As a whole, Rotor is a pure hybrid enterprise that delivers social impact via a sustainable business model. With the spin-off Rotor DC, the original non-profit has streamlined and systematized its impact, thus laying the foundation for upscaling. To finance its growth, Rotor launched a crowdlending campaign in 2022, taking out interest-free loans both large and small from citizens and impact-investors. Although Rotor is not directly pursuing an endgame, the non-profit undeniably has a multiplier effect. This fuels the hope that circular construction will be routine in the future. However, the scaling-up of their impact could be further accelerated by replicating or open-sourcing the marketplace model, or by commercial or governmental adoption.

BC architects & studies operates along similar lines. Like Rotor, it began life as a conventional design practice, researching ecological building materials which they started to use in their own architectural projects and to sell through a spin-off, BC Materials. BC has organized itself into three legal entities: BC architects (a private limited company), BC materials (a cooperative company) and BC studies (a non-profit). Together, these three initiatives are not only profitable but also good examples of the hybrid model. BC materials has also recently overseen an investment round whereby large and small investors could inject capital into the company and become co-operators, with a tax benefit as incentive (via the Tax Shelter).[10]

Buurman Antwerp also launched a crowdfunding campaign in 2021. It is an anomaly in the roll call of social enterprises because its model is based on replication via

10 'Tax Shelter voor startende ondernemingen', Flanders Innovation & Entrepreneurship (Vlaio), 30 May 2022, www.vlaio.be/nl/subsidies-financiering/subsidiedatabank/tax-shelter-voor-startende-ondernemingen.

Bioklas Fort V, Edegem – BC architects & studies

Buurman, Antwerp

franchising. Buurman was initially founded in Rotterdam by two architects who poured their business model into a script that could be utilized in other locations. Buurman has been launched in Rotterdam, Utrecht, Amsterdam and, just last year, Antwerp. The scaling-up strategy – the geographical replication of the model – makes it an interesting addition to the list of case studies. Buurman Antwerp has opted to be a non-profit that derives its income partly from the marketplace for recycled materials, partly from workplace training sessions, and occasionally also through grant-funded projects (for example, via a citizens' budget). The Buurman Antwerp model is thus an income-generating non-profit that also receives subsidies on a case-by-case basis.

CONCLUSION

This modest study into socially enterprising architects sheds light on the business models that help them to fulfil their social missions. The central issue is the selection of a model that allows the social impact to be combined with healthy entrepreneurship. Architects have historically demonstrated a deep-rooted commitment to society and this is no less evident in Flanders. But how sustainable is that commitment in itself? The importance of sustainable business models is not costless. In *De stad als casco* (The city as shell), Eva de Klerk describes Amsterdam as a place where young creative people dedicate the best years of their lives to socially and spatially innovative entrepreneurship, only for their initiatives to typically be hijacked by developers who expand the sites commercially.[11] Strong economic and organizational models are a prerequisite if these social and impact-driven associations are to survive.

11 Eva de Klerk et al., *Make Your City: De stad als casco – NDSM-Werf, Amsterdam* (Amsterdam: trancity x valiz, 2017).

This accords with Eisenman: to realize a true *project*, you need a business model. After all, we note that alternative spatial projects have also become a conventional *practice* (in Eisenman's term). If we see that large commercial agencies (or practices) are also engaged in temporary infill work, then there would seem to be a market for it. But that also implies a danger, because there is a good chance that those commercially oriented agencies will ultimately prefer the developer or pure profit over the sustainable social impact (mission drift). It will then have become a 'fashionable' phenomenon.

This does not mean that entrepreneurship and social commitment are mutually exclusive, on the contrary. One only has to look at social entrepreneurship in other sectors in which income-generation and impact are mutually reinforcing. Socially entrepreneurial architects can learn much from one another, but they must also have the courage to use their creativity to shape their social enterprise, make it sustainable and scale up its impact – without losing sight of the team's well-being, I might add.

This article concerns projects, but one can also question the sustainability of any business model, in any sector, that relies upon underpaid self-employed staff with little job security. Whether you are leading a project or a practice, a healthy business model is vital for both your company and staff. Thinking about what kind of world we want to inhabit is inextricably linked to a consideration of how this goal is achieved, and architects and architecture firms bear a huge responsibility in this respect. My proposal, therefore, is to make social entrepreneurship a compulsory subject in all architecture courses and for everyone involved in the discipline to think deeply about sustainability – not only in terms of what we do, but also in terms of the actions we take. Or as Ella Fitzgerald sang, 'Tain't What You Do (It's the Way That You Do It)'.

STAMEUROPA

Office
51N4E Acte with Chevalier Masson, Mathilde Pecqueur and Salomé Corvalan
Websites
www.51n4e.com
www.chevaliermasson.be
Address
Rue d'Arlon 104, Brussels
Clients
European Quarter / City of Brussels / Belgian Buildings Agency

Design
February 2020
Delivered
May 2021
Surface area
200 m²
Volume
800 m³
Total building cost
€ 100,000 – excl. VAT
Total building cost per m²
€ 5,009 – excl. VAT

Main contractor
Openair, Overijse
Landscape design
Plant & Houtgoed, Overijse
Stability engineer
Bollinger Grohman, Brussels
Sustainability studies
Facilitator Duurzame Gebouwen, Brussels
Design office
Vraiment Vraiment, Anderlecht

FLOW PUBLIC SWIMMING FACILITY

Offices
Decoratelier Jozef Wouters and Pool Is Cool
Websites
www.jozefwouters.be
www.pooliscool.org
Address
Klein Eilandstraat 14, Anderlecht
Client
Pool Is Cool
Design
January 2021

Delivered
May 2021
Surface area
540 m²
Volume
12 m³
Total building cost
€ 113,000 – excl. VAT
Total building cost per m²
€ 210 – excl. VAT
Structural engineer
TA Pollemans, Groesbeek[NL]

Production and construction, surrounding structures
Decoratelier Jozef Wouters, Brussels
Pool Is Cool, Brussels
FIX, Brussels
Production and construction, pool
Ecoworks, Vilvoorde
Be-Steel, Aarschot
HAP waterproof, Braine-le-Comte
Water treatment
Weeloc City, Neuville-en-Ferrain[FR]

BROEI DUIVELSTEEN

Office
ConstructLab
Website
www.constructlab.net
Address
Geraard de Duivelstraat 1, Ghent

Client
Broei
Design
June 2020
Delivered
June 2021
Surface area
1,600 m²

Total building cost
€ 68,000 – excl. VAT
Total building cost per m²
€ 42.5 – excl. VAT
Stability studies
Mouton, Ghent

Critical Factors for Urban Regeneration Projects

Marc Martens

Architecture in Flanders boomed in recent decades: this was a necessary step in the reassessment of our living environment. However, one of today's biggest spatial challenges remains unanswered: the safeguarding of open space in urbanized regions. How do we retain sufficient space in which to produce short supply-chain food, to store and retain water, and to give biodiversity a chance? And what does the necessary complement to this open space – the compact metropolis – look like: a democratic city of engaged citizens, a healthy city with water and green space, an affordable and inclusive city, a caring city? We will not answer these questions by simply continuing to graft onto our historic settlements: full-blown city development projects are required here.

TWENTY YEARS OF URBAN POLICY

Flemish Urban Policy began with the 2003 publication of the White Paper *De eeuw van de stad: Over stadsrepublieken en rastersteden* (The century of the city: On city republics and grid cities).[1] In order to accumulate knowledge, the call for urban development projects was devised, a unique laboratory comparable to the Flemish Government Architect's Open Call. Cities had the opportunity to attract a significant subsidy for a strategic urban regeneration project, provided it met a set of strict criteria: it had to be embedded in the city's spatial policy, deliver regeneration, play a catalysing role in local policy, and generate added value for the surroundings. There also needed to be a public-private partnership (PPP) which the city would be in charge of and which the local population could meaningfully participate in.

How difficult it was to establish these kinds of urban regeneration projects soon became apparent. A kind of support was therefore introduced, the 'concept subsidy'. By now, many urban conundrums have been examined using this formula, including participatory development of mixed urban programmes; creating space for the social economy; placing limits on overzealous property developers; strengthening fragile urban fabrics within large urban developments; dealing with sustainability and climate neutrality in urban developments; reusing exceptional industrial heritage; and strengthening the economy in the contemporary city.

This instantly demonstrates the complexity of contemporary urban development. Not only does it consist of multiple conundrums, but the list of involved parties is long and solutions depend on input from many disciplines. After almost twenty years of Flemish Urban Policy, it is helpful to describe a number of critical factors

1   Filip De Rynck et al., eds., *De eeuw van de stad. Over stadsrepublieken en rastersteden. Witboek* (Brussels: Ministry of the Flemish Community, 2003).

that are crucial to the success of urban regeneration projects. As will become clear, there is still a great deal of work to do.

THE SOCIAL ARCHITECTURE OF THE CITY

One question that crops up in all urban regeneration projects is how we design the city. A highly polemical debate on this subject took place in the twentieth century, during the interwar period. At the Congrès Internationaux d'Architecture Moderne (CIAM), Le Corbusier deployed his considerable rhetorical talent in an attack on the Haussmannian city: he denounced the closed city block, which prevented the optimal orientation of homes and stood in the way of creating sufficient green open spaces. During the fourth CIAM congress, participants set themselves the goal of working out a system of demands under the title 'functional city', a city that would meet the needs of an evolving society. However, the CIAM stood for more than purely functional thinking. In its successive meetings, the movement appealed strongly to the social responsibility of architects and urban designers.[2]

[2] Jan Piet Kloos, *Architectuur, een gewetenszaak* ('s-Gravenhage: Staatsuitgeverij, 1985), 54–71.

The construction industry soon adopted the principles of the functional city, without paying too much attention to the aesthetic, social and cultural values that the CIAM movement had emphasized. This led to dispersed, single-purpose sections of the city that did initially work: the Luchtbal area of Antwerp, for instance, offered port workers comfortable and modern homes where they could live alongside their colleagues. However, once the population demographic diversified and social cohesion fragmented, considerable social friction arose.

Public resistance to modernist formulas only truly erupted when familiar neighbourhoods were razed. In the 1960s, politician Paul Van den Boeynants and his developer friend Charlie De Pauw flattened the working-class Northern Quarter in Brussels to build an ambitious, US-style World Trade Center. The urban street became the exclusive preserve of cars, with pedestrians obliged to make their way along esplanades raised ten metres above the ground. In Brussels, the anti-demolition protests fell on deaf ears. In New York, by contrast, the megalomaniac plans of intransigent city architect Robert Moses were countered by Jane Jacobs, a journalist and writer who inspired a true grassroots movement. Her argument was that the city needs public space where people can meet one another. And the buildings must enter into a relationship with that public domain: 'eyes on the street'.[3]

[3] Jane Jacobs, *The Death and Life of Great American Cities* (New York: Random House, 1961).

In 1985 sociologist Sieg Vlaminck published an article entitled 'Woonecologie, de interferentie tussen gebouwde omgeving en menselijk gedrag' (Residential ecology, the interference between the built environment and human behaviour).[4] One of the illustrations showed an elderly person watching the street from behind a window. It was captioned: 'Older people like to have their own space from which to observe the world around them.' Here the window was not only a composition in the façade, but also the translation of 'eyes on the street'.

[4] Sieg Vlaminck, 'Woonecologie, de interferentie tussen gebouwde omgeving en menselijk gedrag', *Ruimtelijke Planning* 14 (1985): 1–61.

When a team of architects and academics were commissioned by the Spatial Development Department Flanders to conduct a study of urban density, they came to similar conclusions: at its core is high-quality public space that subtly segues into private living space with social control and discreet visibility.[5]

[5] Onderzoeksgroep Stad en Architectuur (KU Leuven) and Werkplaats voor Architectuur, 'Onderzoek naar het omgaan met richtdichtheden', Unpublished research report commissioned by the Flemish Community, 1998.

The 2015 concept study of 'spatial safety' in Antwerp by the consultancy Endeavour updated this approach and tried to better understand the connection between the layout of public space and the user's sense of security. Here, I should also cite the essay by anthropologist Ruth Soenen to mark the publication of the Urban Policy White Paper: 'Diversiteit in verbondenheid' (Diversity in solidarity). For anyone involved in urban planning, she insightfully explains how people in the urban space manage or fail to build up their social capital and how they can identify with a place ('bonding'), but also how they can transcend their own environment ('bridging').[6]

6   Ruth Soenen, 'Diversiteit in verbondenheid,' in *De eeuw van de stad. Over stadsrepublieken en rastersteden. Voorstudies* (Brussels: Ministry of the Flemish Community, 2003), 179–207.

Urban space has multiple manifestations. It does not determine human behaviour but offers opportunities and chances. Flemish Urban Policy has recognized this and commendably has built upon historical insights. It is therefore unsurprising that there are a variety of urban renewal projects currently under way in Ostend, Ghent, Antwerp and elsewhere that tackle both spatial and social issues. Thanks to innovative projects and in-depth concept studies, many cities have acquired experience and knowledge (capacity-building) and gained insight into the relation between space and human behaviour. Along the way, the 'social architecture of the city' has become a robustly underpinned discipline with specific characteristics and with a strong connection to architecture.

CO-PRODUCTION

Flemish Urban Policy played the PPP card right from the start. This felt somewhat uncomfortable, despite Belgium's long tradition of such initiatives. Private organizations invest significantly in education, well-being, healthcare and more. These are often non-profit associations, the heirs to confessional orders, civil charity organizations and solidarity movements. Their service provision and financing follow strict rules that are enshrined in laws and decrees. This institutional PPP is widely accepted, provided that public money is used properly and transparently, and that political or ideological balances are not disturbed. Its added value is self-evident. The policy framework is a permanent subject of political and social debate. Inevitably, the regulation that flows from this makes some generic pronouncements about the quality of the service provision. Different world views are given room to flourish. And the fact that the policy framework is developed at a Flemish level also offers efficiency gains in itself.

In the first urban renewal projects, a very direct form of PPP was explored. This involved two 'neighbours' that collaborate on the basis of their own land holdings: the developer that designs a commercial programme and the city that builds new public amenities. Both partners finance their part but develop their own project with the other partner in accordance with jointly devised quality criteria. In this way, the joint project becomes more than the sum of its parts.

Along the way, another form of collaboration came to light. Although not every project can be loaded up with public facilities, this does not mean that a council cannot or must not make a co-productive contribution to large spatial interventions. Indeed, urban programming may not take shape purely in function of speculative property intentions, but must also give shape to public interests: housing for all, sufficient green and open space, cost-effective infrastructure, the prospect of good management, etc.

In recent years, therefore, there has been considerable experimentation with new forms of PPP, whereby plans are developed in close consultation from the start, and the right balance is struck between economic and public imperatives. This demands a completely different attitude from both parties: the developer and its staff must want to step outside a purely financial mechanism while the city council and its civil servants must now fully embrace their involvement in the design process, as opposed to simply passing judgement.

From the council's perspective, these kinds of partnerships enable them to have greater control over the quality of developments. But citizens generally see things differently. They are prone to exaggeration in their objections and appeals, deploying terms such as 'megalomaniac', 'mobility attack', 'madness', 'profit maximization', 'harmful to the environment', etc. Well-meaning collaborations between councils and private parties are now used as arguments to complain about council bias.

These objections are easy to dismiss as a NIMBY reaction, but are they not rather the sign of an existential malaise? People have an indeterminate sense of dissatisfaction; they do not feel heard, they see their familiar environment change at a rapid pace and fear for their future and that of their children. A concrete project in the local area then becomes a perfect outlet with clear enemies: politicians lining their pockets, financial money-grabbers, lazy civil servants, out-of-touch experts, and so on.

Laid down in Flemish Urban Policy from the start, the preconditions for securing a subsidy are still highly relevant today: an urban regeneration project must be embedded in the urban spatial policy, have a leverage effect on upgrading the spatial environment, be directed by the city and, above all, must offer ample scope for participation. There have been many attempts to involve residents through all kinds of city discussions, communication campaigns, events, meeting days, etc. But in the current social context of dissatisfaction and fear of change, more is needed. The city is highly tangible and this makes it suitable as a basis for a 'city republic', as the Urban Policy White Paper suggested: a place with room for an exchange of views about a communal future. This is an ambitious and unruly process, which demands a completely different mindset from management, civil servants, urban designers and citizens.

THE CITY OF THE FUTURE

A tour of recent projects does not always inspire hope. Progress has certainly been made with regard to implementing urban development and the mixing of functions, there is a particular focus on the public domain, and the introduction of green space and water into the city is now well established. Several projects have also resolutely opted for green energy, and we sometimes see more modest attempts at a better definition of co-ownership. But in most cases, the housing offer continues to be inspired by what could be described as 'market conformity': scant experimentation as regards housing layouts, few alternative housing forms, and negligible inclusive mixing of resident groups.

The battle by developers to maximize profits undoubtedly plays a role, but it is not that simple. Self-evidently, a developer prefers to build what it is best able to sell.

In the meantime, councils place heavy burdens on urban regeneration projects – exacting requirements for parking, green space provision, amenities, certain residential mixes, etc. – which must often be 'paid for' with excessive housing densities. Some architecture firms are happy to go along with this development because it allows them to consolidate and scale up their businesses, a trend worthy of note and one which we are already seeing in technical engineering firms too. Ultimately, high-quality architecture is reduced to façadism in the glossy sales brochures that trumpet: 'a residential temple', 'prime architecture at the coast', 'world-class housing on the Scheldt', etc.

And so we reach the crux of the matter: our one-sided production of housing. In iconic cities such as Basel, Copenhagen and Zurich, it is housing cooperatives that produce trendsetting urban renewal projects, and this is the result of a completely different financial balance. Although Belgium was a leader in terms of housing legislation, savings banks and cooperatives in the late nineteenth century, we have increasingly and narrow-mindedly focused our housing production on unalloyed property acquisition since the rise of the welfare state. All parties involved are caught up in this market logic which only leaves a marginal space for fundamental architectural depth.

A newspaper article on *Composite Presence* (the Flemish contribution to the recent Venice Architecture Biennale) suggests that you can make a city with high-quality architectural objects. However, curator Dirk Somers sketches a more nuanced picture: 'The foundations for urban planning are so weak in Flanders that an architect always needs to ask themselves what role they can play and what they can do for the city. We often talk about this with self-directed scorn. With this model, we want to demonstrate that with this informal, jumbled urban situation you can create exciting architecture if you listen carefully to one another. In fact, it is a negotiated city.' [7] And in the Biennale catalogue, nine architects and chairs of quality forums argue for an integrated approach in which architecture, urban planning and spatial planning come together.

Undoubtedly more is needed to construct the city of the future. The efforts of Flemish Urban Policy with subsidies for urban renewal projects and concept studies must be steadily continued: in order to expand our knowledge, share experiences, provide support to councils, and so on. The organization of the urban debate is of crucial importance to this process.

Above all, there is a need for a broad forum in which all parties involved help to seek out a more diversified housing offer, each from their own discipline. Today's one-sided focus on housing ownership is unsustainable in the long term given the greying of society and declining household sizes. Moreover, we must not only concentrate on urban renewal projects. In the average central Flemish city, an equal number of new homes are given planning permission through striking urban renewal projects as through the regular planning permission policy (the replacement of a few houses by an apartment block here, filling in an empty space in the city fabric or transforming a school into co-housing there). In the former case, there will be an intense negotiation about a new park, about variety in the housing offer, perhaps even about space for business start-ups. In the latter case, the rules of the special plan or by-laws will apply, but the new homes must draw on the city's scarce existing facilities.

---

[7] Geert Sels, 'De stad van de toekomst ligt voor ons neus', *de Standaard*, 21 May 2021, S2, 2–3, https://www.standaard.be/cnt/dmf20210520_97864566.

The challenge is urgent because we have been postponing things for decades. J. P. Kloos wrote the following prophetic sentences as early as 1985: 'The liveability of our planet is in danger. We are using it wrongly. We are overexploiting Mother Earth and one another. We need to be courageous, to familiarize ourselves with the symptoms, and to dare to dig up the backgrounds in order to make a diagnosis of the world that we have ruined.' [8]

[8] Kloos, *Architectuur, een gewetenszaak*, 15.

Designing for an Open City

Livia de Bethune

Many people felt compelled to break the restrictions that were imposed during the Covid pandemic and the successive lockdowns, or even attempted to escape them. Windows, balconies and rooftops were the first things to be appropriated in the city, for example. Then café and restaurant terraces usurped public squares and car parks, while cyclists and joggers claimed the streets and local residents discovered the possibilities afforded by roadsides and riverbanks, or even the green hearts of roundabouts. These shared experiences reinforced an awareness that has long been present in our inner cities, particularly in the nineteenth-century districts, and that is the desire for more open neighbourhoods, with facilities close to home: play areas for children, picnic spots, green spaces for cycling and walking… and above all, places that make chance encounters possible.

I am thinking of an 'open city' with the potential to evolve further, of the kind Richard Sennett describes in *Building and Dwelling: Ethics for the City*. I am thinking of neighbourhoods with multi-use spaces that also attract a diverse public, of locations and buildings with porous borders that encourage a dialogue between inside and outside. I am thinking of incomplete, flexible sites or buildings that local residents can appropriate and continue to develop, thereby creating a collage of varied and recognizable places. In this essay, I examine a number of projects and their starting points that contribute to the concept of the 'open city' in terms of public space and parks.

THE 'OPEN CITY' CONCEPT

Running counter to the 'open city' concept is the prevailing trend for capsular space, as described by Lieven De Cauter in *The Capsular Civilization: On the City in the Age of Fear*. In today's society, which is characterized by growing uncertainty about the future, people seek safety and control and tend to retreat into enclaves with other like-minded people. The tendency is fuelled by ignorance of the 'other' in an increasingly cosmopolitan urban environment. De Cauter fears the Covid crisis and the ensuing lockdowns will exacerbate the move towards capsular space. He sees the walkable city as a potential solution: the city of short chains and local production. This not only implies a shift towards more sustainable urban lifestyles but would also encourage us to leave our familiar, protective bubbles and seek out interaction. De Cauter advocates tactical urbanism: creating temporary projects that allow new practices and places to be trialled and discovered, respectively. It is striking to note that many of the recent high-quality public spaces were preceded by temporary occupations or appropriations that also helped to shape the final results. This is true of the Thurn & Taxis Park in Brussels and the Kapitein Zeppospark in Ghent, both of which are discussed in detail in this essay. The spontaneous appropriation of public space during the lockdowns can also be seen as a form of tactical urbanism. My students from the Faculty of Architecture and Urbanism at KU Leuven made an inventory of many of these initiatives, in which local residents claimed public space at the expense of the car, and subsequently used these examples as inspirational starting points for their own designs for a more liveable city.

The transition from the car-based city to the walkable one becomes more appealing via an important tool: allowing residents to test it out for themselves. This has a motivational effect: people prefer to be convinced by their own experiences. The advantages of this kind of feedback loop, as it is known, are twofold: designers benefit from persuasive dynamics of the residents' impressions while being nourished by their own conscious experiences. All this enriches their personal design library and plants the seeds for innovative, creative designs.

Designers and administrators are faced with the challenge of creating public spaces (in consultation with local residents and users) that attract a diverse public and can be used in various ways. Certain types of quality public space, such as markets and parks, have their own distinct atmospheres, encourage spontaneous encounters and are places where everyone feels at home, depending on the moment, the company, the mood. The age-old concept of the marketplace is an inspiring reference for designers seeking to create accessible, inviting spaces. They sell everything while also offering a rich sensory experience – a visit to a traditional market remains an informal pleasure despite the boom in online shopping. French architects Anne Lacaton and Jean-Philippe Vassal based their design for the Palais de Tokyo art centre in Paris on the Djemaa el-Fnaa market in Marrakech. The architects dismantled the interior of the interwar exhibition palace, retaining only the basic structure of the building, which can be used freely by artists. The architect duo, who were awarded the Pritzker Prize in 2021, are known for generating the maximum social impact with minimum resources in every project – in this case, by applying the market concept to a contemporary arts centre. After all, the open, relaxed atmosphere of a market attracts a highly diverse public, with individuals meeting and greeting one another and engaging in exchanges. It is a place which people regularly return to. These are all qualities that we would love to see in our urban spaces on a daily basis.

The creation of a multi-use public space that residents can appropriate requires a layout that strikes a balance between diversity and specificity, greenery and paving, flexibility and connection to the porous perimeters. Urban space that is freed up by removing parking spaces can once more become multifunctional and shareable: a public domain that accommodates both a greengrocer's fruit and vegetable display and overspills from workplaces, for example.

The Dynamo metal workshop by phalt Architekten on the banks of the river Limmat in Zurich is a successful example of an open workspace. An open fablab – or fabrication laboratory, a public workshop with tools for developers – was built as an extension to the local youth centre, comprising a mushroom-like structure with a closed core for the tool area and a spacious canopy to shelter the young metalworkers who can give free reign to their creativity in the open air. This intermediate spatiality between inside and outside ensures a minimal threshold effect. It attracts the curious and leads to surprising exchanges between the active youngsters and the casual passers-by.

A similarly interesting approach was taken on the Île de Nantes. Here, in addition to an urban development grafted onto the character of these former industrial sites, space was also set aside for artistic and imaginative projects. Giant poetic machines such as *Le Grand Éléphant and Princesse* were built in the Parc des Chantiers, for example. They are paraded daily and enter into dialogue with a wide audience. Creativity is a spearhead of the Île de Nantes, building bridges between education and research, between the economic world and the art scene, combined with an ambitious programme of affordable housing. This is not a construction plan, but a project governance approach with various actors working together in a coordinated way on a project-by-project basis. An inspiring, intense, open approach that transforms the island into an evolving project with room for the unexpected.

Multi-use public spaces featuring restful and quiet areas and green zones are essential in dense urban environments. The greening and softening of inner-city areas helps to reduce urban noise and water issues, provides cooling on hot days and promotes a sense of well-being. Residents and passers-by can appropriate small-scale public green spaces by sitting or lying down on them or creating flower beds as well as herb and vegetable gardens. But the reintroduction of urban greenery is often an extremely technical undertaking: in the reconstruction of Anspachlaan in Brussels (a project I co-designed with the SumProject-Greisch team), the incredibly complex subsoil, including large collectors and utility pipes, required an unshakable handling of the technical infrastructure and rainwater management in order to transform this busy thoroughfare into a green city promenade.

A NEW GENERATION OF URBAN PARKS FOR A COSMOPOLITAN SOCIETY

At the end of the twentieth century, certain urban planners queried the usefulness of metropolitan parks. Underutilized urban squares and public parks were left to decay or became capsular spaces. In recent years, however, relentless urban expansion has revived the allure of historical public urban gardens. In a metropolis like Brussels, for example, they more than proved their worth during the lockdowns. The Jubelpark was created by Gédéon Bordiau at the end of the nineteenth century as a world's fair ground. In 2020 and 2021, its many garden 'rooms' were spontaneously and simultaneously claimed by numerous impromptu or organized activities such as keep-fit classes, volleyball and baseball matches, birthday celebrations and corporate drinks parties.

No less popular were the landscaped parks of Ter Kamerenbos (1861) and Vorst (1876), designed respectively by Édouard Keilig and Victor Besme on the initiative of Leopold II. The king sought to embellish the capital while simultaneously offering residents of the densely populated neighbourhoods greater quality of life. The model adopted was that of the *Volksparken*, which were then in vogue in Germany. A century and a half later, it is fascinating to see how intensively these parks – the green lungs of the city – are used. On sunny days, thousands of urbanites settle on the gentle slopes, which form a theatre of nature. Weary young people held an open-air party in the park as an April Fool's joke during the Covid pandemic, but it soon turned into an angry demonstration against months of restrictions on freedom. For several hours, the peaceful Ter Kamerenbos became the scene of fierce resistance, a place of civil disobedience more commonly found in the city centre.

Contemporary designers are increasingly opting for flexible set-ups and experimental approaches when creating green environments in order to attract a broad and diverse public. The urban parks laid out in recent years on former industrial terrains, harbour sites, car parks and residual spaces in Ghent, Antwerp and Brussels not only respond to the ecological urge for a more climate-robust city, but are also designed as shared spaces that provide a sense of security for a growing group of users. As Jan-Hendrik Bakker explains in *Nabijheid: Filosofische essays over toenadering* (Nearness: philosophical essays on proximity), these parks correspond to a genuine publicness and a public sphere.

The Kapitein Zeppospark in Ghent is part of the Oude Dokken redevelopment. After the port activities moved northwards, the City of Ghent recognized the area's potential for development. Based on a master plan by OMA, many building projects have been realized in recent years. At the same time, the inhabitants of Ghent discovered the place for themselves: they organize temporary events that immediately demonstrate the power of the disused harbour environment, akin to an inspiring *terrain vague*.

↦ See p. 248

In many locations in the late twentieth century, the quality of such harsh environments – silent witnesses to a past of hard human labour – was recognized as an opportunity for developing a new kind of landscape that was grafted onto the history of the sites. An early example is Derek Jarman's poetic approach to Prospect Cottage in Dungeness (Kent) in 1987 or, on a larger scale, the realization of the Landschaftspark in Duisburg. In the latter case, which dates from the 1990s, the Peter Latz agency added simple natural elements in-between the industrial ruins, thereby transforming a former steel factory into a powerful park with a distinctive aesthetic. Numerous industrial-archaeological relics have similarly been incorporated into the park at the Houtdok in Ghent, akin to follies in eighteenth-century landscaped gardens. These artefacts reference the neighbourhood's lost industrial identity. The harbour landscape, with its remarkable aspects and artefacts, contrasts with the new planting and the sober wooden play-and-rest furniture. An urban ecological landscape with different 'park rooms' has thus been created, a landscape whose unpolished beauty has been appropriated by a broad range of Ghent residents. If you cycle through the new park on a sunny spring day, you will see groups of teenagers hanging out on a lawn by the water, parents and toddlers in a playground, families celebrating a child's birthday in a picnic area, couples on the sandy beach overlooking the docks, local girls listening to music on a wooden pontoon while ducks build nests in the reeds ... The designers have clearly gone for a user-oriented approach at the site.

A comparable approach can be seen in the Brialmont Park in Antwerp, where the designers at Cluster landschap en stedenbouw redesigned several residual green areas between the hard traffic infrastructures dotted along the length of the Antwerp ring road. To transform these into a quality park, the designers defined specific places that reference the basic archetypes of landscape architecture. In the dense forest, for example, they created clearings that unconsciously transport the visitor back to one of these landscape archetypes, emphasizing the contrast between open and closed and between light and dark. The terraces that descend to the pond create an amphitheatre in the landscape, where it is possible to come into close contact with the water. Through the topological approach, inspired by the historical fortifications, the Brialmont Park encapsulates itself in the terrain and strengthens the connection

Brialmont Park, Berchem – Cluster landschap en stedenbouw

with the neighbourhood. It has become a spacious park with room for nature and biodiversity, an invitation to linger. Punctual interventions in robust materials recall the former function as a fortress and create places to relax amidst the greenery, despite the proximity of the traffic, the noise of which is partially buffered thanks to newly constructed verges.

The Thurn & Taxis Park serves as a green corridor between the Brussels Canal and the centre of Laken. Built on the former customs railway site, it is now a powerful urban motor. The park is constantly evolving, both through the plants that continue to flourish and via numerous additions. Bureau Bas Smets provided slow- and fast-growing trees. In the short term, the pioneer trees provide a green view and improve the quality of the soil through their roots. These will later make way for the slow-growing noble trees that will determine the shape of the park. Its ongoing development is also reflected in the additions that will gradually introduce recreational and sports infrastructure and thus meet the demands of local residents. These will not be a detraction, however, because the Thurn & Taxis Park has such a clear structure. Bureau Bas Smets achieved this by connecting it to the existing Brussels hydrographic system of parallel tributaries. The area that had been flattened to accommodate the former customs station was given a new gentle slope, like an additional tributary valley. This careful topological engineering provides concrete benefits for rainwater management and soil quality improvement, and above all generates a coherent park landscape in a fragmented environment. The topological

Thurn & Taxis, Brussels – Bureau Bas Smets

landscape approach is now being employed with ever-increasing frequency, particularly because of its ability to create dream-like images and new landscapes through the integrated construction of functional elements.

The Thurn & Taxis Park attracts a diverse public: residents of the neighbouring working-class districts of Molenbeek and Laken, employees from the offices both on and next to the site, and new residents from one of the surrounding housing developments. The bustling atmosphere of today contrasts with the park's history. For a long time, Thurn & Taxis was a forgotten part of Brussels. The rediscovery of the site thanks to, among others, the Couleur Café festival (which set up shop there for more than twenty years), seemed like a harbinger of today's multicultural street scene. In addition, the park forms an important green corridor for small fauna and flora, which are supported by neighbourhood initiatives. Non-profit organizations like Parckfarm T&T promote ecological practices via urban agriculture. The shared maintenance of an orchard, vegetable garden, neighbourhood compost and beehives not only promote biodiversity but also strengthen social relations both within and between different communities.

The creation of urban parks areas is a positive movement. However, the spaces that are considered tend to be old and difficult-to-access industrial sites, some even being located between busy traffic infrastructures. When redesigning such residual spaces, great attention must be paid to accessibility and the safety of all possible users:

Bockstael bicycle and pedestrian ramp, Brussels – Baukunst

from the buggies and tricycles of the very youngest to the elderly with walking frames. Thurn & Taxis is thus increasingly becoming an attractive link for hikers and cyclists thanks to new connecting axes. The footbridge by Baukunst and Util, for example, joins the lower park and the upper district in one flowing movement. It forms, as it were, an inviting 'red carpet' for the local residents.

CONCLUSION

Now that urban traffic is returning to pre-lockdown levels, the battle for public space is flaring up. Yet the pandemic has made us realize all the more clearly the importance of high-quality and flexible public spaces that respond to the needs and challenges of contemporary society. The question is whether this crisis will prove to be a catalyst for a more open city, and how the new vision on the use of space that has grown out of it will inspire designers in the twenty-first century.

As a citizen, but also as a designer, I am often amazed by how long public projects take to get off the ground, despite the urgency of the problems confronting society: climate change, decreasing biodiversity, air quality, quality of life and traffic safety. Activism can shake up administrators and alert them to the hard figures. But sophisticated participatory actions such as CurieuzenAir can be just as effective. Thanks to the commitment of 3,000 Brussels residents, this large-scale citizen survey offers concrete data on air pollution while raising awareness of the issues involved. Car-free days (on Sundays) have also been contributing to a widespread mental shift for some time now and could be organized more often. The power of tactical urbanism is equally tangible in recognizing the potential of residual spaces. Both locals and tourists in the capital are discovering and enjoying the quays of Brussels thanks to several temporary projects, ranging from the provisional opening of the Kanal arts centre to the creation by the non-profit association Toestand of 'Allee du Kaai', a meeting place that is primarily aimed at vulnerable youngsters.

It goes without saying that the design of accessible high-quality public spaces that meet society's needs is not a challenge with obvious solutions. However, the layout of the 'open city' is not just the responsibility of designers. A passionate, courageous and alert city council is vital: one that encourages experimentation and imagination while promoting a shared-use approach. It must also be fully committed to strengthening social relations and cooperating with all the actors involved, from council members, local service providers and non-profits to local residents and designers.

LITERATURE

Jan-Hendrik Bakker, *Nabijheid: Filosofische essays over toenadering* (Amsterdam: Atlas Contact, 2020).
Lieven De Cauter, *The Capsular Civilization: On the City in the Age of Fear* (Rotterdam: NAi, 2004).
Lieven De Cauter, 'Postcorona City: City of Capsules', *Desired Spaces*, 2 July 2022, www.desiredspaces.be/contributions-projekten-projects/postcorona-city-city-of-capsules.
Christophe Girot, *Le Cours du paysage, L'histoire d'un projet sur le monde naturel de la préhistoire à nos jours* (Paris: Les éditions Ulmer, 2016).
Arielle Masboungi and Antoine Petitjean, *La ville pas chiante: alternatives à la ville générique* (Paris: Le Moniteur, 2021).
Carlos Moreno, *Vie urbaine et proximité à l'heure du Covid-19. Collection Et après?* No.30 (Paris: Éditions de l'Observatoire, 2020).
Richard Sennett, *Building and Dwelling: Ethics for the City* (London: Allen Lane, 2018).
Bas Smets, *Landscape Stories* (Brussels: Bureau Bas Smets, 2015).
Hans Tindemans and Els Brouwers, 'Nabijheid is echt iets anders dan bereikbaarheid: gesprek met filosoof Jan-Hendrik Bakker', *Ruimte* 50 (2021): 18–21.
Enrique Walker, 'Anne Lacaton and Jean-Philippe Vassal in Conversation with Enrique Walker', in: Moisés Puente, *Lacaton & Vassal: Free Space, Transformation, Habiter* (Barcelona: Fundacion ICO, 2021): 12–40.
'Livre Blanc n°2. La Ville du 1/4 d'heure: du concept à la mise en œuvre' (Paris: Chaire ETI – IAE Paris, Université Paris 1, Panthéon Sorbonne, 2020).
Guillaume Vanneste, 'Verdraaid goed gevonden', *A+ Architecture in Belgium* 286 (2020): 82–85.
Joachim Declerck, Roeland Dudal and Élise François, *Bouwen voor Brussel: architectuur en stedelijke transformatie in Europa, 44 projecten* (Marseilles: Parenthèses, 2011).

| KAPITEIN ZEPPOSPARK | See p. 248 | |

BRIALMONT PARK	Client AG Vespa	Total building cost € 1,300,000 - excl. VAT
Office Cluster landschap en stedenbouw	**Design** June 2017	**Total building cost per m²** € 23 - excl. VAT
Website www.clusterlandscape.be	**Delivered** May 2020	**Main contractor** Hertsens Wegenwerken, Zwijndrecht
Address Grote Steenweg - Binnensingel, Berchem	**Surface area** 56,000 m²	**Technical execution studies** Witteveen + Bos, Deventer[NL]

BOCKSTAEL BICYCLE AND PEDESTRIAN RAMP	Client City of Brussels (Urban Planning Department)	Total building cost € 280,000 - excl. VAT
Office Baukunst	**Design** September 2018	**Main contractor** Melin, Ottignies-Louvain-la-Neuve
Website www.bau-kunst.eu	**Delivered** March 2021	**Stability studies** UTIL Struktuurstudies, Schaarbeek
Address Charles Demeerstraat, Brussels	**Surface area** 62 m²	**Landscape designer** Landinzicht, Brussels

Sepideh Farvardin

Lucien Kroll

Brussels, 17 March 1927 – Brussels, 1 August 2022

Lucien Kroll died as he had lived, I was told by his family, moving forward through life. And so the career of this hardened survivor came to a coherent close at the age of 95. Besides being an incredibly productive architect (with more than 200 projects to his name), both he and his wife Simone played a pioneering role in the areas of participation and ecology. In the many controversies he was obliged to navigate, he always managed to keep a cool head, and in recent years he was even able to rejoice in the growing interest in his work.

Lucien Kroll was born in 1927 to a family of Walloon industrialists. After completing his architectural training at La Cambre in 1951, he worked with Charles Vandenhove. They co-designed a number of single-family homes but eventually parted ways: Kroll received his first commission from Maredsous Abbey in 1957. From his intense dealings with the Benedictine monks, he learned the advantages of attentive listening and of participatory and incremental programming. That same year he met Simone Pelosse, an assertive potter from the Ardèche who was incredibly skilled at connecting people. The fruit of their collaboration was the Atelier d'Urbanisme, d'Architecture et d'Informatique Simone et Lucien Kroll. Their first big project was inaugurated in 1964 in the Brussels municipality of Oudergem: the building contained fifteen dwellings that had been developed in collaboration with different families, and it had a wild garden designed by Simone. In its early years, the office primarily worked on private homes in Belgium (from 1957) and various urban development studies in Rwanda (1966–67). Kroll's interest in the dynamics of consultation grew steadily. For the design of a school in Eigenbrakel (1965), he called on the expertise of psychologists and pedagogues, and organized many meetings with the future users. In this period his combativeness became apparent: by listening to *la parole habitante* (the voice of residents) and responding to it with the utmost diversity of spaces, Kroll became a fierce opponent of modernism, a movement whose authoritarian and repetitive nature he denounced as alienating. He began to develop an alternative vision of urban development, based on the humanistic ideas of Henri Lefebvre and on Louis Le Roy's 'wild' garden architecture.

Kroll had been attracting the attention of architectural critics for some time, but his most discussed project was undoubtedly Mémé, a collective housing project for the Faculty of Medicine at UCLouvain in Brussels. This titanic commission (1967–78) – which comprised a metro station, a garden, a restaurant and two other residential dwellings – was the result of intensive consultation with the medical students. Mémé is the only large-scale elaboration of Kroll's interest in the theories of John Habraken and Stichting Architecten Research (S.A.R.) on supporting structures and reversible functions. Despite these groundbreaking innovations, reactions to the building were mixed: the reviewers of the time were shocked by the heterogeneous aesthetic and the turbulent participation process. What's more, the project became embroiled in an open conflict with the client, which more or less meant the end of Kroll's career in Belgium. In the years thereafter, he continued his career abroad. From 1977 onward, he often worked in France and the Netherlands, where he designed various communal housing developments: Les Vignes Blanches in Cergy-Pontoise (1977–89) and Admiraalsplein in

Dordrecht (1998). In this same period, he realized a number of schools – the Don Milani School in Faenza and the HQE *Lycée* in Caudry (1997) – and he developed a participatory methodology for the renovation of low-income dwellings (1978–94).

It is striking how prescient Kroll's early concerns proved to be when we look at them in the light of today's challenges. This was confirmed recently when Kroll's studio received the Lifetime Achievement Award of the 2021 Brussels Architecture Prize. Seeking a balance between nature and buildings, the conversion of modern architectural heritage, the reversibility of light components and participation as a means of empowerment: these are all priorities that now seem desirable. Like an omen, Kroll wrote in 2013 in *OASE*: 'Let us imagine ourselves in 2060, when there will be no natural resources left. In order to plan a habitat, we will have to start with participatory groups and test the most radical non-consumption possible.'[1] He already prefigured the greatest contemporary challenge facing our profession, which is undergoing a profound revolution.

Elodie Degavre

1 Lucien Kroll, 'Respect for the Planet: Notes on Good Architecture', *OASE* 90 (2013): 29.

La Maison Médicale (Mémé), Lucien Kroll, Sint-Lambrechts-Woluwe, 1970–76

The people who worked on this book

Livia de Bethune is an architect and urban designer with a master's degree in historic building conservation. A lecturer in the Sint-Lucas Faculty of Architecture and Urban Design, KU Leuven in Ghent and Brussels, Bethune developed a broad expertise in architecture and urban design with Manuel de Sola Morales in Barcelona and at SumProject in Brussels. Six years ago she established the office Multiple with Abdelmajid Boulaioun. She has designed numerous public spaces as well as infrastructure and landscape projects, such as two new tram lines in Brussels, the area around the College bridge in Kortrijk, the reappraisal of the banks of the Somme in Amiens (FR), the development of the public space in Elsene's Atheneum quarter, a master plan for the Brussels marina BRYC, and a global spatial vision for the town of Le Touquet-Paris-Plage (FR).

Sofie De Caigny is the director of the Flanders Architecture Institute (VAi). She holds a PhD in architectural history from KU Leuven (2007). From 2006 to 2018 she was the coordinator of the VAi's heritage department, where she was responsible for the conservation, digitization, dissemination and publication of architectural archives. De Caigny writes about contemporary architecture in Belgium and has also curated exhibitions on the development of architectural culture in Flanders (for example, at the Deutsches Architekturmuseum, Frankfurt, 2016). From 2014 to 2022 she served as secretary general of ICAM (International Confederation of Architectural Museums). De Caigny was the commissioner of the Belgian Pavilion for the 2021 Architecture Biennale in Venice.

Maarten Desmet is an architect and social entrepreneur. He is the author of the book *Gross National Happiness*. A co-founder of Endeavour, an agency for people-centered urban planning, he is responsible for management, partnerships and innovation. Whether in his work for Endeavour, For Good or Stadsform, he always tries to make complex social themes such as sustainability and the city accessible.

Hülya Ertas is the coordinator of exhibitions and publications at the Flanders Architecture Institute. She graduated from Istanbul Technical University (Department of Architecture) in 2005, completing her master's degree in architecture at the same school in 2011. From 2004 to 2020 she worked at the monthly *XXI Architecture and Design Magazine*, becoming its editor-in-chief in 2013. Based in Brussels, she is a PhD candidate in the KU Leuven Faculty of Architecture (Campus Sint-Lucas, Brussels).

Sepideh Farvardin is an Iranian visual artist currently based in Brussels. She holds a master's degree in photography from LUCA School of Arts. Her work has been exhibited in Iran, France, Germany, Morocco and Belgium. Her projects mainly focus on the cityscape and street photography. With a keen interest in the interdependence between personal identity and urban identity, she attempts to uncover the moments when the two meet.

Miles Fischler lives in Antwerp and works for various cultural institutions, including Het Bos, Beursschouwburg, Zeno X, M Leuven and Minigolf Beatrijs. The main subject of their work is the interaction between people and their environment. Fischler observes how individuals personalize spaces, how they behave in them and what they leave behind. Fischler makes images driven by astonishment, curiosity and sometimes also confusion, as a way of relating with and connecting to the world around them.

Marleen Goethals is a senior lecturer in the master's degree course in urban design and spatial planning, and a researcher with both the Urban Development Research Group and the Interdisciplinary Studio for Territories in Transition at the University of Antwerp (Faculty of Design Sciences). Until 2013 she worked as a designer on landscape and urban projects for various design bureaux. In 2005 she began researching socially inclusive urban production and how participatory design processes can enhance social spatial quality. As a researcher and supervisor of master's theses, she deploys design-driven participatory action research (DD-PAR) to find cultural and ecological solutions for concrete needs in rapidly transforming residential areas in post-colonial contexts (Suriname, Brazil) and super-diverse areas in Flanders.

Ward Heirwegh graduated in 2007 from the Graphic Design Department of the Ghent campus of LUCA School of Arts. In his design practice, Heirwegh devotes particular attention to typography, visual language and the editorial process. He collaborates with artists, curators, writers and architects on a variety of projects, including books, exhibitions, record sleeves and websites. In addition to teaching at Sint-Lucas in Antwerp, he is the founder of Sleeperhold Publications, a research platform for artist publications that offers room for experimentation with collaborative opportunities, including with the carriers and conventions of his discipline.

Petrus Kemme obtained a master's degree in engineering sciences and architecture from Ghent University. He worked at the Copyright Art and Architecture Bookshop in Ghent before becoming a project manager for publications, lectures and symposia at the Flanders Architecture Institute in 2018. He has been the project coordinator and editor of the *Flanders Architectural Review* since 2019. Kemme is also the curator of *Table Setting*, an exhibition series for young architects on the square in front of De Singel.

Patrick Lennon has been a full-time freelance Dutch and French to English translator and English copy editor since 2010. He specializes in the arts and culture: architecture, art, music, dance, literature, performing arts, etc. Based in Brussels, he works with artists, publishers and institutions.

Marc Martens is an architectural engineer who qualified in the specialist field of urban design and spatial planning at KU Leuven in 1974 and 2001. He is the director of bureau voor architectuur & planning. From 2003 to 2016 he was a tutor in spatial planning and urban design study in the Architectural Engineering Sciences professional group (VUB). Active as an architect and spatial planner, he is also a member of various commissions and quality forums: the municipal commission for spatial planning in Bierbeek and Leuven, the Flemish Brabant's provincial commission for spatial planning, a member of the Team of Directors for Flemish Urban Policy, and the quality forum be-MINE Beringen.

Mark Pimlott is a university lecturer in Interiors Buildings Cities at Delft University of Technology (Faculty of Architecture and Built Environment). He is the author of *Without and Within: Essays on Territory and the Interior* (2007), *In Passing* (2010) and *The Public Interior as Idea and Project* (2016). His practice incorporates photography, installation, art for public places and architectural design, particularly of interiors. Notable works are *World* at BBC Broadcasting House, London (2013); *La scala*, Aberystwyth (2003); and interiors of the Red House, London (2001 and 2011), in collaboration with Tony Fretton Architects. He publishes and lectures widely, and lives and works in The Hague, the Netherlands.

Eva Pot studied art history at Ghent University. After her studies, she worked for the nomadic and cultural platform Gouvernement in Ghent. Since 2019 she has been working as a production manager at the Flanders Architecture Institute.

Maxime Schouppe studied Romance philology at Ghent University and journalism at the École supérieure de journalisme de Lille. He was a reporter for newspapers in the French overseas department of La Réunion and for the French press agency AFP (The Hague office). He subsequently worked as a communications adviser for ING Group in Amsterdam and as an information officer at the International Court of Human Rights in The Hague. In 2011 he settled in Brussels, where he has since worked as a freelance copywriter and translator, chiefly for the cultural sector. For the Flanders Architecture Institute he collaborated on the reissue of the book *Juliaan Lampens 1950–1991* (2020).

Helen Simpson studied ancient history and Egyptology at University College London before completing a master's degree in museum studies at the University of Leicester. She worked in the UK as a museum registrar before specializing in the organization of large-scale exhibitions, including for the Hayward Gallery in London. After moving to Belgium in 1994, she worked for the Museum of Fine Arts Ghent before embarking on a freelance career as a translator and editor in 2012.

Marie Sledsens is a graphic designer with an independent design practice in Antwerp. She focuses on the design of books and magazines, visual identity, editorial design and scenography. She works closely with various parties in the broad cultural sector and puts the accent on research, experiment and materials. A graduate of the Graphic Design Department at the Sint-Lucas campus of LUCA School of Arts in Ghent, she teaches at the Academy in Berchem, Antwerp.

Martino Tattara is an architect and associate professor at KU Leuven (Faculty of Architecture). His theoretical work focuses on the relation between architecture and large-scale urban design. His critical reassessment of Lucio Costa's project for Brasilia is in preparation. Over the past decade his work has centred on a research-by-design trajectory that focuses on the domestic space and its potential for transformation. Together with Pier Vittorio Aureli, he is the co-founder of Dogma, a Brussels-based architectural practice.

Kiki Verbeeck is an architect. She was a guest lecturer in architectural practice at KU Leuven from 2010 to 2014. In 2002, together with Yves Malysse and Joost Verstraete, she founded the office UR architecten, which was renamed URA Yves Malysse Kiki Verbeeck in 2009. The office creates unexpected architectural puzzles for a wide range of projects in which archetypes are sculpted, in a contemporary way, into a precise identity for a specific context. URA has received multiple award nominations, including for the Mies van der Rohe Award. Their first retrospective exhibition was *Solid Senses* in 2020 at Bozar (Brussels), on which occasion the monograph *Architectural Projects 2002–2020* was published. Kiki Verbeeck studied architecture at Sint-Lucas Ghent and architectural sciences at KU Leuven. She gained experience in Paris at uapS and LABFAC, in Rotterdam at OMA, and in Brussels at Georges Baines and Advisers.

Collaborating in enduring beauty

True beauty is something you'd rather not let go of. That is why your projects are not only about aesthetics, but also about sustainability. This way your customers can enjoy your realisations for a lifetime. Together with Reynaers Aluminium you can give your project that timeless touch. Our high-quality aluminium solutions will inspire you in countless ways and will effortlessly stand the test of time. So your creations will provide long-lasting living pleasure.

ZNA Cadix - ©Frank De Brabandere

Reynaers Aluminium

Windows.
Doors.
Curtain Walls.

Together for better

Looking for comfort-enhancing, creative construction solutions that are also sustainable?

Look no further!

Visit Studio Gyproc® and discover our sustainable construction solutions

- Acoustics and indoor climate regulation
- Aesthetics and comfort
- High-end finishing

IN COLLABORATION WITH

https://discover.gyproc.be/studio-gyproc

Wasserstrich Special, characterful elegance

Discover the six new shades in the Wasserstrich Special collection. Available exclusively in the narrow Eco-brick format.

The slim Wasserstrich Special is longer than the average facing brick. This enables you to create horizontal lines in your architecture. And the weathered, slightly abraded look gives your façade extra character. With the Wasserstrich Special collection now expanded by six new shades, the colour palette gives you free rein to create the look you want. Available in the Eco-brick format that leaves more room for insulation. A great-looking and sustainable choice for both new-build projects and renovations.

Come and see the Wasserstrich Special collection for yourself in our showrooms in Londerzeel or Kortrijk.

Eco-brick®
- ☑ Narrow facing bricks
- ☑ More room for insulation
- ☑ Sustainable choice

Terrazzo since
Natural 1923
Ceramics

Flagstones Terro | Arch & Teco Architecten
Securex Gent | Photography Valerie Clarysse

STONE Olsene
Grote Steenweg 13, 9870 Olsene
T. +32 (0)9 388 91 11
info@stone.be

STONE Londerzeel
Autostrade 30, 1840 Londerzeel
T. +32 (0)52 31 76 03
info@stone.be

www.stone.be

STONE

Forster Presto XS:
Slimmest profiles for doors and fixed glazings

The slim profiles of Forster Presto XS allow intricate designs to be constructed to create an elegant, timeless look, while the high transparency of the glass elements ensures plenty of light is admitted to create a sense of spaciousness and comfort.

Profiles with minimal face widths from 23 mm are available to create modern looks or designs that will fit well in protected historic buildings. The newly developed range of profiles, matching accessories and fittings are easy, convenient and very safe to use.

forster presto XS

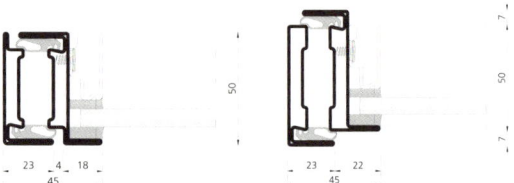

Ultra-thin interior doors made of steel

forster

Reynaers Aluminium SA
Oude Liersebaan 266, B-2570 Duffel
Tel 015 30 85 33 / luc.hermans@forstersystems.com
www.forstersystems.com

Subscribe to A+!

"Where other publications have a niche character or are more biased, the bilingual character and the cultural purpose of A+ in the broad sense make the magazine an essential publication in Belgium".

Harold Fallon, architect AgwA

Discover all our subscriptions on https://www.a-plus.be/nl/abonnement/ or go directly to the website via the qr-code

Questions? Reach us at abonnement@a-plus.be

Building with Concrete

FEBELCEM, the Belgian Cement Association
- documentation and in-house publications
- communication and events
- technical assistance

Vorstlaan 68 b11| 1170 Brussels | www.febelcem.be | info@febelcem.be | +32 (0)2 645 52 11

Parking Building – Ledeberg – Havana i.c.w. L.U.S.T. architecten, Bollinger + Grohmann, VK engineering   © Stijn Bollaert

Flanders Architecture Institute at work

The Flanders Architecture Institute (VAi) is the main contact for architecture from Flanders and Brussels. It provides a meeting place for everyone who wants to make, share and experience architecture. Exhibitions, lectures, debates, an extensive website, events and publications such as the biennial Festival of Architecture and the *Flanders Architectural Review* are important additional instruments. The VAi also represents Flanders at international events such as the Architecture Biennale in Venice. Moreover, it can count on a broad international network, within which it transmits knowledge about architecture from Flanders and Brussels to international forums and vice versa.

The VAi manages a magnificent collection of ever-expanding architectural archives. With this growing collection, the institute is building a bridge between the present, past and future of architecture. In addition, the VAi plays an active role in caring for design heritage. It maps out this patrimony, offers advice on it and informs a wide audience about it through publications and exhibitions.

Follow us on Instagram, Facebook, Twitter, LinkedIn and YouTube.

www.vai.be/en

LUC DELEU & T.O.P. OFFICE. FUTURE PLANS 1970–2020

In 2020–21, the VAi celebrated fifty years of unsolicited practice from Luc Deleu & T.O.P. office. To mark this anniversary, it launched *Future Plans* with De Singel, M HKA / CKV, CIVA and Argos. The VAi's aim with this project was to keep alive the potential of T.O.P. office's reflection on society from the perspective of design practice and to preserve, perpetuate and disseminate design education.

Future Plans also served as a perspective from which to conduct a thorough exploration of T.O.P. office's analogue and digital archive. Which archival material retains the promise of a future plan? Curators Peter Swinnen and Anne Judong translated this question into an archive exhibition, a publication and a documentary.

Via two educational and participatory projects, *A Studio for Orbanism* and *Futurum*, the VAi took specific steps to activate the living archive and to pass on this intellectual legacy to upcoming generations of designers who represent the future.

Luc Deleu & T.O.P. office. Future Plans 1970–2020, Flanders Architecture Institute at De Singel © Olmo Peeters

40 YEARS OF COMPETITION CULTURE

With the double exhibition *Coming of Age. Architectural Competitions in Flanders and Brussels* and *Open Call. 20 Years of Public Architecture*, the VAi shone the spotlight on forty years of architectural competitions. The period between 1980 and 2020 undoubtedly played a major role in the development of architectural culture in Flanders and Brussels.

Based on ten projects from the 1980s and 1990s, *Coming of Age* offered a unique insight into the competition climate prior to the introduction of the Open Call procedure in 2000. The cases were the result of research into competitions published in Dutch-language architectural journals. Each one provided a different perspective on the competition process. Together, they uncovered the key trends from that period.

Open Call picked up the story where *Coming of Age* left off. This touring exhibition, which the Team Flemish Government Architect staged to mark the twentieth anniversary of the creation of the Government Architect role, used archival material and architectural installations to demonstrate how the Open Call works as an instrument. New videos with testimony from former Flemish Government Architects and project managers in the Team Flemish Government Architect completed the final presentation.

The VAi took an even closer look at the Open Call in two publications. *More Than a Competition. The Open Call in a Changing Building Culture*, a joint publication of the VAi and Team Flemish Government Architect, looks back at two decades of public architecture in a series of essays and offers contemporary reflections on the period. The Berlin-based publisher Jovis Verlag, together with the VAi and the Team Flemish Government Architect, published *Celebrating Public Architecture. Buildings from the Open Call in Flanders 2000–21*, in which Florian Heilmeyer studies the built results of the Open Call and presents a selection of seventy public buildings realized as a result of the procedure.

Coming of Age. Architectural Competitions in Flanders and Brussels, Flanders Architecture Institute at De Singel © Olmo Peeters